FRANTZ FANON

FRANTZ FANON

A PORTRAIT

ALICE CHERKI

TRANSLATED FROM THE FRENCH BY
NADIA BENABID

CORNELL UNIVERSITY PRESS
ITHACA AND LONDON

This translation has been published with assistance from the French Ministry of Culture—Centre National du Livre.

Originally published by Editions du Seuil under the title *Frantz Fanon, Portrait* © Editions du Seuil, 2000

English translation first published 2006 by Cornell University Press
English translation first printing, Cornell Paperbacks, 2006

Printed in the United States of America

Library of Congress Cataloging-in-Publication Data

Cherki, Alice.
   [Frantz Fanon. English]
   Frantz Fanon : a portrait / Alice Cherki ; translated from the French by Nadia Benabid.
      p. cm.
   Includes bibliographical references and index.
   ISBN-13: 978–0–8014–4038–0 (cloth : alk. paper)
   ISBN-10: 0–8014–4038–6 (cloth : alk. paper)
   ISBN-13: 978–0–8014–7308–1 (pbk. : alk. paper)
   ISBN-10: 0–8014–7308–X (pbk. : alk. paper)
   1. Fanon, Frantz, 1925–1961. 2. Intellectuals—Algeria—Biography.
3. Revolutionaries—Algeria—Biography. 4. Psychiatrists—Algeria—Biography.
5. Algeria—Biography. I. Benabid, Nadia. II. Title.
CT2628.F35C4713 2006
965'.046092—dc22
[B]

2005032182

Cornell University Press strives to use environmentally responsible suppliers and materials to the fullest extent possible in the publishing of its books. Such materials include vegetable-based, low-VOC inks and acid-free papers that are recycled, totally chlorine-free, or partly composed of nonwood fibers. For further information, visit our website at www.cornellpress.cornell.edu.

Cloth printing   10 9 8 7 6 5 4 3 2 1
Paperback printing   10 9 8 7 6 5 4 3 2 1

Deafness and muteness lodge

behind the eyes.

I see the poison flowering

in every kind of word and form.

Paul Celan, "The No-Man's Rose"

Contents

Preface and Acknowledgments

Born in Fort-de-France, Martinique, in 1925, buried in Algeria in 1961—three months prior to Algeria's independence—and trained as a psychiatrist in France in the immediate aftermath of World War II, Frantz Fanon today no longer enjoys the recognition in Europe he did at one time. He died young; he was only thirty-six. In recent years, his persona has become synonymous with decolonization and Third Worldism. His books are still being read by students everywhere, and Frantz Fanon societies, some in name only but others quite vital, exist the world over, in Algeria as well as in the Antilles, in South Africa and Iran. His status in American academia is quasi-heroic and, on occasion, manipulated. In Britain, they've made films about him and in the English-speaking world, philosophers have written books about him.

To speak of Fanon today, regardless of how old or young one's interlocutor may be, always entails the risk of entering uncharted territory. Reactions are not always easy to predict and generally fall into one of two categories. There is the "Who's that? Should his name ring a bell?" response; or there is the sudden rush of meaningful memory: "He really helped shape my adolescent perceptions of the books I was just beginning to come across at the time." Known to some, unknown to others, never as universally known as Che Guevara or Sartre or Camus, Fanon was, nonetheless, a precursor, and his writings on racism, colonialism, the relationship between oppressor and oppressed, and the prospects of developing nations were groundbreaking. His writings sound an alarm and raise a plea for caution and engage with the realities of the present day.

By one of those fortuitous twists of history, I was given the opportunity to work closely with Fanon from 1955 to 1961, during the critical years that bracketed his involvement with the struggle for Algeria's independence. The confluence of our joint political and medical work brought us together from the moment Fanon arrived in Algeria until his death.

A work belongs to its readers, and each new generation of readers is free to interpret Fanon's work as it sees fit. That being said, it is also true that revisiting the journey and conditions behind the work can, at times, cast it in an altogether new light, altering the perception of its established identity and of the passions that helped shape that identity.

My thanks go to the many people who lived and witnessed those times and who shared their memories with me. Their names appear in this book.

I would also like to thank the younger ones, those under thirty, especially Stany Grelet and Olivier Cherki-Thorent. I owe much both to their know-how and to their ignorance. The fact that despite great academic qualifications in the field of political science they knew so little about Fanon and the historical period in which he lived persuaded me to undertake this project. And the know-how they acquired in their scholarly pursuits helped me bring it to fruition.

A.C.

FRANTZ FANON

Introduction

Every time Jean-Paul Sartre wanted to know some particular concerning Fanon's life, Fanon avoided answering by dismissing the information as extraneous. Yet Fanon felt a bottomless admiration for Sartre and was ready to go to great lengths to secure the great man's recognition and approval. He, in fact, showed a rare candor in his dealings with Sartre and an exceptional readiness to reveal much about himself. But speaking about oneself and narrating one's life are not necessarily the same thing; for Fanon, self-disclosure meant speaking about his commitments, his passions, his battles. "One should not relate one's past, but stand as a testimony to it," is how he once put it to his friend Marcel Manville.

Even if he had wished it, Fanon was consummately incapable of telling the story of himself. He lived in the immediacy of the moment, with an intensity that embodied everything he evoked. Fanon's discourse pertained to a present tense that was unburdened by its narrative past. The little we knew about his personal life had been gleaned from passing allusions, brief glimpses that vanished as quickly as they appeared. It was futile to ask him questions up front; seamlessly, the conversation would be headed off in another direction before we even realized it.

Reexamining the extraordinary trajectory of an extraordinary man by consulting not his writings but fragments of his life is, in a certain sense, an exercise in memory by proxy, a remembering "for another" filled with lacunae, discoveries, encounters, and amazingly few instances of reconstruction.

It is, nonetheless, important to reconstruct the journey if one is to rein in the profusion of attributes that have been imputed to Fanon in recent times. This work seeks to counteract both the unrestrained idealization that holds

Fanon to his heroic image and cuts him off from history as well as the powerless and silent reaction greeting bewildering allegations that dismiss Fanon as an apologist for violence and an obsolete figure linked to Third Worldism. This, then, is my project. If nothing else, I will not have missed an opportunity to exhort the young and ignorant to know the man Simone de Beauvoir described in 1963 as one of the most remarkable figures of his day and to make young Algerians attending the Lycée Frantz-Fanon understand that their school is not just another Maréchal Bugeaud, which is how the largest all-boy *lycée* was known in Algiers before independence, nor is it named for "a French psychiatrist and sociologist" as encyclopedias still persist in identifying him.

In a wider sense, my aim has been to historicize a figure and his epoch. Fanon was an important actor of the day, and there is a sense in which his importance is not diminished today. He was a thinker about violence, not its apologist. The former colonies may no longer be home to the violence of which he spoke, but because we neglected to reflect on it sufficiently and allowed ourselves to forget the stakes of those Fanonian times, violence has made itself a new home, here, just outside the city walls.

Fanon was also a practicing psychiatrist. This is a dimension of his life that has always been underestimated, especially because for the duration of his brief life he worked more in North Africa—first Blida, then Tunis—than in France. I was a young intern at the time and too inexperienced to be a good judge of the breadth of his knowledge or his thoroughness as a clinician. I have had the opportunity since, however, to study his psychiatric writings and the entire unpublished record of his case notes on two talking cures that were conducted in 1959 and 1960. In the process, I came to the surprised realization that Fanon possessed a tremendous intuition about the unconscious and a great erudition in psychoanalytic theory. The innovative boldness he brought to the identification of signifiers and the pertinence of his interpretive leaps are no less amazing in a person who never underwent analysis. The case study in question is very reminiscent of Sigmund Freud's *Rat Man* and of some of the work carried out by Sándor Ferenczi, who, starting in 1958, held a special and acknowledged sway on Fanon. Fanon felt a profound love for his psychiatrist's vocation, and his intellectual life was greatly inflected by his psychiatric work. To construe Fanon as any one thing—psychiatrist, militant, writer, Antillean, Algerian—however, is to misconstrue the profound unity of his project. His life was a journey that, with every passing year, moved him closer to an understanding of his relationship to others and to the world. Naturally, he had his limitations, his doubts, and his fervors. He was a man of extreme intelligence who, at the risk of excess and on premise of excess, threw his entire being into his think-ing. But he was more than a thinker. Fanon had a profound talent for life; he was a man who wanted to be the subject and actor of his own life, and it was for this reason that he was so engaging and disarming—so alive.

I met Fanon in January 1955 when our paths crossed at a conference orga-nized by the AJAAS (Association of Algerian Youth for Social Action). The association was one of the few places where young people from different backgrounds could meet and mix freely: there were Muslims from the youth and scouting movements, progressive Christians, and a handful of Jews who were not associated with any special groups and thus marginalized by most of their peers who had gravitated in far greater numbers to the Algerian Communist Party, which, in turn, marginalized them. The topic of the con-ference was fear in Algeria. Fanon was the last speaker. People said that he was black, that he came from the Antilles. And so he was, but I never saw it. I was so intent on the sparkle in his eyes, of a brown so clear as to seem transparent, on the expressiveness of his elegantly dressed person, on the passionate voice, and, most of all, on what that voice was telling us about fear and anxiety. I do not remember the content of his talk, but I remember the thrilling impact it made on us, all young people at the time. And the whole thing had been carried off in the most impeccable French. After the conference, I was introduced to Fanon and the connection was immediate. Years later, I happened to mention in passing that I had not realized he was black the first time I met him, and he stopped in his tracks, wide-eyed and open-mouthed, before bursting into laughter. He was visibly shaken. He had written page after page arguing for a humanity that would not be ruled by skin color; yet when something did live up to his expectations, it still took him by surprise.

Shortly thereafter, my colleagues at the hospital where I worked as an ex-tern began to ostracize me because of my political convictions. I was being intimidated and harassed on a daily basis; the harassment did not stop at words; it soon took other forms: torn hospital gowns, stolen reports, smashed car windows, punctured tires. . . . I was no longer welcome at the University-affiliated psychiatric clinic where I had wanted to work. Fanon intervened and invited me to join his team in Blida. I accepted.

This book is not an exhaustive biography, and many of the people who had ties to Fanon are not mentioned in it. I did not seek out his Antillean relatives, the brothers and sisters who are still living, because they did not share Fanon's Algerian life and I wanted to view them through the same prism and retain the same refracted reality they had occupied for Fanon during those years. Nor did I make an attempt to track down all the people who are still living and knew him at the time. I did, however, consult the people I knew or came to know in subsequent, numerous meetings, and their testimony has contributed to this work.

This book is not an interpretive undertaking, an inquiry into how motivations allegedly attributed to a person's childhood express themselves in the relationship between the life and the writing. I have no taste for psychohistory. My sole aim is to shed light on a life journey and a specific period in recent history. I have written this book as a countermeasure to the history that is being rewritten as a function of preestablished values and on the basis of absolute misunderstanding. On either side of the Mediterranean, Algerian decolonization has frequently been the object of such studies. This book is a portrait and does not wish to pass itself off as the work of a historian or a biographer. It is an essay, rather, an effort that seeks to convey, despite its shortcomings and incompletion, an epoch, a life, and a body of work often viewed as inadmissible. Let us call it a testimony once removed.

Before Blida

After a happy childhood in Martinique, a young Fanon enlisted in the World War II fight to defend the freedom of Europeans persecuted by Nazism in the name of racial supremacy. Fanon's first encounter with North Africa was as a serviceman when he took part in the liberation of France. After coming home to the Antilles, he returned to France to pursue his education, studying psychiatry in Lyon. He published his first article, "The North African Syndrome." Fanon had his first encounter with institutional psychiatry at Saint-Alban. He published his first book: Peau noire, masques blancs. *He took part in a public debate with Octave Mannoni. He was posted in Algeria as Chief Resident Physician at the psychiatric hospital in Blida-Joinville.*

Who was this recently married young man who turned up in Algeria under clearly circumscribed conditions to join the medical staff of a psychiatric hospital located in a subdivision of the capital city? As noted in the introduction, and will no doubt be noted again throughout the pages of this book, the man was discreet to a fault in all matters that touched on his personal life. Not one person in our group had the least inkling of the events that had shaped his life before he came on board as a member of the French psychiatric public health system. In time, we would learn that the path had been considerable, rich and textured and filled with experiences of many kinds and shaped by intellectual as well as physical struggle. The narrative of the events that had determined the course of his life would emerge piece-

5

meal, in the fragments he chose to share with us. Life before Blida was generally off limits, however, and the same went for his childhood, his family, and almost any other subject of a personal nature. We were not aware, for example, of Mireille, the daughter who bore his name and had been born to the woman he had at one time known in France. Years elapsed, Algeria had already won its independence and Fanon was already dead, before any of us, his colleagues and companions for the duration of his life in Algeria and Tunisia, would find out she even existed.

Certain things were there for all to see: his wife, pretty and understated; their son, an infant at the time;[1] Fanon's brother-in-law, a young artist who lived in Lyon, visited the family for extended periods of time, and loved Fanon for his generosity; and later on, Marcel Manville, the renowned Martinican lawyer, who had been both a childhood friend and a comrade-in-arms and who often traveled to Algeria to defend detained Algerian militants.[2] Guests at the Fanon home were treated to an occasional sampling of *béguine*, the rumba of the Antilles, and served a Martinican culinary treat, and then invited to join in discussions that lasted late into the night. Fanon loved to talk with people who commanded his admiration, or simply with friends, and while his brilliant eloquence was riveting, he was also quite capable of being a generous and sympathetic listener. He was an excellent conversationalist, who never spoke openly about himself.

When Fanon referred in passing to his former stay in Algeria as a member of the Free French forces, he did so merely to indicate his familiarity with the cities of Oran, Bougie, or Algiers. The story of his life, however, remained under wraps. His friend Marcel Manville, to whom he had often remarked that "only those who are done with living their lives write memoirs," has said as much. Of course, the very notion of people who were barely out of their twenties writing their memoirs was an unthinkable one at the time. Fanon, except for rare uninhibited moments, was entirely incapable and would not have known how to begin talking about himself. In those early Algerian days, his name had not yet achieved its later currency. Later, on those rare occasions when he would take someone into his confidence, the exchange would always be one-on-one, brief, and without follow-up. It goes without saying that these intimate lapses did not include the fielding of questions.

What is known for certain is that he was born on July 20, 1925, into a petit bourgeois family of comfortable means. His father, Casimir Fanon, was a civil servant employed as a customs inspector. That Casimir Fanon was a conscientious and discreet man did not prevent him from remarking on the occasion of Bastille Day celebrations that while the siege of the Bastille was underway in Paris, there were still slaves in Martinique. Fanon's mother, who ran a shop in Fort-de-France, was a mulatto woman whose maternal forebears were Alsatian, the Hausfelders; this ancestry conferred a high status on an island that was home to 250,000 inhabitants and where racial mixtures were the object of a complex system of organization that was an essential component of the society and its hierarchies.[3]

Fanon was the third son and fifth child of six surviving children; two had died. There were four boys and two girls. Biographers tell us that the sensitive and impressionable child grew into a contentious and stormy adolescent, that his mother was distant and lacked affect.[4] That he may not have been his mother's favorite son does not come as much of a surprise. He lacked that imperceptible but very real core of serenity that is instilled in the sons of unconditionally supportive and loving mothers, mothers whose love is something beyond, as in the case of Amalia and Sigmund Freud. Even in later years, in Tunis, when Fanon had become somewhat more open with his friends, he hardly, if ever, mentioned his mother, but his father would come up from time to time. All the same, his letters to her, even after his father's death, were invariably warm and spontaneous.

Fanon was born into a large family that, as far as we know, appears to have remained relatively unscathed by tragedy, at least insofar as his parents' generation is concerned. It seems safe to assume that he was well cared for, surrounded by affection, and enjoyed an all-around happy childhood. His friends and his older brother describe him as a boy "like any other," generous, warm-hearted, and besotted with sports and other boyhood games. His parents had him and his brother, who was three years his senior, pegged as a pair of rascals always up to some mischief, sneaking into movie houses, filching marbles and candies wherever they could find them and especially from their mother's small establishment. He was, in other words, exactly what one would have expected of a boy who lived in keeping with his times. Had he been a Parisian boy, he would no doubt have tagged along with the gaggle of harmless neighborhood troublemakers—ringing bell-pulls and rousing the concierge before scattering like sparrows down cobblestone streets. Fanon shared only one episode, imparted with telling emotion and disproportionate solemnity, from that period; I can only refer to it as the "Schœlcher episode."[5] When Fanon was ten years old, he was taken together with his peers on the customary school excursion to the *Schœlcher Monument* to pay tribute to the great man who had "freed the slaves from their chains." Why, the boy suddenly wanted to know, had this man been so great—a hero? What was this thing that had transpired *before* and about which no one ever spoke? His heroism stemmed, no doubt, from that *beforehand*, that unspeakable time when men and women were enslaved, subjected to the "Negro Laws" (*Code noir*). The man, speaking about the boy he had once been, was still overwhelmed by the emotion that had come over him that day. Maybe it was an instance of screen memory, a memory resurfacing to signal another mystery, a deeper unspoken truth, but that is beside the point. The man, speaking of the child, remembered that day as the "first time I saw that the history they were teaching us was based on a denial, that the order of things we were being presented with was a falsehood. I still played and took part in sports and went to the movies, but everything had changed. I felt as though my eyes and my ears had been opened." Was this an instance of embellished memory, an event recast as a fable in keeping with Fanon's penchant for stories and their ability to disarm his interlocutors? Although it is difficult to say for certain, one thing is sure: this memory was at the center of the self he had forged himself.

The Second World War would alter the young Fanon's life forever. The arrival of Admiral Robert and the French military fleet that had made the crossing under his command from Brest to Fort-de-France in late 1939, early 1940, brought disruption to Martinique. For Fanon, it spelled the end of a relatively carefree childhood and the beginning of a conflicted young adulthood. A few years later, in *Africains Antillais*, Fanon would refer specifically to this period. Fanon's countryman and near-contemporary—he was, in fact, three years his senior, an important difference at that age—the Martinican lawyer Marcel Manville, who took part in almost every major political struggle of the century, would also view this as a landmark moment.

Manville had been a classmate of Joby's, one of Fanon's older brothers, at the Lycée Schœlcher, but a shared talent for soccer and an enthusiasm for sports in general had helped cement the special bond that existed between Manville and the younger Fanon. Their friendship would endure, despite the geographic distances that separated the two men, until the end of Fanon's life.

When Admiral Georges Robert, high commissioner of the Republic who would later align himself with Henri-Philippe Pétain, arrived in Martinique in October 1939, Manville as well as his friend Mauzole (Édouard Glissant was part of a later promotion) had already met Aimé Césaire, their recently appointed French literature teacher at the Lycée Schœlcher. Fanon was too young to be attending senior-year literature courses, but thanks to his friends he, too, was able to engage, albeit by proxy, in this new encounter, which, in Manville's words, was a "kind of rebirth" for their little group.[6]

In September 1939, Fanon was fourteen. His life, like that of the other children of the Fort-de-France bourgeoisie, had been largely sheltered and free of hardship. There were the *békés*, of course, the descendants of white Creoles who owned all of the country's wealth, but they were few in number, 2,000 at best, and they lived in their own separate world. The awareness of being a second-class citizen, however, living in the shadow of the *dix familles*[7] who represented the power of the old colonial structure, must have left some kind of mark, but it did not significantly alter the well-entrenched realities of day-to-day life, school, sports, adolescent discoveries, and familiar landmarks.

The first significant break occurred at the beginning of the Second World War with the Pétain-supported landing of Admiral Robert and the ten thousand troops under his command. The local youth viewed this prestigious fleet with great admiration, and it soon became their only topic of conversation as they strolled up and down the Boulevard Savane.[8] There was talk that the fleet included not only the *Émile Bertin* but also the *Béarn*, an aircraft carrier, and, especially, the *Surcouf*, reputed to be the "largest submarine in the world."[9] The departure from Brest had been a measure to protect the national fleet from the German invasion, and the word on the Boulevard was that all of the gold of France was on board those ships. What's more, the fleet had managed to slip through the net of American controls at a time when the popularity of the United States was at a low ebb in the Antilles. After an obligatory call to port in New York, the admiral had set sail secretly and under cover of night for the French Antilles. The feat became the object of great pride among the young men, but before long, they were taken aback by the overt racism and contempt expressed by the sailors who displayed the expected disdain of white men toward indigenous populations, augmented by the arrogant behavior of occupying forces in occupied territory.

This unabashed racism was compounded by severe food shortages and the discrepancy between how these were experienced by the soldiers and by the general population. The Antilles, as had also been the case in North Africa between 1939 and 1942, had been cut loose by the metropolis and forced into overnight self-sufficiency. Salt had to be manufactured, oil extracted from coconuts, and the diet consisted almost entirely of manioc meal and bananas from Guadeloupe. Meat was out of the question for the civilian population, and the little that could be had was reserved at exorbitant prices for the white soldiers of the French fleet. People speak of how they had to bury their dead wrapped in sheets, not the custom among Christians, because wood was in such short supply that caskets had become unthinkable. Furthermore, the manner in which the French soldiers and petty officers swooped down on the local women, destabilizing familial, communal, and romantic attachments in the process, cannot be underestimated.

It was around this time that young Martinicans began to opt for *l'entrée en dissidence*[10] and to travel north to Borne Rouge or south to Saint Lucia or to the British Caribbean and Dominica in order to join the anti-Nazi struggle.

Manville, whose father had died and whose seven siblings were all girls, had promised his mother he would not leave. Fanon, on the other hand, barely eighteen at the time, chose *l'entrée en dissidence*, and in January 1943, he picked his brother's wedding day to make his getaway. He simply ducked out while the meal was being served.[11] He had already prepared the two bolts of cloth, stolen from his father's closet, that he planned to sell in order to meet the smugglers' asking fee.[12] There were many who organized these clandestine crossings to Dominica, enriching themselves in the process. Fanon eventually reached his destination and spent the subsequent three months being initiated into an entirely different kind of education.

His departure coincided with a popular uprising against Admiral Robert. Henri Tourtet, the Gaullist commander of a land army composed primarily of Antillean troops, backed the revolt. The Pétainist Robert was forced to withdraw, to abandon his position or turn his weapons on the crowd.[13]

In compliance with the laws of occupation, Charles de Gaulle appointed a new general to the post. At the same time, Tourtet was organizing a new battalion; Battalion 5 as it was called included mobilized troops from Martinique, Guadeloupe, and Guyana as well as civilian volunteers who joined the Free French Army. Shortly upon returning from Dominica, Fanon joined up as well.

Césaire, who was still teaching at the high school, had already published *Cahiers du retour au pays natal* in 1939 and was trying to revive interest in *Tropiques*, the journal that had been banned in 1943 by Admiral Robert. He and his colleagues at the school were less than thrilled to see their students joining the ranks of Battalion 5. This was not their war, they reasoned, and "blacks had nothing to lose and everything to gain when white people took into their heads to kill one another." Fanon's response was loud and clear: "whenever human dignity and freedom are at stake, it involves us, whether we be black, white or yellow. And whenever these are threatened in any corner of the earth, I will fight them to the end."[14]

Éléonore Fanon, concerned about her son, sought out Manville to ask him to keep an eye on his young friend. Fanon, as Manville related later, was hardly the kind one could keep an eye on. For Fanon, this period marked the beginning of a long series of disjunctions between prized ideals and prosaic realities, between the human dignity he invoked as a universal value and the institutionalized segregation and racist practices that had become his daily fare. The other volunteers in the battalion came from a wide range of social backgrounds. Many were from the elite, the scions of well-known families who had graduated from the Lycée Schœlcher. But the sons of fishermen and sugarcane workers had also joined up. All were united in their desire to fight Hitler and liberate European nations that had been crushed in the name of racial superiority.

Disappointment quickly set in. The young men had expected March 12, 1944, the day on which they were to set sail, to be a day of pomp and military honors and family leave-takings. The truth was an altogether different matter. The men were taken on board the *Oregon* in the dead of night, stowed away like fugitives or lepers, most of them sent down into the hold. The incongruity of the situation was not lost on these young men who had set out to fight for freedom; and the shadow, distant but real nonetheless, of slavery and the slave transports weighed heavily over them as they set off on their journey. That first dawn out at sea, Fanon emerged on the deck and, shouting at the top of his lungs, cried out: "They should have named this ship the *Banfora*."

After putting into port once in Bermuda, the troops docked in Casablanca. Even though the inherent pleasures of the crossing itself and the first glimpses of the Moroccan city had done much to awaken the senses and generally raise spirits, more disappointment soon followed. The troops stationed at first in the vicinity of Casablanca and later in Guercif formed a genuine Tower of Babel. The men from the old colonies (the Antilles) were assigned to the same group as the European volunteers; sub-Saharan African soldiers were grouped with the Senegalese infantry; there were also the *tabors*, most of them Moroccans from that country's mountainous regions; the Algerian infantry; French fighters from North Africa; and finally, French deserters. The international makeup notwithstanding, there was an extremely rigid hierarchy in place in which the Senegalese infantrymen found themselves consigned to the bottom of the heap. This hierarchy was reflected in every last detail, down to the distribution and quality of the tents that housed the soldiers. The Antilleans qualified as *European*, and unlike their African comrades, whose headgear was the *chéchia*, they wore the *calot*. And pity the man who returned to camp minus his headgear; the color of his skin determined just how brutally he would be dispatched with kicks to the backside in the general direction of his tent. Fanon and Manville, both, had occasion to sample this medicine.

Fanon, Manville, and Mauzole had the audacity to complain about the dismal state of affairs during the inspection tour of a delegate of Guyanan origin who had been assigned by de Gaulle to the Algerian Consultative Assembly. Their daring won them the label of *intellectuals*, and the three soon found themselves on their way to Bougie where they would attend cadet school.[15] Bougie was the first stop in a long journey that would culminate in the liberation of France. It was also the stage of Fanon's first encounter with Algeria and the Algerians.

Fanon was incensed to discover that the local population was picking through the leftovers that were left for waste outside the barracks. When well-meaning friends advised him not to meddle, his admonishment to them was that "human dignity was at stake." In June 1944, the cadets were transferred from Bougie to Oran and its outlying areas in preparation for their crossing to France. Their contact with the local population during this period was insignificant, but this brief passage through a North Africa that was simultaneously revealed to them and concealed from them by the filter of the army left a lasting impression on all of them.

Their journey proceeded according to the well-known itinerary of the Free French Forces or, rather, of the Second Division B that had set out from North Africa. Fanon and his friends were among those who disembarked at Saint-Tropez, and they stayed a few days in the region guarding abandoned farmhouses. Fanon was stationed at the house of Paul Bourget, who, along with everyone else in the area, had vacated the premises.[16] Fanon spent all his time in Bourget's library, perusing not only the books but also their various dedications and adding his own signed remarks to their end papers.

Before long, the troops were on the move again.

Fanon, together with his two companions, was assigned to the unit that marched up the *route Napoléon*. In the Doubs region, near Montbéliard, they ran into enemy forces and Fanon was wounded in the fighting that ensued. He received treatment for a back wound, but he was so intent on being reunited with his battalion that he cut his hospital stay short. In 1945, in compliance with an operation dubbed the "whitewashing of the Free French Forces," men from the colonies, darker skinned as a rule, were not being stationed in the North. Fanon and seven of his Antillean comrades, however, were among the few who were sent North, to Colmar or the "Colmar pocket" as it was known. They all took part in the Battle of Alsace. The Allies needed proof that French troops had indeed taken part in the liberation of France. Aside from the extreme conditions of the battle, Fanon and his companions also had to withstand the bitter northern cold. Fanon's state of mind at the time is evident in a letter he wrote to his parents during this period. If he were to die, he writes, it would not have been in the service of a noble cause. "A year has elapsed since I left Fort-de-France. Whatever for I wonder? To defend an ideal that is obsolete [. . .]. I am having second thoughts about everything, even about myself. If I were to never return, if you hear one day that I died fighting the enemy, comfort yourselves in any way you can, but do not say that I died defending an honorable cause [. . .]; because we must not expect enlightenment from this false ideology, this shield wielded by laymen and stupid politicians. *I was mistaken.* There is nothing here, absolutely nothing to justify my speedy decision to anoint myself as the defender of a farmer's rights, when the farmer, himself, does not care a damn about those rights. [. . .] I have volunteered to take part in a dangerous mission. Tomorrow, we set out. I know I will not be coming back."[17] The character traits that would distinguish Fanon for the duration of his short life were already in evidence in this heretofore unpublished letter. Above and beyond the tragic sense of life and death that inhabited every facet of his existence, there is also his vacillation, his constant back and forth between a disillusionment in humankind and his inability to lose faith in it entirely, to stop loving it; between his suspicion of politicians and his readiness to join the causes they promote despite those suspicions; between uttering the "no" of what we would call civil disobedience today and the "yes" that paves the way of human bonds.

At the end of April 1945, the three men were sent back to Toulon. It was in this city and in relative isolation, that the three men partook in the May 8 celebrations. The women of Toulon were rushing the American soldiers off their feet, but the notion of dancing with a man from the Antilles, war hero or not, never seems to have crossed their minds. Despite the medals and promotions that were conferred on them, all three felt they had been carelessly dismissed by both the army and the civilian population. The war was over. Manville never overcame the feeling of abandonment they had experienced, and Fanon never spoke openly about what had been a painful experience. But it marked him nonetheless: he had fought in a war for racial equality and human brotherhood only to find himself isolated, ignored, the object of contempt even. In the eyes of the high command, the volunteers from the tropics had become superfluous, and arrangements to repatriate them had to be made posthaste. The volunteers could not have agreed more; they, too, wanted to go home. Le Havre was not operational, the men had to travel to Rouen in order to board ships that were headed to the Antilles. During the initial leg of the journey, they spent a memorable day at the dilapidated Château du Chapitre, where they were hosted by an important local family that had expressed a wish to meet these young soldiers who had ventured so far from home to defend a cause that need not have concerned them. War-weary and by all accounts bitter, the men were grateful for the hospitality, and Fanon purportedly spent the entire evening quietly stroking the golden head of a small boy who belonged to the household.

The guests had been handpicked for the occasion. Only the sons of respectable families, well brought-up young men who would soon be attending university, had made the guest list. The other Antillean soldiers were not deemed suitable to dine at the table of such a fine Rouen home. This tailored guest list did not escape the notice of their host Mr. Lemonier, who wanted to know if there had been any fishermen, sugarcane laborers, or unemployed men who had joined up as well.

The journey home on the *San-Mateo*, a cargo ship that had been hastily transformed to transport the colonial army, was long and arduous. They spent more than twenty-five days at sea crowded into unhygienic quarters, with their diet consisting almost entirely of crackers left over from the provisions that had been supplied to the French army in 1940. They were hungry, especially for the foods of home they had not tasted in such a long while, and the moment they set foot on land, they were off in search of their favorite meal.

Fanon's friends were so amused by the pomp with which he requested his dish of *dachin* that they christened him *Dachin* on the spot and the nickname would stick for years.[18] The civilian as well as the military authority responded to this homecoming with utter indifference. Many years later, Manville was still smarting from the pain of this cool reception. Aside from a few oblique remarks about this episode in his early writings, Fanon never revisited it in his later works or spoke about it openly at any time. When a direct question was put to him about his war injuries, he would simply ignore it, or, if he happened to be in a playful mood, say that they were the one thing he and General Salan had in common.

Fanon, as his letter home attests, was disappointed to have taken part in the war, but his opposition to Nazism never wavered and the culture of the Resistance pervaded the whole of his life. "I was mistaken," he had written in that letter, and the overwhelming sense is of a profound misunderstanding. Here was a young man, after all, who had foregone everything, including his studies, to fight against an intolerable doctrine that advanced the extermination of human beings in the name of racial superiority. Yet from beginning to end, his war experience had been fraught with ethnic discrimination and petty nationalisms. He never spoke openly about this disillusionment, but his subsequent writings, especially *Peau noire, masques blancs* and *Africains Antillais* are inflected by the lessons he learned on the European front. The experience had also changed him physically, making him seem mature beyond his years. Later, in Algiers, the interns he supervised were, for the most part, a mere three or four years his juniors, but he was generally perceived as belonging to an older generation. For Jacques Azoulay, Fanon's first intern at the psychiatric hospital in Blida, the perception still lingers to this day.[19]

But let us return to 1945 and to Fanon's homecoming in Fort-de-France. His friends Manville and Mauzole, who already had their baccalaureates in hand, were planning to turn around and head straight back to Paris, where they planned to attend university. Fanon studied and sat for his examinations, which he passed. During this period, he attended classes taught by Aimé Césaire, and in an effort to emulate his teacher, he tried his hand at poetry, but his efforts were never published. He also established a Martinican youth group, and his involvement with this project became the topic of a lecture he delivered at Sainte-Marie. Both he and his brother Joby supported Aimé Césaire in his bid for deputy, but when it came to distributing leaflets or making political speeches, Fanon proved an ineffectual campaigner. His style was of an altogether different sort. His great admiration for Césaire notwithstanding, Fanon did not share the latter's support for the assimilation of Martinique and Guadeloupe as "Departments" of France represented by delegates to the French National Assembly. In time, the political gap between the two men became even greater, but Fanon's love for Césaire the poet never waned.

Fanon, like a countless number of his peers both in Martinique and Algeria, felt suffocated by the narrow-mindedness and stasis of the society to which he belonged; taking Manville and Mauzole's lead, he was soon making arrangements to return to France to attend university. In fact, the decision was a foregone conclusion as there were no universities in Martinique at the time. In 1945, Fanon left Fort-de-France and headed for the Metropolis.

Both Manville and Mauzole had settled in Paris; students from abroad—the "colonial subjects" as they were referred to—had moved in great numbers into the defunct bordellos that lined the Rue Blondel.[20] This arrangement was not at all to Fanon's liking; he wished for something of an altogether different kind and wanted "to see something else"—as he would invariably express it in what was to become one of his signature phrases, even later, in Algeria. Apparently he even told Manville that "there are too many Negroes in Paris, I want something more milky." Joke? Half-truth? Many years later, he told me the real reason had been his wish to attend the courses Maurice Merleau-Ponty was teaching in Lyon at the time. In truth, Fanon did not have much choice in the matter; the scholarships that had been earmarked for medical students from the Antilles were restricted to campuses in the eastern region of the country or in Lyon. Was Fanon yet again rewriting the past? There is little doubt that Fanon did not relish the thought of joining the largely black student community on Rue Blondel or of becoming entangled in the unending Stalinist/Trotskyist debate that was raging in the Antillean community. He wanted to go it alone and experience his encounter with French society on his own separate terms. "The less we see of each other, the better we behave," Fanon would often say in Creole to the friends whom he still visited on a regular basis, at least during the first year. Fanon settled in Lyon.

Fanon's years at university have been reconstructed and documented in great detail by his biographers. The best account by far is Jacques Postel's.[21] Postel, who had spent his junior year as a classmate of Fanon's, has the advantage of having experienced the university and psychiatric environments of Lyon in the 1950s first-hand. The other biographers simply are not conversant with the realities of French society in the late 1940s or with the great odds people had to overcome in order to study psychiatry in France at the time.

In 1946, Fanon, despite Mauzole's insistence that he pursue a degree in oral surgery—advice he completely and utterly ignored—enrolled at the medical school in Lyon. His medical studies did not entirely distract him from his study of literature and, especially, philosophy. He also enrolled in the Philosophy Department at the School of Liberal Arts. He attended courses taught by Merleau-Ponty and by André Leroi-Gourhan. His interests ran to ethnology, phenomenology, and Marxism, but existentialism and psychoanalysis took top billing. Fanon was an avid reader with wide-ranging reading habits: Lévi-Strauss, Mauss, Heidegger, Hegel, as well as Lenin and the young Marx. Among the books he had borrowed from the Rue Blondel, he discovered the works of Leon Trotsky, but he put off reading *Capital* and never got around to reading it in the end. In Paris he formed relationships with people who had deep political commitments and who helped pique his interest in Marxist methodology, but he never developed a need for clear-cut political affiliations and with the Communist Party least of all. He was especially drawn to psychoanalytical works and to Sartre's philosophy of the subject. He read Freud as well as the handful of works by Jacques Lacan that were available at the time. His numerous references to the "mirror stage" and the "family complex" in *Peau noire, masques blancs* attest to the influence of these readings. He also liked to read poetry, but to the dismay of his wife-to-be, who was a literature student at the time, he had almost no taste for fiction. His penchant for the lyric stayed with him for the whole of his life, though he made an important exception for the novels of Richard Wright, whose works he found immensely interesting. He also tried his hand at dramatic writing and is responsible for a number of unfinished works as well as two completed plays: *Les Mains parallèles* and *L'Oeil se noie*.[22] Many years later, in the 1980s, Josie Fanon revealed how he had sent the earlier play to Jean-Louis Barrault to no avail. The play, a philosophical meditation, is essentially a discussion of the idea of "action"—an idea that was very much *of the moment* and at the center of both Camus' *Caligula* and Sartre's *Main sales*. The very titles of Fanon's works reveal an intention to anchor thought and action in the body and the senses. In the course of his peripatetic life, that was never as unsettled as during the years he was in Algeria and Tunis, the plays were lost and have never resurfaced. It was also during this period that he wrote for *Tam-Tam*, a journal ostensibly addressed to students from the colonies but which also had a wider audience among supporters of anticolonial movements—people with similar political preoccupations who shopped for their books in the same bookstores.

Fanon did not present himself for the examinations that would have qualified him as a resident, or nonresident as the case may be, in medicine; the preparation such an exam entailed was not foremost on his mind and paled in comparison with his other preoccupations. But psychiatry was something else again, and his interest in the discipline had taken a serious turn by his fourth year of medical school. Psychiatric medicine at the time, in the 1950s, was taught at the Grange-Blanche Hospital by Professor Dechaume. Dechaume was interested solely in psychosurgery, and he viewed things through a neuropsychiatric lens that attributed all psychiatric conditions to organic origins—every symptom had a corresponding therapeutic drug and confinement was a given in any and all therapies. Despite what must have been profound differences, Fanon managed to complete his training with Dechaume before joining the staff at Saint-Ylie in Dole as a temporary intern. After a brief trip to the Antilles, to which we shall return later in greater detail, Fanon returned to France and to a position at Saint-Alban, where he would work with François Tosquelles.[23] The years he had spent working with Dechaume led to the writing of "Le Syndrome nord-africain," one of his earliest publications.[24]

This article, unlike much that was being written at the time, is not a clinical account of a specifically North African pathology. It is, rather, an extraordinary meditation on the rejection and objectification of the other, who is known by the various names of *bicot, bougnole, raton, melon* (all terms of contempt). Fanon exposed the French medical system's racism and dismissal of North Africans who came into its establishments to report their pain. These patients, he argued, *were* their pain and incapable of functioning in a linguistic register that exacts specificity. The physician, whose confidence is precisely bolstered by this specificity, expects the patient to relate a specific symptom, but the patient's suffering follows from his exiled condition as "a man who dies anew every day, living in a feeling of total insecurity, threatened emotionally, and isolated socially," excluded from the agora, deprived of the right to a real existence. The North African worker, cut off from both his origins and his goals, is turned into an object, a thing that has been tossed out into the great mayhem. This text reveals how, above and beyond the expected linguistic barriers, the physician of the Metropolis fails to perceive the ways in which this other has been reduced to the status of an object, and how he fails, as a physician, to set aside irritation, disdain, and hostility in favor of greater openness and genuine receptivity. The essay was as shocking as it was pioneering, and the ideas it sets forth have retained an uncanny applicability to this day. In psychiatric circles, such as the one presided over by Professor Dechaume as well as in other clinics in which

Fanon had served as an intern, these ideas were, needless to say, completely opaque. In a decision that would strike us as surprising today, Fanon did not even attempt to take the entrance exam that would have permitted him to join the staff at Vinatier; a tenure at this most prestigious of Lyon's psychiatric establishments would have entirely compensated for the lacunae in his academic training.[25] Instead, he chose to pursue his training with Dechaume and to hold on to his temporary position at Saint-Ylie in Dole, where he was the only intern for a population of 500 patients. Under the direction of the then-director, Doctor Madeleine Humbert, the experience seems to have been both unhappy and stormy.[26] Shortly after returning from Dole, he submitted his thesis to Dechaume: it was the manuscript of *Peau noire, masques blancs,* and it caused quite a scandal. Dechaume, not unsurprisingly, judged the manuscript unacceptable, and Fanon, on the advice of a lecturer, decided to submit an altogether different and indisputably academic project on Friedreich's ataxia—a hereditary syndrome associated with the degeneration of the spinal cord and perhaps the cerebellum.[27] This is how, in 1951, Fanon obtained his degree as a doctor of medicine well on his way to becoming a psychiatrist.

Fanon's academic career is more or less familiar to everyone. Less is known, however, about how he may have spent his time in Lyon as a twenty-two-year-old with twenty-two-year-old preoccupations or how he experienced French society and felt his marginality as a black man in that society. Even his closest Antillean friends, his war comrades in Paris, were not in the know. Fanon's closeness to them, already undermined by distance, was tried even further by his growing interest in psychiatry. His stays at the Rue Blondel were now increasingly few and far between, and on one of his rare visits, he surprised them by interfering with their attempt to rescue a small child who was having trouble maneuvering one of the notoriously steep staircases that are so characteristic of the buildings that housed those old bordellos. "Allow him to experience it for himself," he advised the young and frantic parents. While this may be a stock phrase in this day and age of generalized psycho-pedagogical knowledge, when even Doctor Spock counsels parents to encourage infants to explore the world, such an attitude was unheard of at the time. Manville did not have the faintest clue that his friend "Dachin" was working on the manuscript of *Peau noire, masques blancs,* and he, together with the others, knew close to nothing about Fanon's personal life. While Fanon spent time with some members of the Association of Black Students in France, his closer ties were to his classmates, the students in his group at the medical school, particularly those who also attended courses in the humanities. He spent quite a bit of time at "Les Nouveautés," the bookstore on Place Bellecour, that was the meeting place of the young, and not so young, who aligned themselves with leftist positions. He took part in a number of demonstrations against colonial occupation. In his classes, he would make the acquaintance of Georges Counillon and of another young man; he would cross paths with both of them again, in 1953, at the psychiatric hospital in Blida, Algeria. By then Counillon was an intern in psychiatric medicine—later, he joined the Algerian *maquis* and was killed in action. The other young man was schizophrenic and had been hospitalized in a neighboring pavilion in the same hospital.

If it is indeed true, as Manville claims, that "Fanon was interested in women," that chapter in his life has remained a closed book, especially as a number of people who were close to him refuse to revisit those times, and such accounts as are available are generally highly subjective and impossible to confirm. What is known for certain is that Fanon met both women, the one who gave birth to his daughter as well as his wife-to-be, in the normal come and go of campus life, in classes, at student demonstrations, and on evening outings to the theatre. In 1948, he became a father to the daughter whom he acknowledged as his child as soon as news of her birth in another provincial town reached him, but he never married the woman who was her mother. He did, however, marry the other woman—Josie to the world and Marie-Josèphe Dublé on her birth certificate—the one he had met on the steps outside the theatre shortly after his arrival in Lyon. Josie was the woman everyone would meet later in Blida, together with the newborn Olivier. The memory of those steps outside the theater was evoked by Fanon in one of his last letters to Josie, sent to her shortly before she left to be at her husband's bedside in the hospital in the United States where he died.

Fanon's ties to his family never wavered, even in the face of the turmoil of his doubts and expectations or in the heat of new encounters, nascent militancy, and the hard work that typified his student days. He had an especially soft spot for his sister, one of the few women who trusted him, or so he said, who was also studying in France at the time. His letters to his mother, though infrequent, were affectionate and extremely well written. Fanon never broke with his family; he simply followed a separate path.

In 1951, after defending his thesis, Fanon accepted a temporary position as a substitute physician at Colson, in the Antilles. The experience proved disappointing, and he returned to France complaining of the close-mindedness and lack of awareness he found there. The pursuit of Antillean autonomy was a thing of the past by then. There were a few, the Guadeloupean poet and militant Albert Béville, for example, who continued to point out the manifestly colonial nature of France's relationship to the Islands.[28] But Martinique had, by and large, acquiesced to the *Départmentaliste* position that had been embraced by Césaire. Fanon still harbored the hope, though he had little faith in the prospect, that change in the Antilles was still possible. When he returned to France, he summarized his experience as one in which he had "met more trousers than men."[29]

Soon after this Martinican detour, Fanon joined the staff at Saint-Alban and began his apprenticeship with Tosquelles. In the superb eulogy he delivered in 1975, the latter spoke of Fanon's decision to go to Saint-Alban as a move toward *a somewhere*, toward a locus that functioned as both a crossroads and an anchor in Fanon's personal journey.[30]

Fanon spent upward of fifteen months on Tosquelles's team. In the process, he would become a disciple of this Spanish psychiatrist who also happened to be an immigrant and an anti-Franquist. Fanon unhesitatingly acknowledged Tosquelles as his mentor, while stressing that theirs was a relationship of difference not consensus. His admiration and affection for his teacher were apparent in the stories he told later in Blida in which his impatience as a disciple, his quickness to differ, his exacting nature as an interlocutor as well as his complete commitment to the project figured prominently. Tosquelles's version, as related in the 1975 eulogy, concurs, and the impression is that Fanon's impact at Saint-Alban greatly outweighs the actual duration of his brief tenure there: "He never really left us; he continued to be present in our memory in the same way he had filled the space around him. He questioned his interlocutors with his body and his voice." He did so not to subject them to a sterile polemic, a round of jousting from which only one would emerge victorious, but in order to engage them. "His mere presence could engage the critical faculties of others, and his acute sense of fraternity allowed him to convey his lucid grasp of difference as a given. As for the suspicious nature that some have qualified as paranoid," Tosquelles continued, "I think it had more to do with a kind of extreme vigilance in the face of any and all normative and reductive discourse."[31] The character traits Tosquelles remembered twenty-five years after the fact are invoked time and again by all who knew Fanon as a young adult. The intense presence of his voice and body, the sustained and demanding attention he showed others, the heightened sensibility he brought to language—the way he worked it and allowed it to work him, to draw him into the most farfetched fictions and to draw him out and onto new ground that held the promise of less improbable ends: these were ever-present traits, recognizable to all those who had known Fanon. Later, when it was my turn to know him, these traits were still glaringly intact.

Returning to the period spent at Saint-Alban, however, we must ask what attraction this psychiatric institution, situated in the Lozère in the foothills of the Massif central and at a significant remove from industrial civilization, consumer society, and the bright lights of urban intellectual life, could have possibly held for Fanon? Nostalgia for a lost paradise was certainly not the motivating factor. Fanon found the place welcoming, especially in light of his previous experiences as a psychiatric intern. Under Tosquelles's direction, Saint-Alban had become an important research hub where the then popular somatic methods were used in combination with institutional psychiatry. The aim was not to muzzle madness but to question and listen to it in order to create the conditions for new structures. The method at Saint-Alban, very new at the time, was premised on a communal arrangement in which sane and the insane lived together as caregivers and boarders inside an institutional framework; the institution, itself, provided a model for the playing out of scenes that had either gone badly or not at all the first time around. Madness was probed in light of its close tie to social and/or cultural alienation. The psychiatric institution was itself subject to inquiry and evaluation, and before work of any consequence could be undertaken, the institution had to be rid of its own alienation and transformed into a space in which the sick and the well could develop appropriate models together. The approach, unlike any he had encountered with Dechaume or during his term at Dole, appealed to Fanon because it allowed for the perusal of mental illness in all its registers by highlighting the nodes between the somatic and the mental and the historical and the structural. Didactic psychoanalysis—as it was then called—was another matter, however, and Fanon, unlike his mentor and most of his colleagues at the time, chose to not take part in it.[32] Years later, in Tunis, Fanon went to some lengths to explain his reluctance, claiming that, in theory, he was no longer opposed to the approach. While at Saint-Alban, however, he had been unable to convince himself of the validity of this approach. Tosquelles, again in 1975, wrote that "Fanon had not resorted to didactic psychoanalysis to cure his normopathy."[33] Fanon, he explained, was engaged in a relentless and agonic relationship to language, and whatever he may have experienced as overwhelming would invariably declare itself where it could be challenged and taken up by language and expressed as a constant refrain.

Years later, Fanon explained his reticence toward psychoanalysis as it was practiced at the time as stemming from what he perceived as its failure to account for the relationship between personal history and history writ large. Psychoanalysis, he argued, disregarded history's "organizing line of force" and the ensuing repercussion on the individual psyche, as well as on the unconscious, when it was destroyed or eradicated.[34] Even though the idea, still an intuition at the time, had not yet achieved its full and clear expression, it already bespoke a certain truth. In *L'Envers de la psychanalyse*, a seminar he delivered in 1969, Lacan described his inability, while treating a number of African patients in the 1950s, to identify any of the constitutive referents of their particular histories. "Their subconscious was not that of their child-hood memories, these had been simply juxtaposed; they were experiencing their childhoods retroactively, taking their cues from our (French) cate-gories of the family. This was the subconscious they had been sold together with the laws of colonial rule."[35] The idea that a master discourse, colonial in this instance, could shape the constitution of the individual subjective un-conscious is of paramount importance to the entire body of work that has been attributed to Fanon, and it is central to his psychiatric as well as his po-litical thoughts on alienation. This idea, although still in a fledgling state to be sure, first appeared in *Peau noire, masques blancs*, the book Fanon was working on at the time. In the late 1950s, during one of those rare afore-mentioned moments of candor, Fanon, on more than one occasion, would say: "When all this is over (by which he meant the Algerian War), I will go into analysis," and he heartily advised at least two of his colleagues to do as much should events ever allow it. And later, when the time and place were right, that is exactly what they did; an undertaking of the kind would have been unthinkable in Tunis during those years.

At Saint-Alban, in 1952, Fanon implemented techniques that are, by and large, associated with sociotherapy. In 1953, he presented the paper he had co-authored with Tosquelles at the Congrès de psychiatrie et de neurologie de langue française.[36] During the same period, Tosquelles served as Fanon's director of studies for the Médicat des Hôpitaux Psychiatriques, the exam that would certify him to practice in public psychiatric institutions. In June 1953, a few months after *Peau noire, masques blancs* had been published by Seuil with a preface by Francis Jeanson, Fanon passed his exams, and on June 2, 1953, he officially joined the ranks of France's psychiatric health system.

While a great number of Fanon's fellow graduates that year have re-mained in the psychiatric profession, they did not so much as mention his death a few years later in their specialized publications. Yet, Fanon had al-ways been their colleague in the truest sense of the word. His political and writing life did not distract from his search for ways in which state-run psy-chiatric services could be improved. Manville reports that it was Fanon's wish to return to Martinique, his recent and disappointing posting there notwithstanding, and he would have if there had been a job available.[37] Manville also hastens to add that Fanon's candidacy for such a job would not have garnered the support of local administrative authorities. Their early and implicit disapproval would, at a latter date, become an official prohibi-tion, barring Fanon from the island. Are we to surmise, therefore, that the French administration in Martinique, unlike its counterpart in Algeria, was familiar with Fanon's writings? Fanon's next step was to look into the possi-bility of a posting in Dakar, where a medical team was in the process of being assembled. He addressed himself directly to Léopold Sédar Senghor;

the two had belonged to the same black intellectual and artistic circles in France.[38]

In the meantime, by September 1953, Fanon was asked to step in as the interim head physician at the Pontorson hospital/hospice in La Manche. Later, Fanon, with customary verve, would remember this episode and his encounter with the physician whom he had come to replace. He recalls a cowering doctor, taking cover behind a barricade of books that had been strategically arranged on the desk. This image would become emblematic of Fanon's singularly unrewarding experience at Pontorson. Fanon, who was unflappable in so many ways, had a difficult time understanding the fear of madness that is the secret bane of so many psychiatrists. *Crazy people*, as they were then called, simply did not frighten him. This did not mean that he was partisan to a more archaic and fundamentalist view that seeks to redress the wretchedness of the mentally ill and their abandonment by God with pity and compassion. Fanon, in point of fact, could be very demanding, often impatient and, at times, even intrusive in his interactions with the mentally ill. He did, after all, prize their dignity as men and women above all else and wanted to hold them to it.

Fanon saw the asylum as an arena in which he could implement the methods he had been taught by Tosquelles. He wanted to shake up the system, to give the patients a voice. He bent many an ear to this end, and his reputation as a revolutionary in the field, which persists to this day, was established in the process. There was one incident in particular that struck him as emblematic of the senselessness that characterized the institution. Fanon had signed a pass permitting twenty-nine patients to go on a supervised outing in order to perform a number of errands at the weekly farmers' market. The hospital's administrative director, who did not quite see things in the same way, refused to add his signature to Fanon's, thereby bringing the hospital to a standstill. It was a common practice for hospital/hospices of this kind to use their patient populations as a supplementary workforce to help run their boiler rooms and laundry and kitchen facilities. Even though the ensuing strike was short-lived, emotions ran high, and a new, and permanently appointed, head physician was swiftly dispatched to take over the helm at Pontorson.

Fanon's letter to Senghor went unanswered. A new position had just been created at the hospital in Blida-Joinville, however. Fanon submitted an application, and on October 22, 1953, he secured the position which fell under the jurisdiction of Algeria's gouverneur général. He was expected to report for duty on November 23.

Fanon was not displeased at the prospect of working in North Africa, and he looked forward to the many unknowns that came with this new turn of events. Some have claimed that Fanon's decision to accept the newly created post at Blida had been a last ditch effort borne of desperation. These claims, however, do not tally with what we know about Fanon's professional and political inclinations. This is not to say that Fanon would not have welcomed a chance to launch his career as an institutional psychiatrist in France; still, his first choice had been the possibility of a position in Dakar. Senegal, he thought, provided an opportunity both to practice psychiatry and to continue his study of societies in which the modern and the traditional exist side-by-side. His intuition was, as it turned out, a sound one, and a number of years later the psychiatric team directed by Doctor Henri Collomb demonstrated as much. In the 1960s, this team set out to show how psychiatry in Africa had to pay particular attention to the ways in which intersecting modern and traditional elements were expressed.[39]

Fanon had, since his university years, already been involved in the anticolonial struggle; he belonged to the inner circle at *Présence africaine*, and he had been a close and attentive reader of the many issues *Temps modernes* had devoted to the colonial situation. While these activities do not exactly qualify him as an activist of the same stripe as some of his early companions who joined the Parti communiste (PC) or the Mouvement contre le Racisme, l'Anti-sémitisme et pour la Paix (MRAP) to express their opposition to the war in Indochina, they do signal his concern and commitment. He had, lest we forget, already authored two works on racism and colonialism that would, in time, become seminal: "The North African Syndrome" had been published in *Esprit*; more important, *Peau noire, masques blancs* had been published at Editions du Seuil on the recommendation of one of its senior editors, Francis Jeanson. On reading the manuscript, Jeanson promptly wrote Fanon requesting a meeting. Both men recall that first encounter as a stormy affair: Jeanson recalls the tense and touchy young man who turned up at his office that day; he had barely started praising the work when Fanon cut him off with a "not bad for a Nigger!" Jeanson, both angered and hurt by the barb, wasted no time in showing Fanon the door, thereby gaining Fanon's immediate respect.[40] After this disastrous first encounter, work on the manuscript progressed smoothly with Fanon agreeing to Jeanson's suggestion of *Peau noire, masques blancs* as the title for the book. The work's original title had been *Essai sur la désaliénation du Noir*, and Fanon's acquiescence to the new title was due in part to his extremely busy schedule at the time. He was hard at work on the thesis that would secure him a medical degree, and his exchanges with Seuil about finding a "more commercial" title were casual at best.[41]

Peau noire, masques blancs was written in Lyon between 1951 and 1952, the crucial year that encloses a triple junction of encounters and experiences. First, there was psychiatry, a discipline Fanon believed was equal to the task of freeing hobbled subjectivities and would become his chosen vocation. Fanon had wished to submit *Peau noire, masques blancs* as his doctoral thesis, and while such a proposition is easier to envision in present-day academic culture, even now, it would hardly qualify as the norm. Then, there was his discovery of phenomenology, existentialism, and psychoanalysis and the influence these schools of thought had on his early work. Finally, there was his encounter with an overwhelmingly white French society and the way in which he assimilated this experience, both in the army and during his years in Lyon, as a black man and a minority.

During the years in Algeria, Fanon did not speak much about this work or its publication. Was it already, in 1955, a mere three years after its publication, a closed chapter in his life? A phase in his personal and professional history that now belonged in the public domain and that he had simply left behind him? On closer reflection, Fanon, at least in 1955, did not seem to attach much importance or express a particular regard for this work. It is true that at the time every aspect of daily life was entirely in the shadow of the events that were unfolding in Algerian politics. The colonial situation was compounded by violence, the objective of which was Algeria's independence. To those who were caught up in the daily fray of this reality, this book, as well as the debate it had spawned, were in all likelihood mistakenly dismissed as obsolete.

There are some today who view the work as juvenile, and there is little doubt that its conceptual framework is somewhat dated, especially with respect to psychoanalysis. That said, it remains a fact that from the moment of its publication in 1952, the work was revolutionary in both form and content as Jeanson so rightly pointed out in his preface. Albert Memmi's *Portrait of the Colonizer and the Colonized*, a work that was subsequently frequently compared to *Peau noire, masques blancs*, did not appear until 1957.

Insofar as questions about blackness figured at all in the discourse of the early 1950s, their discussion, as Jean Daniel has shown, was the purview of a white intelligentsia.[42] While the world of ideas could contemplate such a debate, this same world was deeply unsettled when a black man took it upon himself to enter the discussion.

Peau noire, masques blancs has been an object of special scrutiny among Fanon biographers. There have been countless studies in a great many languages devoted to it; it is not my intention to add to that list here. I simply want to underscore the way in which the radically innovative approach of this work fell outside the bounds of the rational debates of the day.

Fanon's preoccupation answers to two absolute values that exist in a permanent and mutual tension. While he did not wish to diminish the importance of political and economic factors, Fanon's main aim in this work was to communicate black subjectivity in the context of an overwhelmingly white society that takes its supremacy for granted. Fanon wanted to reach beyond ideas in order to instill an awareness in his reader of the most incommunicable aspect of this condition. Fanon's analysis of this subjective experience relies on sociological, political, and psychoanalytic elements to provide an analysis that accounts for the condition while simultaneously trying to surpass it, for black and white alike.

What is this condition we speak of? Specifically, it refers to the Antillean man, the black man from the colony in France but also in the colony, who finds himself caught up from the moment of his birth in a white world that functions both as the rule of law and the frame of reference. This white world rules and exists as the sole referent, not only in political and economic terms but in all other registers as well: linguistic, cultural, mythical, while supplying the values that constitute the subject from the moment he enters the world.

Fanon launches his work with a discussion of the Master's language, French in this case, and the colonized's problematic and alienating relationship to the colonizer's language. "To speak a language is to take on a world and its culture [. . .] and the Antillean who wishes to be white will have a far easier time imagining himself as such once he has made that cultural tool which is language his own." The experience of finding oneself trapped in the Master's dominant and exclusive language was one that was deeply shared by Algerians of Fanon's generation. A number of Francophone Algerians—Malek Haddad, Kateb Yacine, and countless others—bear witness to this dilemma. To these we should also add those "strange Algerian fellows" Albert Camus and Jacques Derrida, who have also addressed this experience and the effects it has had on their person, and, more significantly, on their thinking and writing lives.[43]

By the same token, Fanon also writes about the impasse of resorting to totalizing identities—entirely white, entirely black. The impulse to acknowledge a black world that excludes all others and mirrors the alienating self-identification of the white one, the choice of allying oneself to the idea of negritude is a trap. In his conclusion to the book, Fanon writes:

> I as a man of color do not have the right to seek to know in what respect my race is superior or inferior to another race. I as a man of color do not have the right to hope that in the white man there will be a crystallization of guilt toward the past of my race. . . . There is no Negro mission; there is no white burden. . . . The Negro is not. Any more than the white man. Both must turn their backs on the inhuman voices which were those of their respective ancestors in order that authentic communication be possible.[44]

Fanon formulated these thoughts at a time when the idea of *négritude* was being fervently debated, especially at *Présence africaine*, where opinion was divided between those who championed *négritude* as a recuperation of identity and others, Sartre among them, who saw it as a transitional measure, as a means and not at all an end.[45]

A similar double imperative operates throughout the work and all of the major themes this book touches on can be understood in this double register—the choices in love, relationships to the opposite sex, the deadlock of self-identifications that define an individual human consciousness.

Attempts to summarize this essay, to outline its major themes, manage only to dilute its impact and muffle the power of its last words: "My final prayer: O my body, make of me always a man who questions!" The profound singularity of this work, its subject matter notwithstanding, arises from the writing itself. Its originality follows from its urgency to convey an experience by going one-on-one with words. In a letter to Jeanson, Fanon spoke of his wish to go beyond ideas in order to express some part of an experience that the reader would never know firsthand; the connection he sought to establish with this imagined reader is best described as an irrational one.[46] Fanon wished to go beyond meaning, to write inside the sensory dimension of language in order to give rise to a new way of thinking that would depend on something more than conceptual jockeying.

Josie remembers that she took dictation while Fanon, pacing back and forth in the manner of an orator, composed the first draft of this work that is underscored by the rhythm of a body in motion and the cadences of the breathing voice. With the exception perhaps of "Racisme et culture," all of Fanon's books were written in this way, and even if he did revise them at some later stage, they all began as spoken works, works that were communicated to an interlocutor—preferably a close and trusted one.

Peau noire, masques blancs created an immediate stir and the critical response, the positive as well as the scathing, was uniformly passionate. Despite the overwhelmingly leftist views of French intellectuals at the time, French society was not quite ready for this book. The idea of black writers expressing their discontent in poems or novels was just beginning to take root—even if the label of "exotic literature" was still being affixed to these works, and as Jean Daniel puts it, the preference still ran to Gide's *Voyage au Congo* and not to René Maran, Mayotte Capeccia, or even Léopold Senghor and Césaire. But the fact of an analytic book that sought to penetrate the very heart of racism, particularly of the black/white variety, triggered a baffled, even indignant, reception. The progressive Christian publications were a general exception to the rule, but in every other quarter, regardless of political affiliation, this book was a thorn. The arguments against it were, of course, as various as the players. The Right saw *Peau noire, masques blancs* as a call to racial hatred and its author, who was advised to seek psychiatric help, as subject to the very pathology he described inside its pages. The Left invoked the principles of equality and fraternity to dismiss Fanon's argument, writing, for example, that "The recognition of Blacks as human beings is a longstanding one." The Communists argued that an insistence on the existential experience of racism was both archaic and dangerous. Léonard Sainville, who had just received the 1952 Prix des Antilles for his novel *Dominique, nègre esclave*, wrote in *Lettres françaises* that Fanon

> turns away from those Blacks, intellectuals and working men, who for a long time now have resolved their complexes of racial origin not through the transference of their neuroses, but by simply becoming aware of the range of social complexities in its entirety and by having the will to become part of a general transformation thereby integrating racial ignominy into the whole of the social context; nor does he want to acknowledge those less than insignificant sectors of the white working class, all those strata of intellectual and blue collar workers, who refuse point blank to fall into the trap of racist stupidity and distorting myths for the exact same reasons as the former. All these well-adjusted members of the French nation, of the white race, understand perfectly well that the Black, Jewish, or Yellow problem is one and the same as the problem of the society as a whole and that the only way to remedy it is with the implementation of a new regime. This is where the solution lies. And Fanon has turned his back on it.[47]

Peau noire, masques blancs, disturbing though it may have been given the ideas that prevailed at the time of its publication, was quietly selling, not in great numbers but steadily. By the time of the second 1965 edition and the 1971 paperback, it had become a seminal work, a classic.[48] The world had changed by then. The colonies were gone, racism had not; it had, if anything, become more impassioned, and the book that Fanon had written as a young man became known as a prophetic essay on racism.

Even though Fanon was generally reticent about his life and the events that had occurred prior to the writing of this book, he made an exception when it came to his debate with Octave Mannoni. The dispute with Mannoni had a lasting effect on Fanon, and I had occasion to hear him speak of it.

The impact of Mannoni's *Psychologie de la colonization* (*Prospero and Caliban: The Psychology of Colonization*), a work that had been published in 1950—two years prior to *Peau noire, masques blancs*—was underestimated and overlooked even by such close readers of Fanon as Jeanson. Fanon not only set aside an entire chapter to respond to this work, but his entire book is mined with references to Mannoni, whom he respected and whose work he had followed with interest. But Fanon was disappointed, devastated to put it bluntly, by many of the positions that Mannoni advanced in his latest book.

Octave Mannoni, who later became an important French psychoanalyst, had spent more than twenty years in Madagascar, where he had been posted first as a philosophy teacher and later as the head of Information Services. During his years in Madagascar, he became interested in anthropology. In 1945, Mannoni took a sabbatical from a job that was increasingly in conflict with his anticolonial views and went to Paris where he entered analysis. In 1947, he interrupted his analysis and returned to Tanarive for a brief stay that, as it so happened, coincided with the Malagasy rebellion. It was during this back and forth between Tanarive and Paris and in the hiatus that occurred in the early stages of his analysis that Mannoni started to write his essay on the psychological profile of the colonizer and the colonized, the colonialist and the autochthonous inhabitants of the island of Madagascar.

Mannoni, who unwittingly adopted an ethnopsychiatric approach, advanced the idea of two distinct "models" of personality. The Malagasy personality, he argued, is characterized by a dependency complex toward any figure who is perceived as an ancestor or an ancestor by proxy. Relationships that fall into this category are essentially conflict-free. The European colonist, on the other hand, is characterized by traits that predate the colonial situation, namely an inferiority complex carried over from childhood that the adult tries to compensate for accompanied by a desire for a private, uninhabited world that drives him, like Crusoe or Prospero, to search out a desert island. The colony, he continues, is that desert island—a space where drives and repressed fantasies can be projected. Mannoni draws a distinction between the colonizer, whom he sees in a kinder light as an explorer and a pioneer who genuinely believes in his civilizing project, and the colonial settler, as though the first had nothing to do with second. The white "model" and the native one are brought into direct contact by the colonial situation. The white man who arrives as a stranger in the midst of natives is perceived as pertaining to the same realm as the one occupied by dead ancestors. Insofar as the white man is able to fulfill his part in maintaining the culture of dependency, his newly acquired status as an ancestor casts him as a protector.[49] But this scenario is eroded by the colonial situation, where the superiority complex of European settlers and Europeans born on colonial soil is deeply entrenched and not necessarily a way of compensating for feelings of inferiority. Consequently, the idea of the colony as a place of pure projection where others count for nothing is reinforced. The white man's failure to live up to his role as protector in a society that is defined by its dependency complex gives rise to widespread insecurity; for some Malagasies, this societal malaise results in the replacement of the dependency complex by a complex of inferiority.

French works on psychopathology were rare at the time, and psychoanalytic works that sought to conceptualize the individual outcome for victims of collective psychological traumas even more so. And this, especially the latter, was what interested Fanon; like any student embarking on new research, he read the available literature for evidence to support intuition. While Mannoni's work may have had other aims, Fanon respected it for its attempts at understanding the psychologies of colonialism and racism. It is difficult to imagine how Mannoni's project could have escaped Fanon's interest; earlier pieces by Mannoni published in journals such as *Psyché* had already caught Fanon's attention. Mannoni, who was far from oblivious to the political dimension, especially as it applied to "overseas lands" as they used to be called, was interested in exploring a psychopathological approach that would be more nuanced than the ones that relied exclusively on the relationship between economic powers or socioeconomic groups. He and Fanon had been essentially engaged in the same project, but in 1950 there was a parting of the ways, and Fanon found himself unable to subscribe to the theses that Mannoni was advancing.

Fanon's critique accurately reflected the extent of his disappointment; it was passionate, violent, no doubt partial, but also honest and innovative. The faults of Mannoni's work were many. He accused Mannoni of viewing the Malagasy situation through a white expert's gaze that took refuge behind the claims of universal knowledge and consequently failed to identify with the object of its contemplation. He faulted him for his total misreading of the colonial situation—a situation that entails a radical change for the colonized subject and that carries with it his utter negation by the colonizer. He concluded by pointing out Mannoni's failure to emphasize the colonized's desire for liberation, thereby underplaying the centrality of this desire. While conceding that Mannoni does refer to the desire for liberation, he faulted him for doing so in an indirect and dismissive way: the outrage of the Europeans on realizing that the Malagasies are real people who are willing to negotiate for their freedom reveals their inability to acknowledge this "desire for liberation." But the observation is made very much in passing and does not reflect the overall tenor of the book. The very idea that the desire for freedom could be anything but central was unthinkable for Fanon, and he was particularly disturbed by the gaze that was brought to bear on colonial society in general and on Malagasy society in particular.

There is little doubt that *Psychologie de la colonisation* is also an astute analysis of the mechanisms of racism, especially as these apply to the "petit blanc"—the colonial settler who is convinced of his superiority and who re-sorts to authoritarianism and violence to shore up his belief that he belongs to a biologically superior race and is driven by a simultaneous need to negate and scapegoat the other, whom he turns into an object onto which to project forbidden fantasies of a predominantly violent sexual nature. One should also credit Mannoni for briefly raising a rather prescient question about the psychological and sociological readiness for democracy in soci-eties whose structures have been bolstered by complex and traditional belief systems.

Fanon's criticism drew attention to issues that have remained pertinent to this day. "Mr. Mannoni," he protests, "has not tried to feel himself into the despair of the man of color confronting the white man" (BSWM, 86). In the name of universal knowledge, Fanon writes, Mannoni views the Malagasy with an ethnographer's gaze that enables him to bandy about terms such as *dependency complex* and to advance the "passage from the dependency com-plex to the inferiority complex" as a mode of entry into European civiliza-tion. What is worse is the aptitude he attributes to this "dependent person-ality," its desire to be colonized: "Wherever Europeans have founded colonies of the time we are considering, it can safely be said that their com-ing was unconsciously expected—even desired—by the future subject peo-ples" (Prospero and Caliban, 86).

Fanon cannot abide the fact that Mannoni would advance such a proposi-tion and insist on it, writing: "Not all peoples can be colonized: only those who experience this need" (P&C, 85) He is, at the same time, surprised by Mannoni's inability to read into traditions of interaction with the other who, despite being a stranger, is extended a friendly welcome and treated to a cu-rious interest—seen as a stranger but also as a guest. This tradition has a very long history and continues to be very widespread. Fanon is especially incensed by the litany of psychological categories that masks the failure to note the degree to which the colonial situation is a situation of radical and irreversible damage.

> What we wanted from Mr. Mannoni was an explanation of the colonial sit-uation. He notably overlooked providing it. After having sealed the Mala-gasy into his own customs, after having evolved a unilateral analysis of his view of the world, after having described the Malagasy within a closed cir-cle, after having noted that the Malagasy has a dependency relation toward his ancestors—a strong tribal characteristic—Mr. Mannoni, in defiance of all objectivity, applies his conclusions to a bilateral totality—deliberately ignoring the fact that, since Galliéni, the Malagasy has ceased to exist. (BSWM, 94)

What Mannoni fails to perceive is that "the Malagasy alone no longer exists; he has forgotten that the Malagasy exists *with the European*. The arrival of the white man in Madagascar shattered not only its horizons but its psychological mechanisms. As everyone has pointed out, alterity for the black man is not the black but the white man" (BSWM, 97). In Mannoni's book, however, alterity for the white man is always another white man, never a black man. The black man is only a space of projection. And it is this alienating asymmetry that Fanon proposes to break in *Black Skin, White Masks*.

Mannoni failed to pay sufficient attention to the denial of otherness and to the consequences of that denial, especially as these relate to the colonial psychology that is his subject. The European is the only point of reference in Mannoni's account of the sought-after world, without others, where drives, including the drive to dominate, are given a free rein. Mannoni does not consider the possibility that this other could be the Malagasy, the native, the indigenous inhabitant; it is understood that the Malagasy as other does not exist. There is no one there. The black man not only wishes for some heaven-sent universal law as acknowledgement of his humanity; he also wants to be acknowledged by virtue of his difference, a difference that cannot be dismissed because it bears the mark of history, including the history of domination.

The world of the Malagasy other is negated and that is the peculiarity of the colonial structure. Mannoni, Fanon stresses, is doubly wrong because he underestimates the racism of the colonial structure, and, especially, because he fails to perceive that all parties, metropolitans as well as colonials, the absent as well as the present, are equal partners in this venture.

The other for Mannoni, at the time he was writing this book, was basically the European other. Speaking from the position of the Malagasy other was patently out of the question. Given the impossibility of this identification, which, incidentally, Mannoni genuinely believes can be surmounted, the Mannoni who was writing in the 1950s spoke and wrote from a Western model and from his own subjective experience as a white man in a colonial situation, a fact to which he alludes perhaps too discreetly. Despite his anti-colonialist views, Mannoni, by his own admission, reflexively identifies and participates in the latent identity that defines the other by pointing him out and assigning him to an ethnopsychological category that is entirely dependent on outward indices. This perception, moreover, is based on the presumption of universal categories that bypass singularity.

In light of the prevailing political climate of the day, Fanon was dismayed by the way in which psychology and psychoanalysis had been introduced, despite Mannoni's good intentions, as a new form of expert legitimization. Fanon took great issue with approaches that used psychology to exploitative ends. He, too, was trying to find a way of expressing the situation, of making it readable, and he did not wish to see the tools of his trade, tools to which he expected to resort, serving ideological ends, instead of being used for the advancement of our understanding of human beings and their freedom.

Fanon's response to Mannoni's book may have been brash and impassioned; he was, after all, twenty-five when he wrote it, but it was not mistaken. Mannoni probably did not intend his book to play into the hands of the colonial project, but given the mood of the day, the book's message was unacceptable. It did not grant colonized peoples the respect to which they are entitled, and it did not foster any dialogue of substance between the Malagasies and the representatives of the French nation. It must be acknowledged that it was a youthful and easy to misunderstand work by an author who was struggling with his "own position as a White man in a colonial situation."[50] Written in an awkward prose, it presents psychological as well as sociological concepts that are often contradictory, lacking in rigor, and naive to the point of confusing the registers of desperation with those of culpability.[51] The tone of the book is largely responsible for giving the impression that the author, regardless of what he may have intended, is writing from a position of complicity with the dominant society—he is the observing anthropologist, the Parisian man of letters for whom civilization is Western by definition.

Later, Mannoni spoke quite openly about all this. When the book was published in an English language edition as *Prospero and Caliban: The Psychology of Colonization*, Mannoni acknowledged the book's inadequacies, its failure to consider difference and the unfortunate choice of terms like dependency. While we are on the subject, why did he settle on this term in the first place? In the English-language edition, he attributes the choice to the fact that he was in the early stages of analysis. The implication is that he projected his own dependent relationship onto his field of study. But "transference" in psychoanalysis is not the same thing as dependence; the dependence associated with "transference" is temporary and related to childhood. It manifests itself in the context of a sudden regression: the analysand is momentarily a child but at the same time also an adult. "Transference," moreover, attributes feelings to an unknown and neutral other. It is difficult to imagine how a colonizer, or even a colonial administrator could fill the shoes of this unknown and neutral other, this independent and well-disposed individual who is receptive to an arrangement of temporary dependence.

One more thing: the terms dependence and independence share a close linguistic connection. Independence was the word that was in the air in those days, hovering as something muffled, repressed, unbelievable. To speak of independent colonies was not an easy thing and imagining them in actuality was even more daunting, even for someone like Mannoni who admitted as much in 1966. Almost twenty years after the publication of his book and of *Black Skin, White Masks*, and more than five years after Fanon's death, Mannoni, who had become a well-known psychoanalyst in the interim, wrote an article on *Psychologie de la colonization* that was published in the journal *Race*, bearing the title "The Decolonization of Myself." In this article, he turns the criticism that was leveled at his book upon publication against himself: he admits to a distanced view that highlights the Malagasies' otherness; to an unwieldy conceptual approach borrowed from contradictory psychoanalytic theories; and last, he concedes that he may have unconsciously portrayed himself as more conservative than he in fact was and that while he wished for the end of colonialism, at least in the form that he had experienced it, he also found it hard to contemplate the idea. He concludes by further implicating himself when he critiques universalizing ideologies for perpetuating a form of self-colonization and abolishing difference—the difference that is the footing on which life must proceed, the difference that Fanon viewed as a necessary station in the pursuit of universal goals. But Fanon was gone by then, and he never did find out about his impact on Mannoni. We can, however, speculate as to whether Mannoni's brand of ethnopsychoanalysis may have had something to do with Fanon's reticence to undergo analysis.[52] The debate has not been laid to rest even though its protagonists have. The traits that Mannoni attributed to colonial racism continue to be present in France today, at the very heart of the Hexagon.

Fanon's vehement response to Mannoni places the stress on the radical acculturation that the colonial situation imposes. In so doing, Fanon demonstrates that he is really at odds with the culturalists with whom he is often grouped.[53] In fact, *Prospero and Caliban* is a far better example of culturalism than *Black Skin, White Masks*. Culturalism, a movement that originated primarily in the United States, places the onus on cultural diversity and difference, even going so far as to distinguish between mentalities, to answer its questions about humankind. Difference, in the hands of the culturalists, is posited as a challenge to the universalism that informs the great systems of Western knowledge. Fanon, on the other hand, views culture as a point of temporal and spatial reference that is also a conduit to the universal; moreover, his insistence on the way one culture can radically alter another clearly sets him apart from the culturalists. This idea may be only an intuition in *Black Skin, White Masks*, but it becomes more fully fleshed in later works.

In his sociotherapeutic work at Blida-Joinville, Fanon, as we shall see later, became increasingly convinced that psychopathological expression is grounded in cultural forms; to provide his patients with structures that would be relevant to their daily reality, he made it a priority to become familiar with a culture about which he knew little at the time. This experience was one of the subjects of *L'An V de la révolution algérienne* (Tunis, 1959). In that book, he argued that culture cannot be mistaken for bred-in-the-bone tradition; rather, it is inscribed in everyday behaviors, and as these behaviors unfold and new situations arise, culture is continually being defined and redefined. In the debate that took place between Fanon and Mannoni in the 1950s, it is apparent even in hindsight, that of the two, it was Mannoni who was more aligned with the culturalist position and its eighteenth-century appetites for the exotic. Fanon, on the other hand, comes across as very much a child of the times.

When this controversy occurred, Fanon was already a practicing psychiatrist and had firsthand knowledge of the direct interaction with the suffering body and alienated self of another human being. Mannoni had yet to encounter this daily confrontation with the cries and sufferings of the embattled psyche.

Fanon was a helpless believer in humankind. He believed that human beings, provided that they were in possession of language and of their own history as subjects, could progress from difference to the universal. His later involvement with the political is a logical, if strangely contemporary, outcome of this initial premise. When we consider the evolution of his thought, the idea of his affiliation to culturalism appears all the more remote; culturalism does not interest itself in the alteration of cultures, the different ways of entering into modernity, or with the political dimension.

Fanon's association to culturalism was, if anything, too tenuous, if we are to believe his Algerian contemporaries or the retrospective critique of those who, at one time, had been his fellow militants. "He was too universal," they said, as though they wished to distinguish themselves from him in what was fast becoming the age of insular identities. "He underestimated our Arab and Muslim mentality," they added, and "he did not know our ways, our ancestral traditions, our religion."

Fanon never directed his students to culturalist works. We never heard him mention Gardiner, the theorist of culturalism, and he could not abide Margaret Mead, who belonged to the same tradition. He was, on the other hand, very interested in Alfred Adler, Helene Deutsch, and fascinated by Wilhelm Reich, the Austrian Reich, about whom he would say, with bemusement and genuine concern, "what could have befallen that man in the United States to make him come up with the theory of the Orgone? A biophysical byproduct of the libido that manifests itself as a form of vital energy in the cosmos!" And then, he would spell it out: "What did the United States *do* to that man to drive him to Orgone theory, and especially, to the invention of the Orgone Accumulator?" Fanon was interested in Reich's study of the mass psychology of fascism; he thought that Reich's theory on the effects of social repression on the evolution of human instinct was a valuable one, but he was totally baffled by the work that this Austrian Jew carried out after he had to immigrate to the United States in 1939.[54] Reich's later work rested on the "natural and metaphysical" idea of an atemporal and mechanically generated vital force that he called the "Orgone."

When Fanon arrived in Algeria, very few, if any, of the people there were aware of his past as a fighter and thinker on racism, and Fanon was not given to talking about himself or his past, even to those who worked with him on a daily basis. Jacques Azoulay, who was his first intern, reported, forty years after the fact, that he was entirely unaware of Fanon's history.[55] Azoulay was so uninformed, in fact, as to assume that the only revolution Fanon was interested in was the one in psychiatry, and he never considered the possibility of a past that may have predated Fanon's exploits at Saint-Alban. Which is not to say that interns who came on board later were better informed; none of them had read "Le Syndrome nord africain" or *Peau noire, masques blancs.* Whatever they may have heard about the debate surrounding *Psychologie de la colonisation* was much too vague to involve them in any significant manner.

Fanon was perceived primarily as a psychiatrist, an institutional psychiatrist to be specific, and the qualification was not an irrelevant one. The idea of a private practice seems to have never crossed his mind. The specialists in North Africa who were working out of offices and private clinics at the time were, for the most part, intent on turning their nosologic and descriptive knowledge into financial gain. The psychiatrists who did practice in the asylums and institutions, at a time when the trend in drug-based treatments had not yet occurred, were primarily practitioners of "descriptive psychiatry." A new movement was beginning to take shape in the immediate aftermath of World War II, however. Openly leftist and left-leaning psychiatrists were responsible for a new approach that focused on the asylum itself as an alienated and alienating institution.[56] First we must treat the asylum, they argued, reinvest it with the humanity that it and the patients it ostensibly protects have been denied. The work of dis-alienation became, when seen from this perspective, a collective effort that involved the doctor-patient binome. The mentally ill patient was released from simply being an object of contemplation, a butterfly pinned to the blackboard of classical nosology and became a subject in his/her own liberation; and the doctor ceased to be a demiurge-know-it-all and was reinstated as a human being and equal partner in the fight for freedom, "his hand and his voice always ready and extended toward the other and that other's pain."[57]

These were the ideas and this was the training that Fanon brought with him to Algeria, where ideas of this kind could not have found a more anti-thetical society and psychiatric community. Despite his previous wartime sojourn there, he really did not know much at all about the country and the society he was about to encounter.

Algiers, 1953

Fanon arrives in French Algeria where he learns firsthand about engrained European racism, the glass wall of partition, the singularity of the Jewish minority, and the political, economic, and cultural oppression of colonized Algerians. Algeria is not France.

When Fanon arrived in Algeria in 1953, he set foot in territory considered French since 1830; a corner of France, as the popular claim went, older than Savoy or Nice. The three departments of France that constituted Algeria at the time were a pure fiction that never succeeded in masking that this was a colonized territory. It took the recently arrived Fanon very little time to understand that Algeria had, in fact, never been French. One needed only to look at the demographic makeup—more than 90 percent of the population was not European. At the end of the 1940s, Algeria's population was slightly above ten million. The Europeans, not yet designated as *pieds-noirs* at the time, were about a million strong and the product of the various and successive migrations of French, Spanish, Maltese, Italian (and Corsican, as Ferhat Abbas bitingly noted).[1] There were also 30,000 Jews, indigenous for the most part: they were the descendants of ancient Phoenician, Palestinian, and Roman migrations or of the autochthonous Berber communities that had converted to Judaism before the Arab conquest or of communities that had sought refuge in Algeria after being ousted from Spain in 1492. Rightly or wrongly, they were classified as European by virtue of their political status.[2] The close to nine million remaining inhabitants constituted what was generally and vaguely designated

38

as the Arab population—the fact that some were Arabized Berbers while others were not was never taken into account. The Arab designation did not consider linguistic differences or social stratification or even the degree to which some had assimilated to French culture—so completely as to obviate the very notion of a dual cultural identity; they were Arabs for no other reason than that they happened to be Muslims who did not hold French citizenship. These nine million, with very few exceptions, made up what was known as the *deuxième collège.*

The political status of these peculiar "French departments" had nothing to do with the Fourth Republic, despite the very new "Algerian Assembly" that had been instituted in 1947. This latest body, amended to the traditional deliberative institutions, borrowed the principle of the two colleges and perpetuated, as a result, the masquerade of universal suffrage. Half of the Assembly was elected by Europeans and those Jews who were French citizens,[3] while the other half was selected by the so-called indigenous population: one European ballot was equal to nine Muslim votes. Moreover, executive command in the person of the *gouverneur général* was designated by the French State. Even from the point of view of the institutions of governance and despite the claim that figured as a daily mantra, "Algeria was, in fact, not France."

This masquerade was acknowledged and shored up by political practice: the same administration that was responsible for overseeing the fairness and legality of elections regularly tampered with election results. The practices of stuffing ballot boxes prior to the official opening of polls or of electrical outages at the closing of polls, timed to serve as cover for the switching of ballot boxes, were commonplace. In fact, they were the rule. The protestations of the scrutineers, both Muslim and European, were never heeded, and those who complained were often threatened or harassed. Charles Géronimi[4] recalls how

> on the occasion of the first elections of the Algerian Assembly in 1948, a friend of the family who was a radical-socialist and well-regarded in the small community of Mitidja, shared his worries with us on the occasion of a visit to our home: "It's a disaster," he reported, "the Arabs will all vote for the separatists,"—no one referred to them as nationalists in European circles—"their half of the Assembly will vote unanimously and we can always count on a couple of Communists in the French half, so we may as well pack our bags."

At the time, the nationalist candidates of the *deuxième collège* were handily winning the primary elections, which, exceptionally, had been run more or less on the up and up. Their victory in the second round was widely thought to be a matter of course. But when the final results were announced, there wasn't a single nationalist candidate among the winners—in some cases, the electoral voices had plummeted from a solid 50 percent to 0 percent. On the following day, Algerian Radio and the printed press reported with unflinching arrogance that the Muslim electorate had come to its senses before the second round of elections and not succumbed to the "siren call of the Communist-separatists, thus demonstrating to the world their attachment to the French motherland." No one in Algeria was fooled, the French least of all. The handful of calls for more democratic proceedings were lost in the general clamor of the European community that followed the lead of one of our provincial notables and congratulated itself on the fine trick it had pulled on the Arabs. "It was well organized," he crowed,

> we managed to distract the attention of the MTLD[5] scrutineer and switched the ballot box with another one that had been carefully stuffed in the right way and that looked exactly like the original—they both bore the same strategic ink stain. You should have seen the expression on the face of those *melons* when it came time to count the votes. Our worries are over.[6]

The same tactic was repeated from polling station to polling station, giving rise to the expression "Algerian-style elections," always fraudulent during colonial times and the only form of democratic election that anyone bothered to transmit to the Algerians.

It goes without saying that these political injustices were deeply entrenched in the day-to-day of Algeria in the 1950s. The society had for a long time been structured and compartmentalized, almost branded into its three major components: Europeans, Jews, and natives, which is to say Christians, Jews, and Muslims. These religious markers were the best expression of the inner boundaries, impalpable at times, the present albeit invisible walls of glass around which the society was organized. The only real exchange between these three groups was economic, and even this was carried out on the basis of extreme inequality. At the social and political level, the divisions were airtight. Marriages were almost exclusively endogamous, mixed marriages almost unheard of, and those that did occur were, at least in the 1950s, always rife with family tensions.

In the colonial society of the day, partition was a non-negotiable fact. The word "community" held no resonance whatsoever and adherence to one's identity by birth was held to be a self-evident truth, as natural as breathing; the violence of these tacit rules was as entrenched and oblivious to itself as any drive. The partition was implacable, its barriers unspeakable, beyond formulation. The cultural hierarchy mirrored the political one: the French language and culture, dominant and frequently exclusive, came first. The other languages, namely Arabic and Tamazight, the cultural and historical referents of nine-tenths of the population were marginalized, not to say excluded. In the face of this disdain, the predominant cultures could either persist in a semiclandestine fashion or assimilate.

In May 1945, when high school students in Algiers, who had been equipped with little flags and urged to take part in the "victory" celebrations, wanted to find out more about the "events"[7] that were rumored to be taking place not even 300 kilometers away, they were stopped in their tracks and silenced. Despite the prohibition, the "events" in question would be of major political significance. Students who chose to write about the great and beautiful ruin of the Mansourah Fortress in the Tlemcen region instead of some hypothetical and distant chateau in Chenonceaux when asked to "discuss a historical site that has affected you in a profound way" did so with the trepidation of sinners and transgressors. Even when transmission, of both the good and the bad, may have been the rule at home, in public people put up a rigid facade that did not stray from the identity they had been assigned.

In both Algiers and Blida, the two cities Fanon came to know well during his three years in Algeria, these separations were physically inscribed in the urban topography. In the 1950s, Algiers was a midsized city, and even though it was the cornerstone of the colony, it hardly qualified as a metropolis.[8] The city, in those days, slightly overflowed the hills that flanked the bay and the port to the west. At the foot of the hills, two large horizontal thoroughfares served as conduits for the creaking streetcars; trolley buses operated on the hillsides. In the new town center, hemmed in by the main post office and the Boulevard Victor Hugo, the European community congregated in its cafes, comfortable cinemas, and fine shops. The hills were home to the "right kind of people." The avant-garde architecture promoted by the *gouvernement général* housed and signified colonial power. The old colonial neighborhoods—Place du Gouvernement, Square Bresson, Rue Bab-Azoun, the Rovigo and Vallée inclines—were already in disrepair. The European working class lived in Bab-el-Oued and Belcourt.

Algerians rarely ventured outside the three areas in which they were concentrated: the rundown and overpopulated Casbah was still home to some of the oldest families as well as to migrants from the interior and to the marginalized and the dispossessed; immigrants from other places lived in the "petite Casbah" that abutted Belcourt; and, finally, there were the vast slums, groaning with misery, that cropped up in the interstices between established neighborhoods: Cité Mahieddine, El Kettar, Fontaine Fraîche, on the slopes of the Femme Sauvage ravine, Clos Salembier, the hills of Hussein Dey—it was in these places without public works or services of any kind that the rural poor came to settle. There was not, strictly speaking, a clear demarcation between the European city and the Muslim one; instead, there were different neighborhoods and a keen awareness of boundaries felt by everyone. Though the segregation was not official, Algerians, unless their jobs required it, rarely ventured into the European areas. They made a point of not lingering unnecessarily, passing through like furtive shadows before a piercing gaze that did not see them. Algerian women would venture into the European neighborhoods only if they absolutely had to, always taking care to go there veiled. Young Algerians were virtually unseen on the Rue Michelet where young Europeans of both sexes spent hour after hour strolling or sitting at the terraces of the brasseries that lined the street. The bars of Bab-el-Oued and Belcourt where anisette was served with portions of *kémia* were also off limits. The quasi-totality of Europeans, both the young and not so young, never set foot in the Casbah and never "saw" the slums. These were the very slums, however, where a bond of sorts began to emerge between young French and Algerian men and women who came together to try and address some of the health and social problems that plagued these communities. This movement laid the groundwork for the associations that some years later contacted Fanon and provided him entry to the struggle for Algeria's liberation.

In the vicinity of the Place du Gouvernement, where a statue of the Duke d'Orléans reigned over the plaza, there were a handful of transitional spaces: the steps that led down to the port and the fisheries, and behind these, the Casbah and the old Jewish quarter in the Place de la Lyre. In the normal comings and goings of daily life, this was a difficult area to circumvent; it functioned as an unavoidable intersection—a crossroads where different social sectors crossed paths but did not necessarily meet. This is where the Archdiocese stood alongside the superb edifice that in 1941 housed the Jewish Lycée, also attended by a handful of Muslim students. In a strategic move, it was also the home of the headquarters of the various nationalist organizations: the Democratic Union of the Algerian Manifesto (UDMA), established in 1946 and whose most prominent figure was Ferhat Abbas; the Movement for the Triumph of Democratic Freedom (MTLD), the main nationalist party that evolved out of the Algerian Peoples Party (PPA);[9] the offices of the newspaper *Algérie libre;* the headquarters of the Algerian Muslim Scouts (SMA), almost single-handedly responsible for providing education to Algeria's youth. Those who lived in the fine neighborhoods beyond the central Post Office or in certain areas of Bab-el-Oued had little or no reason to venture into this part of town.[10] At the beginning of his stay in Algeria and until he became aware of the different elements that constituted the Algerian nationalist movement, Fanon had little opportunity or cause to visit this crossroads. His first encounters in Algiers took place in the more upscale parts of town; in those early days, he met only members of the European and Jewish communities.

The "European community" was by and large stereotypically colonial, racist toward Arabs and Jews, and conservative. André Mandouze, a Latinist and Saint Augustine scholar who arrived in Algeria in 1946 to join the University faculty and was also the editor-in-chief of *Témoignage chrétien* and a lifelong militant, captures this European society perfectly when he reports in his memoir that its hero was not de Gaulle but Pétain and relates how the chaplain of the Catholic Student Association (ASSO) impassively informed him on the occasion of their first meeting that when it came to Arabs, the machine gun was a far superior tool to the word. Racist is an understatement; this European enclave simply viewed the world as divided between Europeans and all the rest, with Arabs at the very bottom of the hierarchy. An Algerian proverb put the matter this way: "the French spit on the Spanish who spit on the Italians who spit on the Maltese who spit on the Jews who spit on the Arabs who spit on the Blacks." North African racism toward blacks was quite well entrenched. Fanon would feel the brunt of it, even though he did his best to avoid the subject; he felt it most sharply in Tunisia, where the behaviors and attitudes of his psychiatric colleagues at Manouba were particularly shocking.

The European community was racist from top to bottom, regardless of sociocultural background. The following exchange between a pair of school teachers, entrusted to teach civics and convey moral values in a public and secular institution, serves as an apt illustration: "a transfer from Boufarik to Orléansville wouldn't be so bad, at least your kids won't have to go to school with little Jews." "Yes, but there'll be plenty of Spaniards—not exactly what I'd call a great improvement."[11] Or, the reaction of a future doctor of psychiatry, who on reading the roster for the incoming class at Algiers' Medical School, "Benmiloud, Benghezel, Benaïssa, Chibane, Aït Challal, Boudjellal," exclaimed, "we are being invaded by Arabs. To say nothing of the Jews, who consider themselves at home everywhere and anywhere they please."[12]

The recent arrivals, the "metropolitans," were taken aback at first, but they soon realized that unless they were willing to lead completely marginalized lives they had little choice but to accommodate the norms the society imposed. A handful tried to stand their ground, but the majority, including university professors and psychiatrists as well as bureaucrats working for the *gouvernement général*, succumbed. The Algerian French, who considered themselves more French than the French, did not hide their contempt for the French from France, the *Frankaouis* as they called them, and social friction between the two groups was not uncommon at the beginning. Were not these the same so-called French who had fled the Germans in 1940, while our brave infantry valiantly fought them off? The reasoning among Algerian Europeans was that "we were the ones who liberated them in 1944, we were the ones in de Lattre de Tassigny's army. They don't understand the first thing about the Algerian problem." This claim generally failed to mention that this brave infantry was almost entirely made up of indigenous Algerian Muslims, or that Algerian Jewish resistance fighters played a major part in the preparation of the November 8, 1942, U.S. landing that stopped the German advance.

The racism was habitual; it was unperturbed, understood, and viewed as entirely natural. As far as the Europeans were concerned, the attitude arose out of common sense: "The Muslims are not like us," they would say, and, without missing a beat, and in absolute good faith, "but we love them all the same, and we are good to them. Aren't we good to you, Fatma?" And if a bewildered *Frankaoui* asked them, "but why do you invariably address them in the familiar form?" they would answer that "Arabic does not distinguish between formal and familiar forms." Anyone who took the trouble to know the Algerians even slightly would soon realize that Arabs who spoke French were perfectly aware of the distinction between the polite "vous" and the condescending "tu," and that when these Arabs happened to relate a conversation they had had with their spouse or their parents, the "vous" form was the usual mode of address.

The university, which under normal circumstances would have been Fanon's port of call, was not exempt from this unacknowledged racism. In early March 1956, the European community was up in arms and had recently mobilized against Professor André Mandouze for speaking out on his anticolonial views. The European students, with very few exceptions, had formed a common front to successfully oust him from the classroom and strip him of teaching privileges. In the aftermath of this event, the following conversation took place between a professor who held a chair in philosophy and a student: "How can anyone claim that there is racism in Algeria?" the indignant professor wanted to know. "There are no racists in Algeria!" To which the student replied, "But Sir, I've met many." "Well then," the professor dismissed him, "you must be mixing with the wrong people!"[13]

This racist climate, in its paternalistic as well as in its more aggressive forms, made it all but impossible for Europeans and Algerians to have meaningful relationships. A handful of institutions tried to promote intercommunal exchange, "Amitiés franco-musulmanes" and the "Cercle franco-musulman," for example, but these were official forums that served the prominent and the powerful, who were the foregone "accomplices in the exploitation of the colonial situation." A more authentic bond between the two communities, insofar as such a bond existed, was more likely to grow out of relationships that were formed in the context of social and political movements: within the ranks of the various parties—especially the Algerian Communist Party (PCA); in the offices of the various newspapers—especially at *Alger républicain*; in a number of associations with links to the PCA; and, most of all, in the unions.[14] Increasingly, after 1951, there were also youth movements that rebelled against the unspoken segregation and launched a dialogue and started to cooperate on a number of projects. Emerging in succession, these were the Association of Algerian Youth for Social Action (AJAAS), *Consciences maghribines* (a small militant journal), whose Muslim and European editors went to great lengths to spread the word about Algerian realities,[15] and, at a later date, Amitiés algeriénnes. These movements played a key role in introducing Fanon to the Algerian cause; it was through them that he made his most important contacts and formed his most important attachments. These attachments would prove to have a far greater impact on him than those he formed with more militant hardliners associated to the PCA or inside the framework of the unions, a fact that did not diminish his unwavering respect for unions or compromise his support for the union that operated inside the hospital where he worked.

Attempts at cultural rapprochement were another feature of this period. After 1948, little remained of L'École d'Alger, the pre-War Algerian literary movement that had included writers of "Muslim origin." But even though the movement had more or less become a thing of the past, the friendships and relationships it had given rise to were still very much alive, albeit separated by the Mediterranean Sea. It was Paris, after all, that led the way when Francophone Algerian literature finally gained recognition in the 1950s. In 1952, the Centre régional d'art dramatique (CRAD) opened its doors under the direction of Geneviève Baylac. This self-described multilingual institution sought to bring the Muslim and European communities together through a variety of cultural and creative projects.[16] The experiment remained marginal. Europeans residing in Algiers were much more inclined to troop off to L'Opéra lyrique, especially when groups from Paris happened to be touring the region or to attend the "galas Karsenty" and classical music concerts held at the Pierre Bordes Hall. Muslim participation at these events was practically nil, and European curiosity about Arabo-Andalusian or Berber music was similarly nonexistent—as these forms of music were, as a rule, held in contempt by "les Français."

The same tacit segregation also occurred in hospitals, on sports teams, and even in schools. Despite Pierre Goinard's claim to the contrary in 1984, thirty years after the fact, that "separation in the wings of urban hospitals and on sports teams did not exist," there were, in fact, a number of clinics that were closed to Algerians.[17] Segregation in some of the hospitals to which they did have access was glaring: the shared wing was divided down the middle into Arab and European sections, and if all the beds in the Arab section happened to be taken, the Arab patient would be turned away before being admitted to an unoccupied European bed. Furthermore, Algerian externs (Algerian medical trainees were almost always barred from entering the prestigious intern programs and a nonresident status was the most they could realistically hope for) preferred to work in settings where their status as undesirables would not be at issue. They gave a wide berth to Pierre Goinard's service and preferred to head straight to Professor Vergoz's service—the only one to admit an Algerian surgeon[18]—or to seek out Professor Lévy-Valensi.[19]

In the 1950s, quotas were an undisputed reality; they existed as a fact of nature, a given. Medical students who aspired to internships in those days used to have a little ditty that went like this: "If you are male and European, you have a 95 percent chance; if you are female and European (meaning Christian), you have a 75 percent chance; if you are male and Jewish, your chances are 50 percent; if you are female and Jewish, 25 percent; and if you are male and Muslim, you have a 10 percent chance." Muslim women did not enter the equation; they were statistically invisible and the very idea that they would contemplate an internship in medicine unthinkable. Segregation not only manifested itself in actions, it was also a way of thinking.

The setup at sports clubs worked along similar lines; Europeans went to great lengths to keep the Algerians out of their sports clubs, and then expressed surprise when these formed their own teams. Soccer matches between Muslim and European teams were a rare opportunity for Algerian working-class youths to stake their national claim. Anyone who ever attended a match between *Mouloudia*, a top Muslim team, and one of the *petit-blanc* teams from Belcourt or Saint-Eugène will remember the face-offs between the two tribunes of hostile fans, with the Algerians invariably relegated to the cheaper seats and the great number of policemen who were usually on hand to deter potential confrontations that could escalate beyond the usual tussles between avid fans. Finally, there was the Racing universitaire de l'Algérois (RUA), the well-equipped and rich student club that was considered to be a prime training ground for young athletic talent and was officially closed to "Muslims" and implicitly off limits to Jews.

Every school-aged Muslim child who legally resided in the capital was theoretically entitled to some form of schooling. The rule did not necessarily apply to girls, and recent arrivals who had left the countryside to settle in the city slums usually fell between the cracks as well. This rule, however, applied only to primary schooling; and high school was an altogether different matter. The Lycée Gauthier, for example, located in one of the finer neighborhoods, did not include a single Muslim in its student body. A small number of Muslim students were enrolled at the Lycée Bugeaud, located at the intersection of a number of working-class neighborhoods. But most Muslim teenagers attended the Lycée Ben Aknoun, a Franco-Muslim school. A significant number of Muslim girls were enrolled in secondary schools, but not a single one of them ever set foot inside the gates of either one of the two prestigious all-girl lycées, the Fromentin[20] and the Delacroix.

The Algerian novelist, Assia Djebar, still remembers how bewildered she felt, despite the support of some of her schoolmates, when she realized she was the only Muslim girl enrolled in the advanced *hypokhâgne* program at the Lycée Bugeaud in 1953.[21]

Even before the revolt of November 1, 1954, the few progressive Europeans who had forged friendships or struck up mere acquaintanceships with Algerians had to do so against great odds and in defiance of social and, especially, familial pressures. Algerians were faced with a similarly reluctant community and had to argue against the well-founded perception that Europeans, as a rule, held all Algerians in contempt, and most difficult of all, they had to justify their decision in relationship to the still open wound surrounding the events of 1945. The unions and political parties played a minor role in these newly forged alliances. Relationships were more likely to flourish in the context of the youth organizations, the AJAAS for example,[22] or at the university, where one could follow the lead of professors such as André Mandouze, a Christian and a *Frankaoui* who already held the distinction of having served in the French Resistance, and who, as early as 1946, went on an all-out war against the social and political climate that prevailed in Algeria. Mandouze invited his students as well any other young people who wished to be included to Tipaza, where the alleged advanced course on Husserl was merely an excuse to allow students of all backgrounds a breath of fresh of air and an opportunity to sort out their thoughts away from the loaded atmosphere of the university. The retreat was open to students from all departments and always included literature students and two or three students from the medical school as well as a few from the law school, which is how Mohammad Ben Yahia, the future negotiator at Evian and government minister, came to participate in those sessions. He was a slight young man with a sparkle of mischief in his eyes, and on days when the sirocco was blowing in earnest, we used to joke about how we'd have to load down his pockets with pebbles to keep the wind from carrying him away.

Fanon and Mandouze did meet eventually but not while Fanon was posted at Blida. The two had arrived in Algiers within the same two-year span, but it would be a while before these two men who shared a militant past and an unrelenting preoccupation with the bonds that make and unmake human ties would finally meet. One, a Frenchman and a Christian, a graduate of l'école normale who belonged to the culture of the silent body; the other, an Antillean psychiatrist who understood, beyond the shadow of a doubt, that language is born of the body and knew that a code of ethics cannot be reduced to moral voluntarism.

This way of thinking was in itself utterly out of step with the times. The racist climate was compounded by an intellectual mediocrity that drove people away from this provincial city and toward the metropolis. In the early years, this aspiration was shared by all, especially the young: Europeans who felt defeated by the prevailing ethos of their society; the children of the Algerian bourgeoisie who had distinguished themselves in their studies; progressive Jews who wanted to escape the suffocation of their environment. Though few in number, they aspired not only to a superior intellectual life but to conditions that would allow them to make a stand against oppression, to live up to their egalitarian, at times unmitigatedly Marxist, ideals. They all had the same dream—they wanted to be elsewhere, which, at the time, could only mean one thing: France.

Jacques Azoulay and I, as well as others, helped introduce Fanon to the Algerian Jewish community. While in France, he had on more than one occasion claimed that as a minority he identified with the "Jewish condition," but he knew very little about the history and local culture of Algerian Jews.

Despite their relatively small number, Algerian Jews occupied an important space in post-War Algerian society. Their status was not exactly interchangeable with that of the Europeans. The Jewish community was not entirely homogenous, however, as different origins and personal itineraries as well as differences of social status contributed to its diversity. Whatever nuances there may have been, however, were swept away by the implementation of a historical and legislative common denominator that was accepted more than it was embraced.[23] All Algerian Jews were granted French citizenship as a result of the 1870 Crémieux Decree, implemented at a time when the "French presence" in Algeria was nearing its forty-year mark.[24] By virtue of this decree, the Muslims became the only ones to be consigned to the status of "native," and a new momentum sped the Jewish community's assimilation to modernity, civic responsibility, and increased participation in public life. Later, the repeal of this same decree would bring about another common denominator, when at the height of the Vichy government, Jews were demoted to the status of "native Jew" for a period of more than two years. Despite impressions to the contrary, the official reinstatement of "indigenous Algerian Israelites" to French citizenship did not follow swiftly on the heels of the arrival of the Gaullist resistance in Algeria.

This is a very schematic account of the double movement—assimilation, repudiation—that sums up the situation of Algerian Jews at the end of the 1940s. Individual experiences of this situation were, of course, informed by markedly different degrees of awareness and differences in agenda. There were the rich and the poor; those who lived in the fine neighborhoods and others who lived in working-class ones; there were urban Jews and rural Jews as well as those who came from the deep South, from the Laghouat area and who shared much with Arab and Berber Muslims. Especially in the major cities, in Algiers and Oran, there were completely assimilated Jews, generally from the more well-to-do sectors, and Jews about whom other Jews would bleakly joke that "if they hadn't happened to be Jews, they would have been anti-Semites."

But in 1950, in most Jewish homes in the capital, the widely held aspiration to modernity did not necessarily translate into wholesale assimilation and a break with tradition. In a number of families, grandparents figured as a central presence and their way of life, straddling two, not to say three, cultures often held sway. While this older generation may have conceded French as the language of politics and commerce, Arabic and Hebrew, often conflated into the local Judeo-Arabic dialect, were the languages they used to speak about emotions, books, spirituality, and moral values. They lived in Moorish houses cheek by jowl with Arab neighbors whose values and taste in music they shared. Some, though few in Algiers itself, still wore traditional dress and would only don European clothing to present themselves before municipal officials or to attend the wedding of a modern grandchild. Modest Jewish establishments existed side-by-side with those of Muslim shopkeepers and tradesmen in the poorer areas of the capital as well as in more remote towns and villages. This co-existence was alive and well into the 1950s, not only in the cities of the interior such as Constantine and in the Deep South, Laghouat for instance, but also in the capital and its outlying areas. It should also be noted that during World War II, the Muslim population did not, for the most part, succumb to pressure from the Vichy government, which had found great favor among Algerian Europeans, and in some cases even went out of their way to protect their Jewish neighbors. This solidarity has been acknowledged by a number of Jewish families.[25]

The degree of assimilation varied from place to place, as did the degree of religious praxis. In Constantine, for example, there were 10,000 Jews and twenty-five synagogues as well as countless smaller shopfront establishments that catered to the poorer members of the community. In Algiers, however, there were only a handful of synagogues, generally located in the poorer neighborhoods on the other side of the Grande Poste, which marked the cut-off line between rich and poor areas in a categorical manner. Even in the capital, everyone more or less attended services, some with great zeal and knowledge and others for the form only.

Their diversity notwithstanding, the Jews were still all Jews, conscious of their status as a minority and aware of longstanding Muslim anti-Jewish feeling and Christian anti-Semitism. On the one hand, their status as *dhimmis* meant that history had been kinder to them than it had been to the Jews of Europe, but this status offered little protection from the great poverty of the masses or in times of unpredictable political instability; on the other hand, there was the virulent and vulgar Christian anti-Semitism that permeated the history of colonial Algeria during and after the Nazi onslaught. In 1934, for example, the two strains came together in the pogrom that occurred in Constantine and that lives on as a vivid memory to this day.

To the great dismay of their elders, there were some in the younger generation who opted for atheism even though they may not have had a very good grasp of the tenets or outcomes their choice implied. The stance was part and parcel of "modernity," and especially associated to internationalism—the ideal that allowed one to reach beyond the national question and embrace human universalism in any one of its concomitant expressions of the values of 1789: *liberté, égalité, fraternité*. Though they were barred from educational institutions in October 1940, once the ban was lifted in 1943, the young reemerged with renewed faith in the Republic.

But the young were not the only ones who were susceptible to the ideals of the Republic. Even after World War II, most Algerian Jews continued to place their faith in France, a mythical France to be sure, but one whose allegiance to the principles of the Republic and to the idea of citizenship enabled it to bestow equal rights and responsibilities to all, open the doors of knowledge to men and women alike, and provide the only institutional protection against possible persecution. It was this view of things that enabled them to place their trust against all odds not in racist and Pétain-aligned French Algeria but in the institutions of the French Republic that had joined forces with the Resistance to prevail over the French state. Their fear of racism, a fear they shared with the Muslims, generally translated into left-leaning sensibilities that ranged from radical socialism—supporters of Mendès by and large—to adherence to the Algerian Communist Party that counted many Jews from all the social strata among its members. While a handful of Jews may have voted for Gazagne, the former Vichy prefect, in the municipal elections of October 1947, the great majority backed the progressive program proposed by Tubert, the *général de gendarmerie*, who denounced electoral fraud and the injustice to which the *deuxième collège* had been subject, and who, unbeknownst to his electorate, was also responsible for investigating the Sétif massacre of May 1945 and publishing the true death toll. As early as 1936, important Algerian families, concerned by the manifest inequality that was taking root in Algeria, stepped up to express their support of the Blum-Violette proposal that was relegated to the back drawer when the War broke out. Among these were the Benichous, the Aboulkers, and many others; these families included doctors who ministered to poor and young militants who took part in the November 1942 landing, and their moral and political courage is now a matter of record.

The national question, however, regardless of political beliefs and union affiliations (unions were the only vehicle available to wage laborers), was hardly front and center, and Algerian nationalist movements were perceived as marginal. The MTLD and the L'Union Démocratique du Manifeste Algérien (UDMA), abbreviations for associations where colleagues and work acquaintances could meet, were generally viewed as peripheral. Indeed, the militants within these organizations, including the students, did not broadcast their sympathies anywhere else, and rightly identified themselves as semiclandestine.

Almost fifty years later, Jacques Azoulay reports that as an Algerian Jew he only became aware of Algeria "in Blida, while working with Fanon. That's when I realized that there were Muslims—Muslims and a Muslim culture." This from a man who in his youth had been a militant, and, as such, hardly in the mainstream of Algerian society. He does not recall meeting any Muslims in his years as a card-carrying member of the PCA, where he formed a close friendship with Maurice Audin, the young mathematician who was tragically tortured to death a few years later.[26] He vaguely recalls three or four Muslim students from his days in medical school and as a hospital extern; they generally kept to themselves, never struck up friendships outside their group and never struck him as particularly remarkable. He remembers one of them as being "quiet and elegant, fair complexioned. What was his name?" Even their names seem difficult, impossible to recall, from another world. Which obstacle of the unknowable does one have to surmount to finally ask a real question? The one who looked like me, the one whose hair was even lighter than mine, whose skin even whiter, where did he come from? What family did he come from? What was his story? His language? The barrier, real, subtle, but impossible to cross was such that it had to be annulled. There were neither words nor fictions to express it. "And yet, I didn't really like the society in which I lived: the ignorant and arrogant medical students who only cared about detective novels and 'women,' the European society, and even the assimilated Jewish society to which I belonged."[27]

But the barrier was there, unbreachable, old, and well entrenched. It was with Fanon that Azoulay discovered that there was such a thing as a "Muslim cultural identity" and that it was important, that there was a link between cultural oppression and aspects of psychopathology. The importance culture played in pathology would be for him, and in this he was not alone, a discovery. "Fanon's intellectual approach enabled me to apprehend a content that I would otherwise have considered folkloric, and from the moment of that realization, I understood it wasn't."[28] Fanon had only been in Algeria for two months when he met Azoulay, who had been born in Algeria to parents, grandparents, and great-grandparents who had lived there all their lives.

Contrary to commonly held perceptions that took hold much after the fact, the creation of the state of Israel did not greatly affect the views held by the majority of Algerian Jews. In 1947, there was undoubtedly a minority, especially among the young, that declared itself Zionist and Communist, and a few who even went so far as to spend a couple of years in the new Jewish state; hadn't the Soviet Union, after all, given it its blessing? Most came back in the end, and some from this group of returnees were sent to the internment camp in Lodi in 1956.[29] While the majority of Algerian Jews were attentive to the creation of the new state, they demonstrated their solidarity mainly by coming to the aid of the Moroccan Jews, much poorer on the whole, who had to transit through Algeria on their way to Israel. The general sentiment, however, was that this new state did not directly concern them, and Jerusalem continued to be perceived as a mythical locus, a place largely unrelated to ideas of territorial appropriation—a view that won them the sharp disapproval of a number of representatives from Zionist governing bodies and organizations at the time.

Basically, in the 1950s, the majority of Algerian Jews did not contemplate the possibility of living anywhere but in Algeria, a sentiment that is not necessarily contradicted by the dream of departure cultivated by a younger generation that found partition intolerable. Even the richer families viewed France as a place for jaunts, excursions to take the waters at Châtelguyon for those with digestive problems, for example, or Bagnèrre-de-Bigorre for those with emphysema, or Vichy for liver troubles; the more adventurous went as far as Abano in northern Italy to seek relief for their rheumatic ailments; some took their children to the mountains to breathe the bracing air, and in the summer, families spent their vacations in Luchon, Évian, or Megève. Families of lesser means went to Bouzaréah, to Yacouren in Kabylia, or to the beach. But even in these places they did not mix, not with the Europeans and not with the Muslims, even in parts of Algeria where the strictures may have been slightly more relaxed.

This was the frame of mind in 1953, and it would last until 1957, with Algerian Jews holding onto the hope of a livable solution for all.

Fanon's ties to this community were casual, but he did form close bonds with individuals within the community. He had strong feelings about the appeal that had been made by the French branch of the Front de Libération Nationale (FLN) to Algerian Jews, reminding them that they were an integral part of the nation, that they were and had always been Algerians and that their rightful place was in an independent Algeria. He did not comment, however, when the Algerian Jewish Committee for Social Action (CJAAS) published its official response to the FLN appeal of November 1956. The CJAAS did not claim to represent all Algerian Jews. The response pointed to the heterogeneity of positions and declared its support for a diversity of viewpoints. The spectrum of opinion was indeed great and included supporters of the Organisation Armée Secrète (OAS), a small number when all was said and done, as well as an equally small number who openly supported and participated in the Algerian armed struggle for independence. The majority took a wait-and-see approach, and most were dismayed that Mendès France, who had negotiated so ably with both Tunisia and Indochina, was not at the helm of the French Socialist government. After 1956 and in the wake of the policies of Guy Mollet and Robert Lacoste, the rift in opinion gave way to profound disappointment. The binary logic of the Algerian War of Independence, later augmented in an oblique way by the conflict in the Middle East, which in its turn would become a prolonged war of Jew against Arab, brought about the quasi-total, albeit reluctant, expatriation of Algerian Jews: "in our heart of hearts, we felt impotent, and we were left with the lingering and at times painful feeling that we had failed to serve as mediators between two clashing worlds."[30]

The three communities were segregated not only in Algiers, or in neighboring Blida, but also in Oran to the west as well as in the eastern regions of the country. The historical saga has it that "things were different in the east," that the different communities in and around Constantine lived in greater proximity and with some degree of cultural exchange and tolerance. There is some truth to these recollections that have become idealized in hindsight. When Jean-François Lyotard,[31] who was a young philosophy teacher in Constantine between 1950 and 1952, talks about this period in his life, the obstacles he describes are the same as elsewhere in the country and the prevailing political reality for him and for everyone else is one and the same: "Algeria is emphatically not France." The author Rolland Doukhan, an Algerian Jew and native of Constantine who left in the 1950s to "pursue his studies" and whose attachment to his hometown has not diminished in the intervening decades, says as much. He recalls how his mother, a woman who spoke only Judeo-Arabic, fretted over the friendships and acquaintances of his adolescence. His closest friend, whose family came from Kabylia, was the son of a teacher of French; later, this friend would become the poet Malek Haddad. Haddad's family was much more cultured than Doukhan's but that didn't count for much at the time. Personal transgression of the social divide only confounded matters and fueled the fires. Rolland Doukhan's sympathies were rudely put to the test by the events that befell Sétif in 1945. "Constantine's Jewish community," he explains,

> was completely unaware of the events that took place in Sétif, despite their proximity. I was seventeen at the time and totally oblivious to the things that were happening around me. I found out about a year later, in my philosophy class at school. I found out that thousands of Arabs had been killed in retribution for a hundred European dead. At the time, I had just joined the Algerian Communist Party, I realized that there were Communist ministers in the government who had given or ratified the order to carry out this violence. In Algeria, in Constantine, I lived through major events which I did not really experience, because I was confined behind glass walls. Paradoxically, it was in France that I finally was able to develop political views, even about Algeria, and to smash those walls of glass to smithereens.[32]

Such was the tenor of Algerian society in 1953, when Fanon discovered it for the first time and utterly misread its various elements. Even though he had experienced racism firsthand, nothing had prepared him for the incredible reality of a world built on "uncontested segregation."[33] As any other psychiatrist in the service of France, Fanon's first point of entry was the European community, which at the time had yet to seriously entertain the possibility of leaving Algeria. Although things were certainly getting worrisome around this time, despite grandstanding to the contrary. Anticolonial feeling was on the rise, and European privilege was feeling menaced. They were, after all, already at war in Indochina, where as the *Écho d'Alger* would put it, "our valiant soldiers have triumphantly safeguarded the values of Western civilization." Consensus pinned the delayed victory on Communists who deigned to call themselves Frenchmen and stabbed our brave legionnaires in the back and on the subversion that was gaining ground in neighboring countries and threatening Algeria's borders: the King of Morocco was seen as a traitor and Bourguiba as a trouble-fomenting agitator. In Algeria, however, there was nothing to worry about after Naegelen and now Léonard had replaced Chataigneau—"the Arab who used to be at the head of the *Gouvernement général.*" And let's not forget Sétif and the lesson we taught the Arabs there; they have been appeased and they really feel quite affectionate toward us now, except for a handful of troublemakers who should be put behind bars, that Ferhat Abbas, for example, that pharmacist who would never have become a pharmacist if it were not for France, and instead of thanking us, he wants to establish an Algerian Republic, as though such a thing were possible. . . . [34] And so on and so forth; this, then, was the dominant discourse, adamant in its refusal to admit that in the municipal elections of April 1953, conducted under the strictest surveillance, the MTLD had been elected in its totality and refusing to heed Mayor Jacques Chevalier, who was neither a Communist nor a Separatist, when he called for immediate and urgent collaboration with these elected officials by naming the lawyer Kioune, the leading representative of the MTLD, as deputy mayor.[35] In other words, as a high official of the day had put it, "In Algeria, we are sitting on a volcano; it just happens to be dormant."

But, for Fanon, the capital Algiers would, in fact, take a backseat to Blida, the place where he lived and worked in the hospital that was located on the periphery of the town. The distance separating Blida from the capital was a mere forty-five kilometers, fifty if one chose to take the road that cut across the Chiffa Gorges to catch a glimpse of the apes that frolicked on the rocks.[36] This town of 60,000 was an administrative subdivision of Algiers and an almost perfect replica of the larger city in its compartmentalization of every aspect of social life, down to its topography.

An Algerian poet had dubbed it "Ourida,"[37] and even though Blida was purportedly famed as the "city of roses," the evidence for this distinction was slim at best, and at least at first glance, there was little to the delight the eye in the city's European neighborhoods. The banal *Place d'armes* and typically colonial and provincial streets that branched off of it did not offer even a whiff of the bougainvillea, the jasmine, and musk roses that could cut the senses to the quick. There was not a single suggestion of the aloes, the Barbary fig cacti, and other exotic plantings whose thorns and rounded shapes, at once gentle and sharp, captured something of the essence of Algeria—sweet and violent, generous and wounded. That Algeria must have existed in the gardens of ancient and local Muslim families or in the villas that housed the teachers and officials who were just passing through.

The European population in Blida was a significant one, and much as in Algiers, its presence determined the public feel of the town. At least a quarter of this population was tied to the military; Blida was home to Algeria's first military base, an airbase, a major communications and posting center as well as a large military hospital. Its administrative status as a departmental subdivision was a reflection of its military importance. The town was also a playground for the rich colonial families who lived in the Mitidja region.

They enrolled their children in local schools and preferred to avoid the drawbacks of the capital by shopping for their clothing and seeking amusement in the smaller town. Blida was also home to Jewish and Muslim communities, with their respective social complexities. A number of well-to-do Algerian families were associated with the town—with respect to the Algerian bourgeoisie, Blida carried the same social prestige as Tlemcen or Constantine. The mark of the local bourgeoisie, where Fanon would make a number of friends, was felt in the public sphere in a way that it simply was not in Algiers. This did not the diminish the fact, however, of the glaringly apparent social and ethnic divisions that existed in this microcosm. The psychiatric hospital, a city within the city, did indeed employ a large medical and administrative personnel made up of Europeans and Muslims who worked side-by-side and were joined by similar union goals. And despite the ethnic segregation practiced in the dormitories, the two major boarding schools, one for boys the other for girls, did indeed exceptionally admit students from all backgrounds. Still, as Assia Djebar and Nabile Farès, who were both children of the elite and student boarders during this period, remind us, the dormitories and dining halls were not conducive to friendship and the only exceptions were the rare exchanges that would occur after lights out. At the Lycée Duverrier, the boy's school that had started out as a *collège colonial*, a "boys will be boys" laxity masked the underlying atmosphere of violence, and students did not mix outside of school; Jewish and Muslim boys were simply not invited to Christian homes. The relationship between Jews and Muslims fared better than in Algiers, however, and there were friendships between Jewish children and the children of affluent and old Blidean families: the Bencherchallis, Aclis, Bengergouras, Fellags, Boucebsis, and Yazids, to name a few. In 1954, however, things began to change, and by 1956, the relationship between communities became openly confrontational. The day students at the Lycée Duverrier remember the name of two families who lived in Blida at the time, the Sainte-Maries and the Lagaillardes. They were the leaders of the *bande de la gare*, an openly and sweepingly anti-Semitic gang. They largely ignored their Arab classmates and routinely picked fights with their Jewish ones who formed the *bande de la place*. The violence of those confrontations is still vivid today among men in their fifties and sixties who had been boys in Blida at the time.

In essence, during his first year in Algeria, Fanon was brought face to face with the European milieu to which all psychiatrists belonged. He tried to make his way into this circle but never at the expense of his philosophical and political beliefs. In Blida he regularly attended showings at the *ciné-club*, also immensely popular among his colleagues, and it was not very long before his comments and contributions drew their attention to him. His relationship to his Algiers-based colleagues was negligible, however, and their almost uniform response to him, as we shall see later at more length, was one of immediate contempt. He did make an effort, however, to meet with French orientalists and Arabic-speakers, most eminently Professor Marçais, who worked in the capital. But when he realized, as Professor Lévy-Valensi put it, that an Arabophone does not equal an Arabophile, he quickly dropped these acquaintances. Azoulay, who often accompanied Fanon in those early months, remembers a number of disappointing encounters, among them one with the members of the philosophy department. The two had attended a lecture on Kierkegaard, delivered by the same university professor who claimed he had never met a racist. Fanon was practically floored by the pomposity, made all the greater by the copious libations, of the speaker and the mediocrity of the paper. At a conference on French existentialism, I have personally witnessed the philosopher in question dismiss Sartre and Merleau-Ponty as "acrobats who will bust our chops until the day they fall on their faces." Fanon, who was a great reader of Kierkegaard and so close to Sartre, had no choice but to walk away from such a personage.

While Fanon had tried to establish a contact with scholars of the Near East, he did not seek similar entry with the "heirs" to the l'École d'Alger and the cultural movement that revolved around them and the Éditions Charlot publishing house. They were the first to publish Camus, and before 1948, their list also included Gabriel Audisio, Jean Grenier, Emmanuel Roblès, as well as Mohamed Dib and Jean Amarouche. Charlot and the quasi-totality of its group of authors left Algiers in 1948. In 1953, however, on the initiative of Jean Senac and Mohamed Dib, with the support of Emmanuel Roblès and Gabriel Audisio, there was an attempt to launch a number of new journals: *Rivages, Soleil, Terrasse* in Algiers and *Simoun* in Oran. Except for *Simoun*, which continued to be published until 1961, the journals were very short-lived. There were local publishers, Éditions Baconnier (a very important private printer and a small publisher with close links to the *Gouvernement général*),[38] for example, that tried to solicit manuscripts from Muslims, and their most significant success in this respect was the 1954 publication of Mouloud Feraoun's *Jours de Kabylie* that stands as a testament to nonconflictual goodwill. Elsewhere, the much poorer En Nahda publishing house and bookstore tried to develop a cultural space that would speak more directly to Algerian Muslims. They were responsible for the publication of Kateb Yacine's first book on Abd El-Kader. They also published the works of the philosopher Malek Bennabi. But at the time, Fanon had not yet met Dib, or Ferraoun, or Kateb Yacine.

Despite the resources of his Antillean experience and his intellectual struggle with the colonial idea, this was the first time Fanon had found himself in a society as rigidly encoded and as free of qualms as Algeria's colonial society.

But an extremely motivated and involved Fanon already had his work cut out for him at l'hôpital psychiatrique de Blida (HPB), the psychiatric hospital in Blida.

Blida

Fanon's reception at the Blida-Joinville psychiatric hospital. The study of psychiatry at Algiers University; the Algiers School and the doctrine of primitivism. Fanon introduces sociotherapy at Blida-Joinville. "Africains Antillais" is written. The year 1955 is a watershed year: Fanon joins the Algerian revolution; psychiatry and politics are profoundly connected. In 1956, Fanon presents "Racisme et culture" at the First Congress of Black Writers and Artists, held at the Sorbonne. In Algeria, the noose is tightening. Fanon resigns from his post and is expelled from Algeria.

The psychiatric hospital at Blida, known to all as HPB or Joinville—people would say "fit for Joinville" in the same way the French say "fit for Charenton"—was a city within a city. It was here that Fanon spent the years between 1953 and 1956, performing his daily rounds, honing his ideas, and making the transition from political commitment to political action.

The hospital grounds were vast. Patients were housed in old prison-like structures as well as in newer, more modern facilities. Staff villas, a dormitory, and various administrative buildings dotted the tree-lined avenues. It was necessary to have a vehicle, of the two- or four-wheel variety, to move about the sprawling campus. There was also a chapel where festivities were occasionally held and a mosque that had been transformed into a basket-weaving workshop.

The large complex also included a farm, partially staffed by patients, that supplied the hospital kitchens. The therapeutic possibilities of this setup

59

were not lost on Fanon, who, soon after his arrival, tried to incorporate the farm into a program of treatment, but the plan was never implemented, neither during nor after Fanon's tenure at the hospital. When Algeria secured its independence, the farm was turned over to the Ministry of Agriculture.

The staff houses, including the one assigned to Fanon, were pleasant, each one with its own garden tended by a patient "worker." The hospital/asylum was essentially modeled, at least in its architectural intent and design, on French public psychiatric institutions for the treatment of the chronically ill. It operated in an enclosure of vast green spaces and on the premise of secluded self-sufficiency.

This image of the psychiatric asylum would undergo a considerable transformation between 1954 and 1956. Rumblings and rumors began to spread throughout Blida about the things that were taking place inside the hospital's walls. High school students from those days remember going to get their culture fix at the *ciné-club* that had been founded and was entirely run by psychiatrists who were attached to the hospital. They vaguely recall hearing some talk about how the hospital had devised a new approach to alienation, something about the relationship of one human being to another human being. They also remember the rumor that surfaced later, after 1956, about the two camps inside the hospital, the rift between supporters of the French camp and supporters of the November 1954 Movement. They will tell you that it was around this time that the hospital started having a reputation as a "breeding ground for fellaghas."

In 1953, the HPB was the only major long-term, which at the time meant indefinite, care facility for the mentally ill in Algeria. A 1938 plan to create similar establishments in Oran and Constantine was shelved when the War broke out. After the War, mental health annexes were appended to general hospitals throughout the country; these annexes teemed with so-called incurables who were sent for a monthly consultation with a staff psychiatrist at HPB.

In 1953, the psychiatric wing of the HPB was home to 2,000 patients; it had been designed to hold 800. There were only four head physicians, each supervising a separate division. The need to create a fifth position and a fifth division to handle the large patient population was fast becoming an urgent necessity. This was the position that Fanon came to fill.

Psychiatric facilities in Algeria, particularly those serving members of the non-European sector, who were too poor to take part in the growing trend of seeking care in private clinics, were generally inadequate and markedly inferior to those of metropolitan France at the same period. In this too, Algeria was most certainly not France.

In 1955, an article detailing the situation of mental health in Algeria appeared in *L'Information psychiatrique;*[1] it was authored by the four chief resident physicians at the HPB in collaboration with the indefatigable Fanon. This article, which Fanon embarked on a mere three months after arriving in Blida, is an accurate and meticulous account, supported by facts and figures, of the prevailing conditions. The problem of mental health resources in the colonies had been raised as early as 1912, but it was not until 1932 that institutional psychiatric reform was introduced in Algeria, largely at the instigation of Doctor Lasnet and Professor Antoine Porot, the latter a product of the military medical system.[2] The reform, shaped by a number of decrees and ordinances that appeared between 1933 and 1934, called for the implementation in Algiers, Oran, and Constantine of three primary care observation clinics, or "*services ouverts*" that would not answer to prefectural authority. In Algiers, this clinic was located in Mustapha, the capital's most important and only university hospital. Most psychiatrists were selected through a national exam that was also open to contestants from metropolitan France, and in 1953, their ranks did not include a single "Arab" psychiatrist. The mental health reform also brought about the creation of Blida-Joinville, a hospital that specialized exclusively in psychiatric treatment as stipulated by the law of 1838. The joint article published by the Blida team stated that conditions had "remained unchanged" since the hospital had opened its doors and that the facility was "glaringly underequipped." It took Fanon's arrival on the premises, however, for the other four physicians whose association to the hospital predated his to make a public statement about conditions at Blida-Joinville.

Still, the joint effort demonstrated by the five physicians and their willingness to put aside their theoretical and political differences attests to Fanon's ability to rally his colleagues in a shared effort toward a common goal. Insufficient attention has been paid to Fanon's gift for bringing people together; he was obsessed with the connection between human beings, the bonds that can quash all differences.

His four colleagues, F. Ramée, R. Lacaton, M. Micucci, and Jean Dequeker, were, in effect, very different: respectable psychiatrists of the classical school who accepted the institutional status of the asylum at face value and restricted their critique to problems having to do with the lack of equipment and the poor training of the personnel. Doctor Ramée was the only one who had studied under Doctor Porot, the founder of the Algiers School of Psychiatry who was responsible for the theory of genetic difference on which he based his conclusions about the primitive nature and deficient mental and physical evolution of the North African *race*. The other three were "metropolitans" and did not share the racist views that were commonly held by Algerian Europeans, but the pressures of the colonial situation had forced them to adapt. The one woman in their midst, Mlle

Micucci, lived an isolated and withdrawn life. Jean Dequeker, who had been Gaston Ferdière's assistant and knew Antonin Artaud as a result, had a very special aura about him and loved film. The *Frankaoui* Lacaton was a more recent arrival and had not yet resigned himself to the status quo; he would, in subsequent years, increasingly align himself with Fanon on both the psychiatric and the political fronts. Fanon's "Letter to a Frenchman," published by Maspero in 1965, is thought to have been addressed to him.[3]

The HPB was radically transformed by Fanon's arrival. Fanon has claimed that his new colleagues were not quick to dismiss him or his methods out of hand. They were quite aware of his allegiance to the new school of thought known as institutional psychotherapy. Curiosity seems to have been the overriding sentiment of the Blida medical team toward Fanon.

But this benign state of affairs disappeared almost as soon as Fanon was there in person. In order to reorganize the HPB, each head physician had to give up one or more pavilions to make up the fifth section that Fanon would oversee. A hospital visit by the administrative director and the senior medical staff was called. The hospital's existing four sections were an archetype of the institutional asylum: the sexual segregation that was a standard practice for this type of institution was compounded by the separation of Europeans and natives (this term was later amended to "Muslims"). In practice, this arrangement translated into separate pavilions for European men, European women, Muslim men, and Muslim women. But what horrified Fanon most of all—and continued to horrify him for years to come whenever he spoke of it—was the dehumanizing spectacle that unfolded before his eyes: wings teeming with idle, unshaven patients, all dressed in the same impersonal hospital-issued uniform that gave them the look of prisoners; the more agitated patients were tied down to their beds, some even to trees in the park. Those who had the double misfortune of being both schizophrenic and tubercular were naked and tethered to iron rings, living amidst piles of straw in isolated cells. Fanon gave full throttle to his disapproval, and his criticism did not let up for the duration of the entire tour. This did not sit well with his new colleagues, and in the meeting that took place immediately after the tour, they were no longer amenable to the idea of turning over their pavilions to Fanon. It was at this point that Fanon, who later would take a special pleasure in recalling the savvy of his strategy, suggested that he would visit the pavilions on a rotational basis in order to train the staff and help introduce the new therapeutic methods that were completely unfamiliar to his colleagues. Naturally, this proposal was immediately rejected, and the fifth section, consisting of one pavilion for European women and three for Muslim men, materialized.

Fanon also met with the nurses and orderlies who helped keep this immense hub of activity on track and with whom he would have to work closely. There were only three Muslims in positions of authority, working as head nurses or assistant head nurses. But shortly before Fanon's arrival, a large number of Muslim nurses' aides had been hired by the hospital's socialist director. The nursing personnel was well organized and belonged to the Confédération Générale du Travail (CGT), a union whose membership was open to both Algerians and Europeans. The impact of a very impressive strike that the CGT had led in the 1950s was felt for a long time in workers' organizations. A significant number of CGT adherents were also politically active, in the MTLD as well as in the Communist Party.[4] This political acumen helped sensitize the nursing staff to conditions within the psychiatric asylum; they were extremely aware of their position as mere guards, hired on the basis of their physical strength and their readiness to keep the pavilions clean and the bed sheets tightly tucked for the doctors' scheduled inspections.

Fanon also had a great many allies among the interns who were in residence during that three-year span. They unanimously supported the new and revolutionary psychiatric trends, and many of them joined the struggle for Algerian independence, some paying with their lives: Slimane Asselah, Georges Counillon (whom Fanon had already met in Lyon), Tirichine. François Sanchez and Meyer Timsit, whose nickname—Popoff—summed up his political beliefs, were detained in internment camps, and others were exiled. But the hour of national upheaval was not yet upon us.

Tragic and dehumanized though they may have been, the conditions Fanon encountered at the HPB still bore the mark of a very human folly. This resilient humanity fell outside the purview of the "front line" care—to use the military metaphor that found favor at the time—associated with the Algiers School. The very same Doctor Porot who had labored to advance the state of psychiatric care in the 1930s and who, together with his students, developed the theory of primitivism had recently resigned his chair in neuropsychiatry because of ill health.[5] Professor Manceaux, who had the distinction of being neither a neurologist nor a psychiatrist and whose brief appearances at the clinic only served to further highlight his ignorance, succeeded him. Despite paltry qualifications as an educator and nonexistent research, this professor was allowed to teach and indeed did so with great enthusiasm in his lectures about his theory of alcoholism. There are, he used to say, two kinds of alcoholism: an "excusable" kind associated with worldly women and scions of society whose participation in cocktail parties and celebratory toasts was a matter of course; and, an "inexcusable" kind practiced by workmen who, with every anisette they downed at the corner pub, were stealing food out of the mouths of their own children. These statements, their vulgar reasoning aside, had a certain piquancy, given the predominantly Muslim environment and a medical setting in which alcoholism was not an especially pressing concern.

This professional wasteland was the occasional destination of a handful of guest psychiatrists: Pélicier, Susini, Lanfranchi. As a rule, these visiting lecturers worked at the more luxurious Ermitage, a private clinic in Kouba on the outskirts of Algiers, from where they sent difficult to resolve cases to the Mustapha Hospital until such time as these could be transferred to Blida-Joinville. As soon as the Provisional Algerian Government was declared in March 1962 at Rocher Noir, the physicians in charge of this luxurious establishment rounded up their European patients and headed for France. They left all their Algerian patients behind in the care of a single Algerian nurse with a rudimentary pharmacy as his sole provision.

Charles Bardenat and Jean Sutter, key figures at the Mustapha Hospital, were both university professors with an extensive knowledge of psychiatry. It was under their supervision that medical students, both externs and interns, were introduced to the rudiments of clinical psychiatry. Bardenat, recently reappointed after having been relieved of his duties at Liberation because of his Pétainist zeal, was the co-author with Porot of the *Traité de psychiatrie médico-légale;*[6] he practiced "bookkeeper psychiatry," a cumulative approach that relied on the number of symptoms as a guide for pigeonholing the patient in one of the categories provided by traditional psychiatric norms. Sutter, on the other hand, was a true psychiatrist, and there were enough differences in his professional experience to set him apart. Formerly at HPB, he had served in the French expeditionary forces and was wounded in the Italian campaign.[7] He had the physical appearance of a strange giant in a tale by Edgar Allan Poe. He kept to himself, practiced in an annex building reserved for pedia-psychiatry and did his best to avoid Manceaux and other staff members. Still, Porot had been his professor as well as his thesis adviser in 1938, and they had co-authored the 1939 paper on "the primitivism of the North African native and its repercussions on mental pathology."[8] Both men stood by their view of the North African as a primitive being, leading an instinctive and vegetative life, primarily ruled by "the diencephalon [. . .], a particular disposition of the architectonic structure, or at least in the dynamic hierarchisation of the nervous centers." In short, by an insufficiently developed brain.

Sutter, who in the 1950s presented himself as Roman Catholic and liberal, had nonetheless blithely endorsed, either out of solidarity with his mentor or out of personal conviction, the Algiers School theory of primitivism.

This theory holds that North Africans are characterized by primitive brain development and that their lives are ruled by instinct, given the absence of higher brain functions. Their abulic condition explains their intellectual apathy, their distaste for work, and their inability to tackle tasks in an attentive and logical manner. They have a proclivity to lie and be insolent and their criminal impulse signals them as potentially dangerous. These traits followed from the genetically determined retarded development of the native brain in which the diencephalon (responsible for lower brain function) eclipses higher cortical functions. In light of these drawbacks, "these primitive people cannot and should not benefit from the advances of European civilization." These advances are beyond their capacities of appreciation and any effort to force the situation can only bring them distress. This theory, which is so closely aligned with both the 1930s and the colonial order, appeared in the 1952 *Manuel alphabétique de psychiatrie*, where it is attributed to Porot and his co-authors: Jean Sutter, Henri Aubin, and Charles Bardenat. Insidiously tenacious, it makes a second appearance in the 1975 edition of the manual authored by the Algiers School. Until the publication of the *Traité d'Henri Ey* around 1959, this manual was the sole, and consequently highly prized, French-language resource available to students of psychiatry.

Fanon did not take the Psychiatry Department of Algiers University head on, but by late 1953, word was out that a different kind of psychiatric training was on offer at Blida, and a number of interns began to quietly make their way there. Jacques Azoulay was among the first, and Charles Géronimi, who was appalled by the Algiers approach, followed shortly thereafter. Fanon's public condemnation of the Algiers School, published in *Consciences maghribines*, didn't appear for another two years, when in a radically altered political climate, he drew a direct parallel between Porot's theory and Carothers's claim that the "average African is a lobotomized European." From the moment he arrived in Blida, Fanon devoted all his energies to introducing a program of sociotherapy that was light years ahead of the ideas that were being promoted in Algiers.

Fanon wasted no time implementing the Saint-Alban sociotherapy model in his division. In a few months time, the atmosphere at HPB was utterly transformed. The nurses, interns, and doctors who witnessed the phenomenon firsthand would certainly agree, some with a smile others with a sigh and regardless of whether they were supporters or detractors of the new practices.

Sociotherapy seeks not only to humanize the institution but to transform it whole cloth into a therapeutic environment in which patients and medical staff work in concert to construct a new social arena in which the broken thread of personal suffering can be salvaged and expressed. The realization of this new environment involves the creation of new points of reference, an open space in which conflict can be accommodated and emotions mobilized in the effort to delve into deep recesses and, by design as much as by chance, allow the catastrophe to be expressed in a different manner. Creative, cultural, and manual projects and activities, encompassing sensorial, affective, and corporeal experience, help reveal the "evolution of a given life, its unfolding narrative." The focus of sociotherapy should not be confused with work programs in which patients, "the most peaceful ones as a rule," are assigned maintenance duties and expected to report back to their pavilions at nightfall.

Jacques Azoulay, who arrived in Blida a month after Fanon, was the first to become involved in helping Fanon implement the new method. Azoulay had been working on Manceaux's team in Algiers and was extremely distressed by the incompetence, racism, and ignorance that were the order of the day. He was not dissuaded from pursuing a career in psychiatry, however, and was studying for an exam that would gain him admission to a facility he had come across in a journal, the Psychiatric Asylum of the Seine. The decision to pursue a career in psychiatry was a classic compromise for someone from his background; it accommodated his philosophical mindset, his pressing interest in human nature as well as familial constraints that saw only medicine, the law, or engineering as apt choices for a son. At the time, Azoulay did not entirely understand the reasons behind his choice. His only certainty was that a stint in Blida would improve his chances of passing the upcoming exam. He arrived at HPB and became Fanon's intern; an earlier candidate had desisted, preferring to follow a safer path. Azoulay did not know the first thing about his new "boss," not even his name. But from the moment the two men met, the connection between them was mutually apparent. It was while working with Fanon that Azoulay came to understand why he had felt so drawn to psychiatry and the reasons behind his questions on alienation. His enthusiasm was boundless, and for an entire year, the two men were unconditionally immersed in a joint adventure. Their intellectual affinity as well as their overlapping experience of racism, anti-Semitic and anti-black, cemented their relationship and enabled a close collaboration.

Fanon's feelings for Azoulay went beyond affection; he felt a quasi-brotherly tenderness for his student. More than forty years after the fact, the emotions of that bond were still vivid for Azoulay as well. But he underestimated Fanon's commitment to the anticolonial struggle. What is all the more surprising is that this brilliant, despite his modest disclaimers, psychiatrist and psychologist still contends today that the only revolution Fanon had been involved with before Algeria was the psychiatric one with François Tosquelles. That Fanon's deep involvement with the anticolonial debate dated back to his time with Tosquelles evaded him completely. The blind spot persisted, even while Azoulay was serving his time in the French military. After his eight month (November 1954–July 1955) posting on a stranded mountain peak, Azoulay turned up at the military hospital in Blida. Fanon sought him out and offered him a place to stay in the psychiatric hospital. When questioned about his decision to become part of the French Army, Azoulay tried to make light of the situation: "But right now it's just words . . . You may talk a good streak, but you're not going to get involved." Fanon remained impassive. This was July 1955. Fanon had already established contact with the resistance and was already providing medical and political support to them. Despite being an anticolonialist, Azoulay, who had been enlisted by the French Army on November 1, 1954, preferred to keep Algerian nationalism at arm's length and to distance himself from his embattled country. And though the distance was narrowing for Fanon, his involvement did not jeopardize the respect and affection he felt for his friend. In 1956, the two men met again in Paris, and though warm, that encounter would be their last. One chose to practice psychiatry in France; the exam which had so filled his thoughts as a young man stipulated a return to metropolitan France. The other chose to distance himself more and more from France, from Paris, and to strengthen his bond to the Algerian armed struggle inside Algeria, at the very moment that André Mandouze, a symbolic figure of the Algerian resistance, was leaving the country after a five-week incarceration to take up a teaching position in Strasbourg. It was a time of dispersals, of permanent and temporary separations, of choices that meant that Azoulay, who was certainly not alone in the France of 1961, was incapable of understanding the Fanon who had written *The Wretched of the Earth*.

The experiment in sociotherapy, invaluably documented in Azoulay's dissertation, took place between 1953 and 1954.[9] Fanon immediately started implementing the modalities he had been taught at Saint-Alban in the European women's pavilion. General biweekly meetings that included the medical and nursing staffs as well as the patients were instituted. Everyone was expected to participate in the open forum in which differing opinions about the hospital as well as other matters could be aired. A program of festivities and holiday celebrations was implemented. Fanon had hardly been there a month when the Christmas party that inaugurated this program took place. And it was quite a party!

Christmas, with its well-established symbolic conventions, provided the perfect opportunity to introduce a new set of expected behaviors. A large dormitory that normally accommodated sixty-five beds was emptied of all furnishings. Patients (Fanon preferred to refer to them as boarders) from the various wards flocked to the event: male and female patients, male and female nurses. Members from the administrative and medical staff also made a good showing. No effort had been spared to ensure that the celebration would unfold in an atmosphere of great solemnity; the evening included religious hymns, choral performances, a crèche that had been painstakingly adorned by hands that shook with the emotion of it all, and a Christmas tree.[10]

Fanon's desire to change the therapeutic approach to madness and his commitment to seeing that change through was evident in the upheaval he managed to cause in such a short time. In this particular pavilion, he had the support of the entire medical staff, beginning with the matron, an intelligent woman who was full of initiative and who, moreover, had a soft spot for him.[11] In no time, committees made up of nurses and patients had been set up for programs in music and film; another group was in charge of writing copy and printing the weekly publication *Notre Journal*. A number of workshops were created, including one for knitting and another for sewing, in which the various parts of garments were parceled out to different patients to teach them how to work as a group. Patients who participated in the sewing workshops were allowed to pick whichever fabric they liked from the stock of fabric that was purchased from a small kitty. This particular exercise also required patients to stand still for fittings and submit to the seamstress's gaze while simultaneously contemplating their own image in a mirror. The positive results yielded by these methods were soon apparent. An early and telling sign was that patient agitation, one of the banes of confinement, was on the decline. A report of the hospital's shortcomings was compiled and submitted to the administration soon after the project was launched.

These positive outcomes did not appease Fanon's detractors. Some of his colleagues, whose habits had been disrupted and routines disturbed, did not mask their hostility, while others, the majority, did not hesitate to express their skepticism. They were biding their time until they could spring their trap: Wasn't Fanon going to try out his methods on the Muslims? How could anyone be so naive as to think that these methods would work on Muslims! They are simply too backward. That's typical *Frankaoui* thinking for you, a newcomer's "pathos" before he "comes around." Fanon knew that the Muslim men would present a tougher challenge. His Arabic was nonexistent, a problem he planned to address as soon as possible. And his Kabyle was equally nonexistent. His intern spoke neither. Despite an effort to prepare the ground by conducting meetings that included only the nursing staff, things got off to a very bad start. Nothing went as planned. Thoughtful effort had gone into preparing the large table covered by an immaculately white sheet and adorned with flowers around which doctors, supervisors, and a carefully selected interpreter were invited to gather. But it was a resounding failure, with the patients indifferent to a man. Further attempts to repeat the strategies that had worked so well for the European women did not fare any better. The male patients did not engage with the collective games that were intended to resocialize them—the ball games and the games of hide-and-go-seek—nor were they interested in the parties or the attempts at choir singing. Even the basket-weaving workshop was deserted.

The atmosphere in the men's pavilion soon became oppressive; the staff became increasingly resistant to Fanon and Azoulay's requests, some went so far as to disregard them completely, and requests for reassignment from Muslim as well as European personnel were on the rise. At the end of the third month, the contrast between the strides that had been made in the European women's pavilion and the dismal failure of the same sociotherapy methods in the Muslim men's pavilion was a striking one. Fanon was subjected to the same litany over and over again: "You're still a greenhorn when it comes to Algeria. You don't know them. When you will have spent fifteen years here like the rest of us, then you'll understand." Fanon, however, was not about to be dissuaded. He knew his failure had nothing to do with the purported biological backwardness of Muslims, their laziness and ineptitude, and more to do with an assumption that "the frameworks of Western society with its established technological evolution" could be applied to a Muslim society that was, furthermore, primarily rural in its makeup. "We wanted to create institutions, but we forgot that any undertaking of this kind must be preceded by a persistent, concrete, and genuine exploration of the foundations of the native society." Fanon and Azoulay went on to say, "Could our judgment have been more impaired than when we proposed to implement a Western-based sociotherapy program that disregarded an entire frame of reference and neglected geographic, historical, cultural, and social particularities in a pavilion of mentally ill Muslim men? Are we not guilty of having thoughtlessly embraced a policy of assimilation?"[12] By embracing assimilation, they had effectively stripped the "native" of cultural specificity and left it up to him to "live up" to the colonizer's model. Assimilation, in the context of colonial societies, does not rest on exchange; it amounts, rather, to the absolute advantage of the dominant culture at the expense of the wholesale effacement of another culture.

The failed sociotherapy trials were not seen in an entirely negative light. They were considered, rather, as a positive sign of resistance by a culture that refused to bend when faced with its own denial. The gap between the two cultures had to be broached and the ongoing mutations in Algerian society accounted for. Fanon and Azoulay embarked on a careful reevaluation of their program. The patients could not abide the interpreter because he embodied the link between them and colonial authority, administrative or legal as the case may be, and because of his inclination to be complicit with that authority. The planned festivities had failed so miserably because the only meaningful holidays, at least in 1953, were the ones that held religious significance. The lack of interest in forming a choir followed from the cultural perception of performers as professionals who do not pertain to the group, individuals who, especially in rural areas, are viewed as itinerant. The basket-weaving workshop had found no takers because the making of baskets had traditionally been women's work.

This rigorous reevaluation gave rise to new institutions, ones that were familiar and culturally suited to the lives of the Muslim patients. The first of these transformations was the creation of a traditional teahouse, the kind of *café maure* that was the customary meeting place for men in Algerian society at the time. This first experiment opened the way for others: festivities to mark Muslim holidays, events that featured troubadours. Abderrahmane Azziz, the musician who taught Fanon so much about *Chaabi* musical forms, became an important contributor to this effort. Algerian members of the staff, whom Fanon had involved in his psychiatric revolution, wholehearted supported the experiment, steadfast to the end, until the day Fanon was expelled from Algeria and the Algerian medical staff was dismantled in its entirety.

At first, the Algerian staff had been both intrigued and circumspect about the new psychiatrist, the black Frenchman who was not really French. Also, he was extremely preoccupied by his appearance and was known to change shirts and even ties twice a day; his tailored smocks sported wide lapels and were buttonless, fastened by a belt, the pocket held a large monogrammed handkerchief which he often produced to wipe his face in the near constant heat. Above and beyond the political beliefs that in time would bring them ever closer to Fanon, his ideas on how to approach the mentally ill soon won him their respect. Makhlouf Longo,[13] a psychiatric nurse and ward supervisor, speaks of Fanon in near-hagiographic terms:

> He was extremely demanding, and he practiced sociotherapy. One day he called a meeting for all the Muslims on the staff, there were eighteen of us. "I would like to know who you really are," he said, "I would like us to help one another for the welfare of the patients." He told us that every single patient could be helped because he saw all patients as salvageable. "Remain open," he said, "remain honest, be sincere . . ." That's how he won us over.

Longo retains a very vivid memory of the man and of their work together.

This is how the Doctor organized his section. There were separate meetings for the support staff and for the supervisors. He insisted that we know
each individual patient, he wanted us to know about their lives before they
became ill. He taught us how to welcome them into the ward. "The patient," he explained to us, "is able to perceive the doctor's attitude, and a
proper welcome can lay the ground for the prospect of recovery." The employees were expected to record their observations of the patients in their
sections. These reports were used to follow the patient's progress. The patient's behaviors and attitudes were detailed in them. We also had meetings
for the entire medical staff, Fanon would be there as well as the interns,
and we aired opinions and discussed treatment methods. After that, we
would have a group therapy session with the patients. In the group meetings, ideas would crop up from every quarter—from the Europeans as well
as the Muslims. After a while, we had visitors, people who came to have a
look at what they could not see from the outside. One day, we organized a
huge party. There was a journalist from *Alger républicain*, and I told him
that we owed all of it to Doctor Fanon. The next day, the Doctor came
looking for me and told me that, "the fact that things get done is far more
important than who does them."

When the police came to arrest Longo in the first days of January 1957, he
asked them to grant him an hour to gather his belongings. In fact, he wanted
to say good-bye to the Doctor, but he could not find him, and he never saw
him again. This is the contribution of a man for whom I have felt affection
and admiration, one of those nameless, faceless Algerians who never lost
their way, even against the greatest odds.

Was Fanon's attempt to impose European "methodologies" on Muslim
patients a genuine "mistake," or had he consciously implemented a plan that
he knew was doomed to failure from the outset? "We were wrong," is how
Jacques Azoulay summed it up. But when Charles Géronimi, another intern, approached Fanon a year or so after the fact to express his surprise that
the author of *Black Skin, White Masks* and "The North African Syndrome"
could have been so wide off the mark, Fanon reportedly smiled and said:
"You can only understand things with your gut, you know. It was not simply
a matter of imposing imported methods that had been more or less adapted
to the *native mentality*. I also had to demonstrate a number of things in the
process: namely, that the values of Algerian culture are different from those
of colonial culture; that these structuring values had to be embraced without

any complexes by those to whom they pertained—the Algerian medical staff as well as the Algerian patients. I needed to have the support of the Algerian staff in order to incite them to rebel against the prevailing method, to make them realize that their competence was equal to that of the Europeans. The burden of suggesting appropriate forms of socialization and integrating them into the sociotherapy process had to be placed on the Algerian staff. That's what happened. Psychiatry," Fanon reportedly said at the end of this exchange, "has to be political."

While Fanon's ideas about psychiatry's direct connection to politics may have been avant-garde at the time, he did not agree with the antipsychiatric trend that denied the existence of madness, to which he ascribed no revolutionary value whatsoever. He was, however, profoundly touched by madness, which he understood as alienation and a loss of bearings, as the burden of an individual human experience. He equated madness with oppression, not liberation, and he understood the sociogenesis of mental illness as an unrelenting and longstanding problem. This view had distanced him from the organo-dynamic theory of Henri Ey, the eminent psychiatrist whom he admired greatly, and it is evident even in his thesis, its classicism notwithstanding, that he had carefully studied Jacques Lacan's ideas. Fanon, in other words, was already greatly preoccupied with the impact of crushing historical factors as well as of language and culture on subjectivity, and Azoulay, still a young student at the time, was just beginning to grapple with these ideas. Fanon in 1953 was still unfamiliar with the customs and values of Algerians, especially those who lived in rural areas, and it was to this end that he invited Azoulay, the other interns would follow in time, to accompany him on extensive and frequent travels to attend exorcisms in Kabylia and to participate in the pilgrimages held at the various shrines on the outskirts of Algiers that housed the *marabouts* who were reputed to reverse sexual impotence and cure other ills. Fanon also turned his attention to the Arab nurses on the hospital staff, and they became the object of his tireless questioning. His methods were unprecedented; his behavior was unthinkable. No psychiatrist before him had ever proceeded in like manner. Such an initiative would have been out of the question for the native staff. And it usually did not take long for those psychiatrists who had been classically trained in France, a number of whom had acquired a solid foundation in "so-called clinical psychiatry" to align themselves on the side of the fence that denied the existence of the native as other. This position was reinforced and bolstered by their secretly held contempt for the mental illness of this other. Fanon, however, was not one to be easily deterred by such attitudes; he simply jumped the fence. While his manner with the patients may have been impatient and even aggressive on occasion, it was completely devoid of contempt (he reserved that sentiment for some of his colleagues), and he looked forward to his meetings with them with passionate enthusiasm. In this regard, he was completely in step with the psychiatric approach, championed by Paul Sivadon, Sven Folin, and especially Tosquelles, that was gaining ground in post-War France and that viewed the patient as a full-fledged other and took special care to not rush the first encounter and to extend a genuine welcome to the patient, regardless of the latter's alterability and violence. Fanon, to whom this approach merely reiterated the obvious, always sought to diffuse the excesses of patients who had been labeled as dangerous by seeking an ever-increasing connection with them, by involving them in an effort of mental reciprocity—and not by calling on the police. He countered the violence of the mentally alienated other by using language and acknowledgment to open a space for negotiation. He also understood the ways in which the personality expressed the psychic wounds that had been inflicted on it by violence, and insofar as it was possible, he tried to avoid a repetition of a similar violence in the therapeutic response. This aim was to remain a constant of his work, at HPB as well as later in Tunisia.

As any psychiatrist working in an asylum setting, however, Fanon had to treat extreme mental pathologies, and he was extremely interested in the efficacy of the entire arsenal of biological therapies that were in use at the time and to which he also resorted. His patients were treated with the most advanced available biological treatments, always in combination with some form of psychotherapeutic component. When neuroleptics, antidepressants, and tranquilizers appeared in 1955, Fanon was among the first to begin prescribing them. New advances in pharmacology interested him immensely; he was extremely optimistic about the benefits of lithium salts, for example. He also recommended and was a close observer of insulin and electroshock therapy, and tried, whenever possible, to be present when the patient regained consciousness. He even spoke up for antiquated methods, as when he used a fixation abscess to enable a patient to relive the stages of an unfolding pregnancy by association; the patient who had been in a state of high agitation did indeed benefit as a result. It was also during this period, despite the demands on his time and his hectic schedule, that he traveled to France to perfect his mastery of electroencephalography. Even though Fanon subscribed to many of the "organic" treatments of the day, he was adamantly opposed to lobotomy, a practice that had been much in favor before his arrival at HPB. Neurosurgeons from the metropolis traveled on preestablished dates to Barbier-Hugo, a private clinic situated in the heart of Bab-el-

Oued, to perform the operation. On the appointed days, those patients from Mustapha and HPB who had been "selected" were sent in convoys to undergo the procedure. Fanon was violently opposed to this practice.

For nearly fifteen months, Fanon devoted the better part of his formidable energy to his psychiatric work and to putting his methods into practice at the hospital. Whenever his schedule allowed it, Fanon, who slept little and was an early riser, kept up his trips into the country's interior, where he sought out Kabyle villages so that he could learn more about local forms and institutions and expand his knowledge of Algerian society and its mutations; to this end, he spent his evenings listening to storytellers and attending ceremonies that commemorated local saints and witnessing exorcisms.

The year 1955 was a landmark with respect to both psychiatry and politics, inside as well as outside the hospital, and for Fanon's personal as well as his writing life.

By the beginning of 1955, the repercussions of Fanon's undertakings were apparent for all to see, not only inside the hospital, where the general atmosphere was much changed throughout, a number of sectors had no choice but to fall into step with the prevailing climate, but outside its walls as well.[14] Fanon's impact on Blida was also being felt beyond the town and his reputation was spreading across the social spectrum. His name was beginning to make the rounds of Algerian liberal and nationalist enclaves and he was fast becoming the object of great interest and curiosity. This was not the case, however, in Algiers, where the academic psychiatric community's hostility toward him took an overtly racist turn: "Who is this nigger who thinks he can teach us about psychiatry?" An eminent member of the faculty and a future leading expert of the former-metropolis spoke of him as "a pretentious idiotic Martinican with a complex." It must be said that the cultural sophistication of the psychiatry faculty at Algiers University was of a piece with the intellectual mediocrity of the society as a whole. Charles Géronimi recalls how his colleagues ridiculed him when he turned up with a volume of collected poems by Apollinaire that he had purchased on his way to the hospital. Only Lucette Sahuquet, who was a member of Centre régional d'art dramatique (CRAD) and worked as a secretary to the hospital's director, expressed her sincere approval. The effects, if indeed there were any, of the malicious chatter in the capital did not distract Fanon from his endeavor, and he did not allow himself to be roped into personal confrontations. Instead, he opted for a different route. His first interest was the hospital where he continued to labor and create new structures that would transform the prison-like character of the institution. His plans for the patients included a new theater and, most excitingly for Fanon, a new soccer stadium, the construction of which he oversaw in every detail until he was forced to leave the country. He submitted a request for a new building to house a nursing school; he had already become heavily involved in the training of the nursing staff. It was also during this period that he established an open clinic that he operated jointly with R. Lacaton. The clinic, to which the coercive 1838 law mandating the hospitalization of the mentally ill, still in effect at the time, did not apply, was intended for the treatment of "mild psychiatric cases." Two rooms had been set aside to accommodate patients who needed hospitalization: a ward for women as well as one for men, but in this instance, there was to be no differentiation made between Muslims and Europeans. The clinic was inaugurated with some fanfare in 1955 by Professor Porot, whose name it bore. Fanon, who was greatly displeased by this turn of events, suggested that the entire hospital be named in Porot's honor.[15] He explained to us that "the naming of a single pavilion is a minor affair to be settled by the medical administration, but the naming of an entire hospital has to be decided by decree from higher ups in the bureaucracy and was bound to take a long, long time. . . ." The unwitting Porot felt extremely flattered by Fanon's proposal, and the medical administration's subsequent petition to rename the hospital was, as expected, irretrievably lost in the thickets of bureaucracy.[16]

The opening of the clinic was an important development. From the moment it was up and running, Fanon began to change its intended function. Almost immediately, he transferred a handful of patients who had been at "de Clérambault," the closed ward under his charge, to the new clinic. He wished to make it perfectly clear that he did not distinguish between those patients who had been labeled "chronically incurable" and others. Delirious and hallucinating patients, as a result, were placed alongside the neurotically depressed. More to the point, however, the clinic's more relaxed admission policy made it possible for Fanon, as well as Lacaton, to use it as a safe house for militants, men as well as women, who were on the run from security forces. The problem of tidying up Fanon's study and cleaning up the trails of mud that had been left by the "pataugas" worn by the clandestine visitors who had to come to the clinic not for psychiatric help but to steal a night's sleep on Fanon's couch fell to the interns.

Fanon set in motion a plan within the HPB for the creation of a nursing program specialized in psychiatric care. The nursing staff he had found on site had not had specialized training of any kind. He began working on developing a curriculum for a degree in psychiatric nursing. He felt that it stood to reason that the nursing staff of a psychiatric institution should have the appropriate training for the job; this view was far from being a widely held one at the time. In due course, the specialized program was up and running, but as there was a shortage of buildings, and until such time as a projected site to house it could be built, classes, taught by interns as well as head physicians, were conducted in the chapel.

The nursing program served as a framework for Fanon to organize seminars and invite a number of "metropolitan" colleagues who shared his commitment to institutional therapy. Tosquelles never participated in the lecture series, but Dr. Georges Daumézon, who was in charge of admitting patients to Sainte-Anne in Paris, spent several weeks in late 1955 and early 1956 at HPB directing a training program that was conducted by instructors from the CEMEA (Centre d'entraînment aux méthodes d'éducation active). Daumézon was extremely fond of Fanon. But when he was questioned by Jean Ayme about the situation in Algeria shortly after his visit there, all he said in his signature paradoxical manner was that "people there were dying in about the same numbers as in the Paris-bound traffic at the end of any given weekend." This was in June 1956. In 1952, Daumézon, who coined the term "institutional psychotherapy," viewed the colonial question in much the same way as did the French Communist Party at the end of the 1940s. In 1957, he, along with many others, including Henri Ey, advised Fanon "to give up politics and to concentrate on psychiatry where he was really needed." The colonial question had been relegated to the back burner, and the link between political oppression and individual psychopathology that was increasingly at the heart of Fanon's work dismissed along with it. More seminars had been in the works, but by 1956, the situation in Algeria had become too volatile.

In addition to his reform within the hospital, Fanon also used his publications as a forum in which to address the Algiers-based psychiatrists. Despite an almost uninterrupted presence at the hospital—the nurses recall running into him at any time of day or night—Fanon continued to publish at a considerable pace, a corroboration of both his professional breadth and his growing commitment to the situation in Algeria. Increasingly, his professional and theoretical research supplied the foundation for his overtly political writings. He started by taking the problem of mental health in Algeria head-on and using it as an occasion to openly criticize the theories associated with the Algiers school. He had convinced all of his colleagues at HPB, regardless of their political views, to present a united front in the extremely detailed report and appraisal of mental health conditions in Algeria that they presented in *L'Information psychiatrique*. During this same period, he collaborated with Lacaton on an article on the ways in which patient depositions and admissions were conducted by North African medical and legal institutions; the paper, which was presented at the *Congrès de psychiatrie et de neurologie*, was an all out assault on the perception of the Algerian as a born liar and primitive.[17] In the absence of a social contract between the criminal and his or her judges, a confession of criminal activity made no sense. This contract had yet to exist, and the refusal of an accused Muslim to admit to his or her actions was tantamount to a refusal to acknowledge a power to which he or she may submit but does not accept.

"Africains Antillais," completed in 1954, appeared in the journal *Esprit* in February of that same year. The text marks an important shift in Fanon's work and seems to close a chapter on his Antillean past. As autobiography, it bears Fanon's paradoxical mark and seems to claim "I am and am not there." He revisits his childhood and youth and the moment at which he became aware that the African, Senegalese infantry man "crouches in the labyrinth of his epidermis." Fanon does not judge, he merely describes, but the metaphors speak for themselves. Until 1945, the African was a Negro and the Antillean a European. After 1945, the Antillean is toppled from "the great white mistake to the great black mirage." In a handful of densely embodied lines, he exposes the identity pitfalls of an all-white or an all-black identity, which he views as so many traps. In the subsequent "man must be set free" of *Black Skin, White Masks*, Fanon's position is shored up, always in search of paths out of the alienation and oppression of all humankind: the solution is not one of "negritude" as opposed to "blanchitude." If difference accrues along the way, as it must, it will serve to build cultures, societies, and nations that are in constant motion. This particular thought was one Fanon cherished particularly, but then, of course, it was also embodied by what he lived in his daily life: people, structures, a society in motion, a historical juncture he had not experienced in the Antilles.

Also at this time, Fanon was contacted by *Consciences maghribines*, a political journal that had been in print since 1945 and sought to fill the void that had been left by *Consciences algériennes*. This was the journal in which he published his "ethnopsychiatric observations," pieces that essentially and in a very straightforward manner denounced the theory of primitivism and its application to the Muslim community. He used this occasion to point out the proximity between this theory and Carothers's view of the black African as "almost identical to a lobotomized European." The journal's editorial board was made up largely of former members of the AJAAS; people who met in the offices of Amitiés algériennes, a humanitarian organization that offered material and tactical support to the families of political detainees. The organization was in reality run by national militants with ties to the *maquisards* of *Wilaya* 4[18] posted in Chrea, a place that had until very recently been considered an elegant ski resort by the inhabitants of the capital and its environs. Situated near Blida and strategically perched in an elevated area, it was one of the first sites of the armed resistance. As early as 1955, a number of Algerian students, all trained in basic first aid and appointed as "political commissars," left their city lives to join the fighters in the mountains. By then, the need for medications and safe havens for the wounded was becoming apparent; a number of fighters were already showing symptoms of emotional and psychological distress. Fanon's first significant contact with the Algerian National Liberation Movement took place through this organization. It was by way of these intersecting networks that Fanon was contacted in 1955.

Fanon's response to November 1, 1954, is not known. What is known, however, is that his support for Algerian nationalists was fast in coming. He had been, since his youth in the Antilles, a supporter of total decolonization. In those earlier times, he had been in disagreement with his teacher Aimé Césaire and held the view, unpopular at the time, that a confederation of the entire Antilles was a necessary step toward Antillean independence. In Algeria, he was in agreement with the liberal opposition to "blind repression" and added his voice to the demands for the liberation of political detainees who had been arrested on preventive grounds; a special emphasis was placed on the release of elected officials who had been subject to the sweeping measures, and Fanon insisted on the importance of establishing a dialogue with this particular group. Fanon had kept close tabs on the declarations that had been published by the FLN, and he was particularly attentive to the ones that were published after the ronéotypé document of April 1955 that called on Algerians to join the ranks of the Front de Libération Nationale "the only political party that provides aid and support for the army." Until that point, Fanon had not had the opportunity to come into contact with the leaders of the insurrection who were still relatively unknown at the beginning 1955. Fanon still did not know that Abbane Ramdane, the man who would later become his friend, was responsible for the tenor of the appeal, of the new political will that would bring the FLN out of the shadows once and for all.[19]

When the time had come toward the end of the winter of 1954–55 for Amitiés Algériennes, whose activities up to that point had been limited to Algiers, to set up satellites in the provinces, Fanon's name came up as a possibility for the Blida area. "There is a new psychiatrist at HPB who has been doing good work and has shown himself to be openly and staunchly anti-colonialist, in discussions at the Blida *ciné-club* for example. His name is Frantz Fanon." The name was not unfamiliar to Dr. Pierre Chaulet, one of the leaders inside the organization. This young doctor, who was closely associated with Mandouze, involved with the "progressive Christian" community, a member of the AJAAS and of Amitiés Algériennes, and an editor at *Consciences maghribines*, was among the few in his profession whose reading habits extended beyond medical literature; he had read *Black Skin, White*

Masks and had brought it to the attention of Salah Louanchi, a young Algerian journalist who also worked at *Consciences maghribines* and who later became part of the leadership of the French Federation of the FLN.

A couple of months later, Pierre Chaulet received an urgent plea from the guerilla army asking him to put them in contact with a "safe" psychiatrist who could address the mental and emotional problems of its recruits. Chaulet immediately thought of Fanon; the two men met; Fanon agreed on the spot. At first, it was simply a matter of treating guerilla fighters for a whole gamut of illnesses. The admission policy at the open clinic Fanon was running with Lacaton was much easier to circumvent than the one that was in place at the hospital. Lacaton was, to all appearances, entirely complicit with Fanon. In the early days of the revolution, Fanon was not approached as a political thinker but as a physician, and while his anticolonialist stance was a matter of public record, his qualifications and readiness to offer practical and medical help to the combatants held far greater sway. The FLN was interested in securing help to address health and hygiene problems in many places throughout Algeria.

Fanon's writing, however, both in its substance and in its perspective, was significant for those who supported this rapprochement, Pierre Chaulet and Salah Louanchi, for example. It was as central as any professional imperative in my meetings and work with Fanon. When I arrived at HPB, in late 1955, early 1956, intensive psychiatric work was matched by an equally important political activity. The hospital was divided between supporters of French Algeria, whose conservatism extended to psychiatric matters, and more recent arrivals who were progressive supporters of psychotherapy and sociotherapy and understood cultural oppression as alienation. The second group was willing to support the November 1954 Movement and the fighters of *Wilaya* 4 and did so on a daily basis. The situation was explosive, and in this, the hospital was no different from the rest of Algeria. All the same, with Fanon at the helm, the psychiatric work stayed on course: morning rounds, afternoon meetings with the staff alternating with group therapy sessions, work sessions in the library under Fanon's direction, evening classes for the nursing staff, and, on a rather regular basis, discussions on assigned readings with the interns. Some of the pavilions, especially in the children's ward, were still in an appalling state: autistic and encephalitic children *existed* there, in a pale semblance of life spent rocking back and forth in the care of a single nurse who couldn't offer much else beside her compassion. In 1956, the amount of work ahead of us at Blida-Joinville was monumental.

Fanon took a great interest in the training of interns and did not begrudge them his time. At his insistence, the hospital had made great strides in improving its library holdings; by 1956, its collection of works on psychiatry, psychoanalysis, and neurology was far superior to the one available at the university-affiliated Mustapha Hospital. The library subscribed to all the major French magazines and journals; its English offerings were not as plentiful, but this did not reflect Fanon's interest and extensive reading of psychiatric works outside the French sphere. He often requested translations of Spanish or German articles, and after he had grasped the gist of the article in question, he invariably took the translator to task for the quality of the translation. He was engaged in a continuous dialogue with the interns and would talk with them for hours on end, if not at a patient's bedside, then in the library, or during the scheduled discussion sessions that dealt primarily with psychopathology. In the politically charged atmosphere of 1956, we spent a number of evenings gathered in the dormitory in order to read and discuss Freud's "Wolf Man." We knew that we could be called away at any moment by the needs of a wounded, mentally exhausted, or fugitive combatant, but, paradoxically, these duties did not qualify as interruptions; it was all of a piece, and it did not feel as though we had strayed from the topic at hand and our inquiries into the sufferings of desire. The degree of enthusiasm or interest that the interns brought to these theoretical discussions was uneven, but they proved to be an enlightening experience for most. Regardless of their Muslim, Jewish, or European origins, and despite their progressive political views, the young Algerian doctors who made up the team were not especially well read, most were uncultivated. In a haphazard fashion, they were discovering psychiatry, anthropology, philosophy, and psychoanalysis for the first time. Fanon's reading list included Freud, Helene Deutsch, Adler, and Reich, the Austrian. He wanted his young charges to learn, to discover new things and produce, and while he was moved by the progress of his more motivated students, he was also demanding and unrelenting with those students who were less gifted or lazy.

We also frequently visited him at his home; these visits were as free of fuss as his unannounced arrival in the dormitories for a chat or a study session. His usual and extreme discretion about his personal life and intellectual achievements did not extend to the great abandon with which he discussed psychiatry and psychoanalysis. On the subject of Tosquelles, he was tireless, publicly expressing his deep admiration, and more cautious about expressing his affection, which was no less deep. His face would relax and his eyes light up at the mention of the psychiatrist who had been a pioneer of institutional psychotherapy in the immediate aftermath of World War II. For the duration of that war, the mentally ill, regardless of where they may have been, had been subjected to horrific conditions. By the 1950s, however, that battle had been eclipsed by the more pressing questions surrounding the collapse of colonial empires and the emergence of world powers. In Germany, the simple fact of being committed to a psychiatric institution was seen as grounds for sending the mentally ill to the gas chambers. This fact, which is now widely known, was suppressed at the time, and Tosquelles was one of a handful who sought to expose it. The subject of the mentally ill who had died in droves from starvation in French psychiatric facilities was even more controversial.

Fanon's secret soft spot for Tosquelles was not just the result of professional admiration; Fanon also admired the Spaniard for his staunch anti-Franco position. Tosquelles, who had lived in France since 1939, had a merry way of mangling the French language. Tosquelles's stubborn refusal to submit to the rules of pronunciation fascinated Fanon, whose own accent in French was impeccable, almost a thing of beauty to his many Algerian students who had also started to shed their regional accents and particular linguistic mannerisms. The *r*, for example, became softer in the mouths of the Europeans; it was no longer burbled by Berbers or throttled by Arabs and Jews. And vowels, over which the Semitic languages tend to run roughshod, regained their distinct enunciation.

The interns worked closely with Fanon on a variety of research projects, all addressing some aspect of psychopathology in the context of Algeria's colonization. One of those projects became the article "L'attitude du Musulman devant la folie"; it had been written by François Sanchez, an intern who was arrested in January 1957 and interned in the camp at Lodi.[20] Most of the projects had to be abandoned midway. One of these projects was exploring ways in which the Thematic Apperception Test (T.A.T.), a test that measured projection, could be adapted to Algerian society.[21] Preliminary findings had already indicated that the standard plates did not work in the Algerian setting. The test was designed around a series of prototypical images to which the patient was expected to respond by projecting his/her personal history. The imagery was entirely drawn from the Western and Christian world: cemeteries dotted with crucifixes, a wooden stairway in a late nineteenth-century European building, a mother, her hair in a low ponytail, bending over a little girl who is holding—would you believe it?—a Stradivarius. These images are not happy ones by any standard, but they were completely outside the orbit of perception of Algerian patients and totally useless as personal narrative triggers as they did not offer a single metaphoric or metonymic hook. The images and the figures they represented were totally alien to the patients, who were Algerian for the most part and rural besides. Confronted with these images that did not spark their imaginations in any way, the patients exhibited reactions of "phantasmagoric paucity" and "lack of symbolic elaboration." These responses partly bore out some of the claims made by Fanon in the "North African

Syndrome." New picture plates had to be created to replace the old ones if the test, which was sound in principle, was to work at all, but the project was never completed and had to be abandoned in late 1956 as a result of the precipitous wave of exiles, expulsions, and arrests; like so many other things, it, too, was postponed until after Independence. It should be said, however, that Fanon was extremely invested in this project at the time.

During this same period, Fanon was supervising two doctoral theses in medicine. His student Ziza was working on a study of the role of *djnoun* (*djinns*) in Algerian psychopathology; specifically, he was interested in how belief in *djnoun* structured and organized life in rural communities and in the repercussions this belief may have had on local expressions of mental pathologies. The existence of *djnoun*, or genies as they have come to be known in the Western tradition, is acknowledged in the Qur'an. They function as agents of good as well as evil. Their dual nature is strangely reminiscent of the ancient Furies/Eumenides who accompany Orestes in his madness. In North Africa at the time, mental illness was generally attributed to *djnoun*. Literally, the Arabic word *medjnoun* (which means "mad" in common usage) means one who is possessed by the *djnoun*. Patients suffering from hallucinations held the djnoun responsible for their torment. Women who suffered from forms of postpartum depression that were much more extreme than the ones we usually encounter in young urban women these days, a condition which was endemic in the rural areas, claimed that *djnoun* had entered their bodies. The other thesis, the work of a student named Asselah, was a study on dreams. Asselah reported that while Professor Manceaux had claimed to be very interested in his topic, he had also said that "Arabs only dream about white horses." These two dissertations were never completed. Dr. Ziza came through the turbulent times that swept the HPB in the early months of 1957, but Asselah never emerged from the interrogation room to which he had been taken by the "security forces."

This double trajectory in which psychiatric and political work were intimately linked lasted until the end of 1956. It was inscribed in our daily lives. In hindsight, it is astounding that we managed to maintain the connection between these two spheres. It would be misguided to conclude that it was simply a matter of events accumulating, a matter of parallel pursuits linked by abstract and tenuous connections. Quite the contrary, these were inseparable pursuits, enmeshed, one deeply engrained in the other. The army and the police understood this perfectly, and they would raid the hospital grounds on a regular basis to search for suspects, people on the run who were being sheltered there as well as members of the hospital staff. In the meantime, the need for medical and hygienic support was becoming more urgent by the day, and the *maquis* was stepping up pleas for psychiatric help. Our days revolved around the nexus of politics and psychiatry and not in an abstract or theoretical sense but in a very real sense that was fraught with danger.

So it was that 1956 was a landmark year. Everywhere and in every way, Algerians wanted to be acknowledged as capable of ruling themselves. But every single space for negotiation was immediately retracted. There was, instead, a brutal and unrelenting repression and a refusal to acknowledge the demands and the existence of those who were making them. Fanon, on whom none of this was lost, was alarmed about the psychological repercussions of these developments. The year 1956 marked the escalation of the armed and political conflict that would sweep the country in its entirety. From that time on, differences of opinion were swept aside, and the FLN and other nationalist movements, including those that had been opposed to armed struggle, formed a united front. Former members of the MTLD, the UDMA, as well as of the Association des Oulémas (scholars and reformers of Islamic law)[22] and the PCA joined forces. New unions were formed: UGMA (students) was the earliest, in July 1955; UGTA (workers) in February 1956; UGSA (merchants) in September 1956; and they all threw in their lot with the FLN and went into action by organizing solidarity strikes and providing logistical support. At the August 1956 Congrès de la Soummam, the FLN published its position and political platform to a wide-reaching effect.[23] In June 1956, the newspaper *El Moudjahid* was created to take the place of the defunct *Résistance Algérienne* and would from that point on become the official organ of the FLN. It was becoming increasingly clear, especially after February 1956, that the new Socialist government in France was not going to live up to expectations and was shutting door after door on the possibility of negotiations. The metropolitan response cloaked itself in the refusal to acknowledge the movement of liberation and in military repression.[24] Prior to February 1956, Guy Mollet had ignored the proposal of the Algiers-based FLN that was personally conveyed to him by André Mandouze and Robert Barrat. After his lightening visit to Algiers in February 1956, it was obvious to everyone that the "tomato" bombardment that had been unleashed on him by militant Europeans had forced him into a hasty retreat. During this same period, the ongoing extensive and secret negotiations with internationally known FLN members were brought to a halt by the October 1956 hijacking of the airplane carrying a delegation that included Mohammed Boudiaf, Mohammed Khider, Hocine Aït Ahmed, Ahmed Ben Bella, and last but not least, Mostefa Lacheraf, an important figure in the intellectual and militant leadership of the FLN. They were headed for a conference in Tunis that had been designed as a forum for representatives from the three North African nations, Algeria and the newly independent Morocco and Tunisia, and was viewed as an opportunity for the FLN leadership to gather in one place. The importance of 1956, with the Section française de l'internationale ouvrière (SFIO) at the helm in France and Robert Lacoste in Algeria, as a critical turning point in the Algeria tragedy cannot be sufficiently underscored: from countless lost opportunities for negotiation to armed struggle and a policy of assassinations and blind repression to the ascendancy of Lagaillarde's troops and an open season on torture.

The war escalated, spreading to every corner of the territory and changing every aspect of our day-to-day lives. The need for medical aid became greater as the armed conflict grew. First, there were the wounded, and for these, Fanon solicited the help of a surgeon who was affiliated with HPB. The surgery facility at HPB was modest; there was a small operating room equipped with a few beds that were used for the treatment of wounded combatants. Later, in Tunis, Fanon told us that the pharmacist at HPB had also assisted the effort by supplying morphine capsules; the doctor did this at a time when most doctors, fearing direct reprisals, refused to sign their name to certificates attesting to the evidence of torture.

This network of medical support soon became something more. Before long, cooperation with the local FLN leaders included arrangements to shelter and transport combatants as well as assistance in the delivery of documents and weapons. Mustapha Bencherchalli, the scion of a "good family" that had made its fortune in tobacco, had entry into Blida's most exclusive bourgeois circles and was Fanon's go-between with the local leadership. In his powerful American convertible, he thoroughly enjoyed carrying on as a playboy and finessing his way past even the most forbidding checkpoints. With almost total impunity and in the comfort of his snazzy vehicle, he ran weapons from the cache that had been seized by Maillot in the spring of 1955. He openly visited Fanon on a regular basis under the pretense that he was in therapy, but no one was fooled.

In time, Fanon's involvement exceeded the local network and came to include the regional leadership. He established ties with the military command of *Wilaya* 4 and had become especially close to Commandant Azzedine and to Slimane Dehiles whose *nom de guerre* was Colonel Saddek. Both men had allowed students, who described themselves as Marxists, and women to join their armies in their mountain hideaways. The practice of segregation that was in force in other regions of the country did not apply to *Wilaya* 4, although it would follow suit at a later date. The better Saddek came to know Fanon, the greater his admiration and affection for the man, and through all the trials and tribulations of the struggle for independence, he never had a change of heart. For his part, Fanon liked Saddek for his ability to combine military prowess with an open mind—at least in those early years.

By late 1955, Manville had joined the team of French lawyers who were taking on the cases of Algerian defendants and had started making frequent trips to Algeria. Whenever he was in Algeria, he stayed with Fanon, and the latter took every opportunity to demonstrate to his friend just how harsh things had become. Manville, a Communist and a lawyer who believed in the legally constituted state, was not always easy to convince. Their exchanges sometimes veered to mutual mockery, but beneath the jesting, something was beginning to take shape. On a day of scorching heat, Manville found himself traveling in the indescribable Peugeot 403 that passed for Fanon's car. His pal Frantz wanted him to see a cement factory that had been shut down in retribution for the strikes. Security had been heightened, and it didn't take much time for the pair to find themselves stopped at one of the ubiquitous checkpoints. Manville, who had left the house in his shirtsleeves and had neglected to bring his identification documents, was detained on the spot. As they took his friend away, Fanon bid him "Farewell," then added, "why farewell, you may ask? Because for all I know you may already be a dead man." Shortly thereafter, Fanon presented himself at the police station with the appropriate documents and the two men were sent on their way. Fanon wanted Manville to have a firsthand experience of the absurdity and arbitrariness to which he had become accustomed. These kinds of incidents had become habitual, and needless to say, they usually did not make for such a good story. This experience was at the root of Manville's suggestion that Fanon speak of the *illegally constituted state* in the letter of resignation he was drafting at the time.

Fanon, who liked to give rein to his imagination, was given to trotting out preposterous scenarios like burning down the Admiralty in Algiers, or killing Césaire, or plotting to assassinate Froger, the president of the all-powerful Association of Algerian Mayors.[25] These suggestions never went beyond the realm of fictional fancy, but by actually enunciating them, he was able to accede to more plausible plans of action. When Meriem Belmihoud, Safia Bazi, and Fadila Mesli, three young and charming students who had joined the maquis, were detained in the area southeast of Blida on July 14, 1956, Fanon and Manville agreed on the symbolic importance of entrusting their defense to a woman, namely Mme Kremerbach, a Socialist and a Jew who had been deported. She accepted, but it was never to be. Political events were too far advanced by then, and the Suez crisis was already under-way. Manville was unavailable at the time, and they were represented by the young lawyer Jacques Vergès.

Fanon's contribution on other fronts was more substantial. In his recent memoirs, André Mandouze relates how he had been forewarned by Fanon about the grisly acts of provocation that were being prepared by a highly placed bureaucrat of longstanding—who had played an important part in the repression of 1945—to coincide with Guy Mollet's visit to Algiers.[26] The blame for these highly organized but indiscriminate attacks, carried out by local hoodlums, would fall on the FLN. Fanon had become privy to the plan because the wife of the bureaucrat in question was one of his regular pa-tients.[27] André Mandouze was able to intervene in a timely fashion and in-form the French government of the plot, thereby averting disaster.

For the whole of that year, Fanon was seldom absent from his patients' bedside when they were recovering from the insulin-induced comas re-quired by the Sakel cure. He continued to attend afternoon group therapies and to conduct evening discussion sessions in the dormitory. He also never stopped writing. In early September, he traveled to Bordeaux, where he pre-sented a paper on T.A.T. and the Muslim woman at the Congrès des Médecins aliéniste.[28] He presented early findings on the inadequacy of the plates that were traditionally associated with the test, concluding that the only plate that elicited any reaction from the Muslim imagination had been the blank one, the one devoid of figures or subject matter of any kind.

Between July and August 1956, he was also feverishly at work on "Racisme et culture," the paper he planned to present at the Premier Congrès des Écrivains et Artistes noirs. Throughout all the paroxysms of that devastating summer, the endless student strikes, the curfew that had been imposed on Blida, the attacks on neighboring farms that were carried out in retribution for the summary executions of nationalist sympathizers, Fanon worked on his paper. It was also the summer of the Congrès de la Soummam, the forum at which the Algerian position was clearly delineated and the FLN officially instated.

Immediately before traveling to Paris, where he presented "Racisme et culture," in September 1956, Fanon attended the Congrès de Bordeaux, where he was introduced to Jean Ayme, an institutional psychiatrist with a long history of anticolonial activism who was very perturbed by the events that were unfolding on the other side of the Mediterranean. The connec-tion between the two men was immediate, and the fact that Daumézon had introduced them was neither here nor there. Fanon and Ayme decided to make the drive to Paris together, stopping along the way to visit the Trot-skyist historian Pierre Broué.[29] The three men talked through the night.

The next morning, Fanon had to be in Paris to present "Racisme et culture" at the Premier Congrès des Écrivains et Artistes noirs that was being held at the Sorbonne. This paper marked a new phase in Fanon's intellectual evolution.

Four years had elapsed since the publication of *Black Skin, White Masks* and its queries into the depersonalization of the colonized subject and that subject's inability to answer the question "who am I?," a question that, in the Antillean setting, was made all the more acute by racial considerations; in this work, Fanon also explored the mentality of "voluntary servitude" that rests on a fabricated identity modeled on the oppressor's identity and the psychological traumas implied therein. The discussion is spurred on by these ideas and Fanon's intimate knowledge of their repercussions. Two years had elapsed since "Africains Antillais," a work that cautions against resorting to the recourse of identity and advances the idea of inscribed difference; the idea of cultures and societies in motion is already present, albeit in sketchy form. In "Racisme et culture," these ideas were more fleshed out as a result of the three years Fanon has spent in Algeria, where he arrived as a member of one society and ended up immersed in another and where he experienced colonial oppression side-by-side with the emergence of a movement of national liberation. This, while the countries of the Antilles were being reinvented as departments of France. With renewed conviction, he revisits the idea of racism as a cultural element—"an element that renews and fine-tunes itself in accordance with the evolution of the cultural whole that informs it." Biological racism, with its scientific aspirations, gives way to cultural racism, which, since 1945 has been quietly bolstered by a modernity that places the accent not on skull formation, or skin color, or the shape of a nose, but on "ways of existing." This racism, Fanon continues, is only part of a whole that is far vaster and that entails "the systematic oppression of a people through expropriation, raiding and plunder while it simultaneously destroys the modalities of existence, ransacks cultural structures, and effaces the lines of force that order the culture." And there was more. Fanon even went so far as to say that the most traumatic thing of all is not the total eradication of a culture but the inevitable survival of a part of that culture. The culture, now diminished, endures an unending agony, lingers on in an embalmed state, encysted, "immobilized in its colonized condition," alive and mummified at the same time, existing as evidence against itself. Kateb Yacine, a contemporary of Fanon's and the author of *Le Cadavre encerclé* and *Nedjma*, relied on a similar metaphor to express the sentiment of alienation and the impossible situation of a culture in stasis; he saw it as a body that could not be laid to rest. This depersonalization, the presence of this *cadavre encerclé*, is a necessary feature for domination to assert itself, and domination is necessary if power is to secure the economic and political upper hand. When the system of oppression is perfectly oiled, it no longer needs deliberately violent methods to sanction its superiority; the violence resides in the institution itself, muffled and implicit to such a degree that the "commercial undertaking of destruction" can be replaced by a verbal mystification that is compatible with an ideology that is purportedly democratic and humane but racist nonetheless. Things are much the same as our century draws to a close.

The trammeled culture needs to be freed, reinvigorated, reappropriated so that colonized peoples and their colonizers may be liberated. Fanon concluded his paper with a statement that, regardless of where one stands on its utopian aspirations, fundamentally illustrates his thinking:

> When liberated, the seized and rigid culture of the occupier opens itself up at long last to the culture of a people who have become true brethren. The two cultures are now in a position to confront and enrich each other. . . . Universality resides in the decision to take on the reciprocal relativism of other cultures once the colonial status has been irreversibly excluded.

Fanon, nonetheless, continued to hold on to the view he had divulged to Mannoni some years beforehand that there was no real difference between the day-to-day racism of the petty colonial settler and the racism of the metropolis. He would never veer from this position, and in his last exchange with Sartre, he faulted the great man for his failure to make a radical break by withdrawing from French intellectual life to express his opposition to the Algerian war. Shortly after the conference at the Sorbonne, Fanon would make his own radical break. At the conference, his paper had caused quite a stir, and Fanon used its success to align himself with the most assertive arguments for independence in Africa as well as in the Caribbean. It was during this conference that he struck up a friendship with George Lamming, the English-language novelist who had been born in Barbados. He and Fanon were the youngest panelists, both opposed Césaire who, despite his militancy, still thought of Martinique in terms of the metropolis. The two men agreed on the necessity of a consolidated Caribbean and shared a similar understanding of the pitfalls of cultural subjugation. Fanon also met Richard Wright, for whom he felt a great admiration. In 1953, while still at Saint-Albain, Fanon had written Wright a deeply respectful letter in which he revealed his intention to adopt Wright's ideas as praxis. In Tunis, three years later, a decidedly more circumspect Fanon published a stinging review of Wright's *Listen, White Man* in *El Moudjahid*.

In October 1956, Fanon returned to Blida to discover that matters at the hospital and in Algeria had taken a great turn for the worse. As the calendar year drew to a close, the political situation in France was shaken by two major events: the Soviet invasion of Hungary and the Suez crisis, in which France and Great Britain, with Israel bringing up the rear, went to war against Gamal Abdel Nasser, the "novice-dictator" who had nationalized the Canal. These developments were, as one would expect, deeply felt at HPB. The PCF's rousing response to the invasion of Hungary revealed the degree to which the Algerian problem continued to be a minor preoccupation for the French. The Suez crisis was vexing on two fronts. The initiative undertaken by Nasser in response to the United States's refusal to finance the Assouan Dam did not strike Algerian nationalists as particularly shocking. French public opinion, including that of the French Left, on the other hand, was indignant and labeled Nasser a "dictator" and "Arab Hitler" but neglected to acknowledge the national economic interest of France as the real stake. The crisis was further proof of Guy Mollet's continued insistence that Nasser was the main orchestrator behind the Algerian Nationalist Movement and of his unwillingness to acknowledge its autonomy. He thought that by bringing down Nasser, he could put an end to Algerian unrest. This line of reasoning further confirmed the Algerian view that the president of the Socialist Council was seriously in the wrong.

Fanon, who had been heartened by the Left's entry into government and who had held out the hope that the tide would turn in Algeria, was astounded by the developments. Algerian nationalists were now in a stranglehold. The reprisal against the UGTA strike had been brutal, and the FLN's call on students, merchants, and workers to participate in a second general strike was countered with a warning of more severe reprisals. The French Authority was shocked and angered to realize that a number of French nationals supported the Algerian Revolution and that their support went beyond humanitarian aid. By the end of 1956, Résident Général Lacoste and Colonel Massu were in agreement that the repression should extend to these French citizens.

The HPB was viewed as a den of *fellaghas*. It goes without saying that Fanon was in the scopes of the security forces. Georges Counillon had joined the maquis. Rumor had it that a major raid was being prepared. It came later than we had expected, in January 1957 during the general strike. A month earlier the policy of escalated repression that had taken its toll even against the psychiatric nursing staff, all of them members of the UGTA and participants in the general strike, had prompted Fanon to resign from his post at the psychiatric hospital of Blida-Joinville. It is difficult to know if

Fanon's resignation was an act of protest against the extreme measures to which the strikers had been subject, motivated by a sense of his own immediate personal danger, or if his ties to the leadership of the FLN were in fact closer than they appeared to be. In all probability, even he did not entirely comprehend the reasons for his action. What we do know, however, is that his letter of resignation speaks of the "absurd gamble" of insisting, at all costs, on the restoration of alienated individuals to "their rightful place" in a country where "systematized dehumanization" rules the day and where "non-rights, inequality and death are advanced as principles of law," where "the native, a permanent alien in his own country, lives in a state of total depersonalization." Given such a context, how can one sustain the subjectivity that is necessary to fight alienation? How can one proceed when this subjectivity is totally at odds with the reality that surrounds it? This is the dilemma that Fanon highlighted in his letter of resignation.

Word of Fanon and of the positions he held, both in theory and in practice, had reached Abbane Ramdane and Ben Youssef Ben Khedda, FLN leaders of the interior front who were clandestinely based in Algiers. Fanon had already expressed his interest in working with the political leadership. Whether Abbane requested or merely agreed to a meeting with Fanon is really neither here nor there. What is certain is that both men welcomed a chance to meet, and Pierre Chaulet made all the arrangements. The meeting took place in late December 1956, postponed by one day, from the 29th to the 30th, because of the demonstrations by European activists following the assassination of Amédée Froger by a feddayeen commando. Fanon had already submitted his resignation letter to Lacoste, the Resident Secretary. We were never privy to what had transpired in the course of that meeting. From all appearances, things must have gone well between Fanon and his interlocutors who, to a man, all ended up in Tunis.

In response to his letter of resignation, Fanon received an order of expulsion. The expulsion, it is safe to assume, saved his life when we pause to reflect on the fate of countless "intellectuals" who had taken up the cause of those who had been labeled as outlaws and brigands. The great distinction of Boumendjel Esq.[30] and the French citizenship of Maurice Audin did not stand them in great stead against their torturers. Fanon, a black man, would not have fared much better. Those who failed to leave on January 1, 1957, namely, most of the interns and the nursing staff that had worked with Fanon were, in fact, arrested; the lucky ones were interned. It was the beginning of the end of Robert Lacoste's final hour.

Fanon, who received his order of expulsion in the first week of January, left Blida by himself and traveled to Paris via Algiers. His wife and son, who had stayed behind with the Chaulet's, joined him a few days later.

In the course of January and February 1957, the noose was tightening more and more. Support networks and safe houses in Algiers, including the ones associated with the highest command, were dismantled. Abbane, Ben Khedda, as well as countless others had to leave the country. By February 1957, they had all left. Using the underground that was in place in the country's interior, they relocated to bases in Morocco or Tunisia. Pierre Chaulet was arrested on the very eve of the day he was supposed to deliver Abbane to a meeting point in Blida with *Wilaya* 4. Claudine Chaulet stepped in where her husband left off, and even though Chaulet was incarcerated, he did manage to hear the news that the *package* had been safely delivered.

Fanon Transits through Paris

Fanon is semiretired in Clermont-de-l'Oise at the home of his colleague Jean Ayme. The French turn their backs on the Algerian War. After spending three years in Algeria, Fanon is convinced that Algerian independence is an inescapable fact. The French Federation of the FLN and Francis Jeanson make arrangements for Fanon's move to Tunis.

While Abbane Ramdane, with the help of the underground, was steadily making his way toward Tunis, and the Battle of Algiers, sparked in June 1956 by the Authority's failure to uphold its promise of staying summary executions,[1] was escalating, and young militants cried—or did not because it was too late even for that—in agony, and Larbi Ben M'Hidi, the historically acclaimed leader of the Toussaint Movement died at the hands of his torturers, Fanon arrived in Paris.[2] In the greater Paris area, to be specific. At first, he stayed with Jean Ayme in the apartment that had been assigned to the latter in his capacity as the chief resident physician of the psychiatric hospital at Clermont-de-l'Oise. Ayme hosted Fanon for two weeks.

Fanon and Jean Ayme had met, as has been mentioned, at the Congrès des Psychiatres de langue française that had been held in Bordeaux a couple of months beforehand. Ayme, who was an institutional psychiatrist and in analysis with Lacan at the time, was a longstanding opponent of the colonial enterprise and a member of the Lambertist Movement. He had been a supporter of the Algerian Revolution as early as 1945. He was not entirely unfamiliar with Algeria, having spent his adolescent years there in the late 1930s. He spent three of those years at the Lycée Mustapha, where he was enrolled as a sixth-grader. Ayme remembered that, even in those days, support for the short-lived Popular Front was quite widespread.

When Fanon and Ayme had met in Bordeaux, they immediately hit it off and discovered that they were of a mind about "the events" in Algeria. In January 1957, Ayme was more than glad to host Fanon at Clermont-de-l'Oise. Fanon arrived alone. Josie joined him a few days later with their very young son in tow, but she soon left again, leaving the small Olivier in the care of Jean Ayme's wife for a few days. By inviting Fanon to stay with him, Ayme was simply being a good friend, but he also wanted to seize the opportunity to discuss more practical matters. He was, at the time, the Secretary General of the Psychiatric Hospital Physicians Union. Given that Fanon had absolutely no prospect of returning to Algeria, Ayme wanted to find a way of helping him retain a salary. The bylaws, however, were very difficult to circumvent because even though institutional psychiatrists were considered civil servants, their salaries had to be directly disbursed by the institutions that employed them. There were no exceptions to this rule, and Ayme's efforts were in vain. Fanon, his exceptional circumstance notwithstanding, did not qualify for payments of any kind and suddenly was facing great financial difficulty. Tosquelles took over the support of Fanon's daughter, as Fanon could no longer afford the payments. This was the fallout of the letter of resignation that Fanon had sent Lacoste—great material hardships that are usually glossed over. Despite the uncertainty of his situation, Fanon remained calm and was able to maintain a relative peace of mind. He still functioned on three hours of sleep and continued to devour books. The reading materials that Ayme had given him included the transcripts, unpublished at the time, of the first four Congresses of the Communist International; these documents had a special fascination for Fanon, and they accompanied him through many long nights.

Fanon, during this period of semiretirement, was free to indulge in marathon discussions of the kind that had always been so dear to his heart. Ayme, who was a seasoned Trotskyist, realized, like many before and after him, that Fanon, for all his philosophical and psychiatric erudition, was basically "politically unformed," both as a militant and in his grasp of major revolutionary movements. Nor was he particularly knowledgeable about Algerian nationalism and its various leanings and factions, at least not at the time. While in Algeria, Fanon had thrown in his lot with the FLN and supporters of the Soummam platform. And while he had a better firsthand knowledge than Ayme of that movement's operational structure and of the major players within that structure, he was only vaguely aware of the uninterrupted historical importance of the Messali Hadj-led MNA, the movement that had emerged out of the PPA-MTLD[3] and that was still thriving in France, where it was better known in certain circles than the newly emerged FLN. Ayme refrained from telling Fanon that a great many members of Messali's movement had used the bed he was sleeping in. Fanon, however, was not interested in tactical politics, and this indifference would often lead, as we shall see, to tactless, at times even naive, behavior in situations that were entirely dictated by the logic of alliances and calculated enmities.

Jean Ayme came away from his long conversations with Fanon convinced of the "clarity of Fanon's position." Unlike Albert Memmi, who in 1971 argued that Fanon as an Antillean should have returned to his native Antilles,[4] Ayme understood that Fanon had "been given the opportunity to take part in revolution. Despite his longstanding support of the Antillean Independence Movement, he was never able to identify a militant structure capable of sustaining a serious contemplation and enactment of said independence." The author of *Black Skin, White Masks* was not one to wait for a better tomorrow; the onus was on the present moment, and the obligation to think and act had to be honored everywhere and anywhere; the Algerian situation had presented a very real opportunity for a concrete effort toward decolonization and the promise of change such a goal implied. Fanon's identification to this project was dual in nature, both collective and individual. This duality is best illustrated in an anecdote that left a lasting impression on Ayme. The encounter took place during the month of Ramadan. Fanon was sitting in his car—the aforementioned indescribable white "pigeot"—smoking a cigarette with the windows down and his elbow resting on the car door, Italian style. An Algerian, who probably mistook him for a local because of his dark skin, approached him out of the blue and said, "We disapprove of people smoking during the month of Ramadan." Fanon demurred, and without a word, extinguished his cigarette. "I felt I had been designated as an insider," he later told Ayme.[5]

This attitude struck Ayme as entirely coherent and in keeping with the cosmopolitan and internationalist character of revolutionary logic. Ayme, to this day, continues to find nothing unusual in Fanon's decision to enlist his proficiencies and beliefs in the service of the Algerian Revolution. This alliance, as the anecdote related by Fanon makes clear, does not in any way reflect a denial or disregard for skin color or even the illusion of a rubber-stamped universalism. What it conveys, rather, is the gist of an internationalist discourse of solidarity that Fanon would continue to explore and develop in his writing for FLN publications.

Fanon continued to bide his time. Uncharacteristically, he did not grow impatient. Tunis had not yet emerged as a possibility, but his involvement with events in Algeria was too great for him to consider a change of course. The atmosphere in France was strikingly different from the one he had left behind, where the War had occupied everyone's mind and impacted everyone's life. While 1956 was a disastrous year, characterized by military and police repression and weekly executions of young nationalist militants at the Barberousse prison, it was also the year that marked the political consolidation of the FLN. Algiers, when Fanon left it, was at the height of a pitched and savage battle. In France, on the other hand, 1956 was the "year of silence and lies,"[6] a year of resignation. The demonstrations that had occurred in the early months of that year at train stations, shipping harbors, and military barracks to protest against the departure of those who had been called, or were being called yet again, to serve in Algeria were largely forgotten. On March 12, 1956, even the Communists sanctioned the implementation of special powers that authorized extraordinary measures in Algeria. The impact of the Soviet Union's invasion of Budapest, and to a lesser degree of the Suez crisis, was having far greater repercussions on the Left and was behind a flurry of resignations that the war in Algeria had failed to trigger. The idea of a "new left" affiliated with Claude Bourdet and Gilles Martinet was beginning to gain ground, but it was largely propelled by events in Hungary and Suez and held little attraction for Fanon. Similarly, he was not drawn to the emerging and small movement "Socialism or Barbary" that had been launched by Claude Lefort, Cornelius Castoriadis, and Jean-François Lyotard, even though the latter had started addressing the Algerian question in 1955.

Fanon no longer thought, as he had previously, that the Socialist and Communists were going to bring the war to an end. He became increasingly aware of their inability to envisage Algeria as an independent nation. The three years he spent in Algeria had convinced him otherwise, and he was persuaded that independence was the only possible outcome. He was already deeply committed to the Algerian resistance and considered himself an insider.

The great movement of popular solidarity he had wished to find never materialized. On the subways and commuters trains he used to get around, the talk among workers was about overtime and paid vacations.

In what way have the people of France and their representatives helped the Algerian people in their battle? [. . .] Why do elected Communists at the Palais-Bourbon, at the Council of the Republic, at general and municipal councils, keep a shameful silence on the countless atrocities committed by their troops and abstain from all actions that would support Algerian independence? Why haven't the leaders and executives of the CGT organized strikes that would inconvenience French imperialists in their colonial war? On a daily basis, dock workers in Marseille, Bordeaux, Nantes, to cite just one example, are loading the munitions and arms shipments that are spreading death in our *douars* and *mechtas*.[7]

Fanon did not write these lines. The text had already been published in Algeria in the second issue of the *El Moudjahid*, in a piece that appeared under the header "The Fiction of French Aid." And even though he may not have written these lines, he wholeheartedly subscribed to their message.

During this period, Fanon also met with some of his colleagues and learned that most of them were in analysis and heralding psychoanalysis as the ultimate system for the resolution of all conflicts. This was a view that held great currency at the time. But Fanon was not especially interested in cultivating these intellectual circles either. At the beginning of 1957, opposition to the Algerian War in the press and in the intelligentsia was still relatively circumscribed. This, despite the disquieting realization of the growing support for the Algerian Nationalist Movement that had been revealed two years prior in Colette and Francis Jeanson's *L'Algérie hors-la-loi* (Seuil, 1955).[8] The newspapers *France-Observateur, L'Express,* and *Témoignage chrétien* denounced the policies of Guy Mollet and demanded an end to the war. In their own way, *Le Monde* and *Le Canard enchaîné* did so as well. *Esprit* and *Les Temps modernes* continued to condemn colonial policy but in a sporadic manner. In the issue of *France-Observateur* of September 15, 1955, Robert Barrat published "Un journaliste français chez les hors-la-loi algériens" in which he interviewed some of the leaders of the insurrection. He was arrested for his efforts. In March 1956, Claude Bourdet was held at a police precinct because he signed a petition, also published in *France-Observateur,* protesting the posting of young French men to the colony. The arrest of Mandouze, held in an Algerian prison from November 19 to December 19, 1956, on the charge of being a "mail box" for young Algerian rebels, gave rise to a number of demonstrations. The solidarity movement also included the Comité d'action des intellectuels contre la poursuite de la guerre en Afrique du Nord, established in 1955, and the Comité de résistance spirituelle, a group that was created in 1956 and that numbered a great many Roman Catholic adherents—Robert Barrat, Henri Marrou, Jean-Marie Domenach—as well as Socialists who, like André Philip, had broken rank with the party. But voices such as those of Mandouze, Bourdet, and Barrat, among the first to raise the alarm and speak out, as early as 1955, in support of Algerian Independence and of the need for negotiations with the FLN— a position that led to their short but symbolic arrest—were on the decline. Later, in 1957, the growing momentum against the war was fueled primarily by accounts of reprisals and torture. Pierre Vidal-Naquet, who devoted four years of his life to opposing this war, believed that support for Algeria's independence took second place to the more pressing need to denounce the use of torture and the intolerable fact of French compatriots using the same Gestapo methods that had been used against the French in the 1940s.[9] By spring 1957, *Témoignage chrétien* had published a brochure containing the posthumous letters of Private Muller.[10] Another document entitled *Les rappelés témoignent* had also started making the rounds. The publication of Pierre-Henri Simon's *Contre la torture* caused a great stir. The young historian Robert Bonnaud, who had objected to his enlistment in the "pacification" of Algeria, published "La paix des nementchas" in the April issue of *Esprit*. In June 1957, *Les Temps modernes* published "Un an dans les Aurès" by Jacques Pucheu. But by that time, Fanon was no longer in France. He had, in fact, already left the country when the scandal broke, in March 1957, about the alleged suicide of the Algerian attorney Ali Boumendjel and when the Audin affair surfaced three months later.[11] He had already spent close to four months in Tunisia when Raymond Aron published *La Tragédie algérienne*—the only book among the many that were published that year to advance a logical and realistic argument for Algerian independence. Ironically, it had been written by a man who was perceived as having right-wing sympathies. Fanon and Aron would eventually meet in Tunis.

Fanon wanted the French intelligentsia to openly declare its support for negotiations with the FLN. While his familiarity with the movement's historical antecedents may not have been perfect, he knew that the FLN was the only nationalist organization that had to be reckoned with at that moment. Fanon was not in the same position as French intellectuals who, with very few exceptions, claimed to have no knowledge of the FLN; he could not very well deny the existence of the experience he had shared and seen at close range of the men and women whose names drew a resounding blank in France. One need only glance at Abderrahmane Farès's memoir to realize that the political leadership in 1957 understood the inevitability of negotiating with the FLN.[12] Representatives of the French Federation of the FLN were not helped by the fact that they happened to be in France; French intellectuals disavowed any knowledge of them as well. Fanon, on the other hand, felt a very close connection to them and sought them out.

It was during this period that he met again with Jeanson. Jeanson came away with the impression that Fanon had become a much more even-tempered man, but he also described him as distant and dismissive of the opposition movement in France, even of the group that Jeanson was responsible for at the time—the group that would secure him passage out of

France, as Jeanson bitterly remarked at a later date. An additional and final encounter between the two men would seal their feelings of mutual disenchantment. A couple of years later, they bumped into each other, entirely by chance, at the Madrid airport. They were saying their good-byes, after the long evening they had spent together, when Fanon, in a parting shot, dismissed the French support courier networks and described them as "duped by the political facade of the French Federation of the FLN that answered to a military leader whose identity would never be revealed."[13] Fanon was, in fact, alluding to his own experience on the Mediterranean's other shore, where he had been witness to an unending conflict between the political and the military factions from the moment he had set foot in Tunis. Jeanson was, despite his disbelief, deeply affected by Fanon's attack. Regardless of how unpleasant their exchange may have been, Fanon, contrary to what Jeanson may have thought, always felt a deep affection for the man. But this was not a time for emotions.

After his stay with Ayme, Fanon spent the remainder of his time in France with Manville. Manville did all he could to convince him to remain in France. Manville confessed that he did not want to lose his friend and added that he wanted to keep him close by in the eventuality of an Antillean front. Manville did his best, introducing Fanon to Senator Ledermann as well as to other friends who belonged to the Communist Party. But Fanon's mind was made up. He left Paris at some point between late February and early March, traveling via Switzerland and Italy to finally arrive in Tunis. Arrangements for his journey had been made by Salah Louanchi, who was responsible, with Mohammed Lebjaoui, for the leadership of the French Federation of the FLN. In addition to his familiarity with Fanon's writings, Salah Louanchi, a former member of Amitiés Algériennes, the group that had contacted Fanon in Blida in 1955, had also met Fanon in person. The FLN "organization" had reached a decision that Fanon would be more useful outside the country, either in Tunisia or Morocco, where the militants who had been on the run were beginning to regroup and organize support systems to provide information and medical assistance to ALN combatants and refugees. Frantz Fanon was the last person whose safe passage to Tunis, via Rome, was organized by Louanchi; by the end of February 1957, he, Lebjaoui, and the entire leadership of the French Federation, were all under arrest.[14]

Josie and Olivier joined Fanon in Tunis shortly after his arrival. The time Fanon had spent in France had been a kind of semiclandestine layover. The Chaulet family, whose departure from Algeria had been postponed until Pierre Chaulet's trial was over, and I, the people who had been in the closest day-to-day contact with Fanon received no news from him while he was in France. Later, Fanon would hardly ever speak of this period in his life. Perhaps he wanted to face this detour alone, without the benefit of family and friends, in much the same way he had left Paris to go to Lyon when he was a newly arrived student from the Antilles.

Tunis

Fanon settled in Tunis at the height of the power struggle within the FLN. During this time, Fanon became a committed activist and struggled with both radicalism and orthodoxy. Activism brought ordeals including dealings with Melouza and the death of Abbane. Fanon also wrote for El Moudjahid *and was involved in the operation of the newspaper. Professionally, his challenges in psychiatry at this time included discord at Razi de la Manouba Hospital and his participation in advances in the theory and techniques implemented at Charles-Nicolle Hospital. He viewed his political commitments as essential and strengthened his ties to Africa. He continued lecturing at the university, kept up his relations with friends, and became involved with Raymond Aron, Jacques Berque, and Giovanni Pirelli.* L'An V de la révolution algérienne *was written during Fanon's time in Tunis.*

Assisted by the FLN in France and its networks in Italy and Switzerland, Fanon arrived in Tunis in late March, early April 1957. From this point forward, Fanon would step up his activism. Like so many others who had been driven out of Algeria, he had little choice but to carry on his work outside the national territory, in the so-called free zone of a friendly nation or brother country to use the preferred terminology of the day. When he arrived in Tunis, he reported at the "Base," as the Tunisian FLN headquarters was called. He met up with Youssef Ben Khedda, who was already on site and, more important, with Abbane Ramdane. Both Abbane and Ben Khedda had traveled overland from Morocco and, assisted by the *maquis*, had managed to cross safely into Tunisia. Their standing within the leadership, however, had been significantly weakened by the failed January 1957 strike and the loss of the Battle of Algiers that had decimated the leadership and destroyed support networks. Even before Fanon had set foot in Tunisia, and while his two comrades were still on their long trek across Algeria, the remaining members of the CCE already had been called to task by Ahmed Ben Bella[1] loyalists who contested their legitimacy and rejected the plan that had been inspired by Abbane and presented at the Soummam meeting. Debate and dissent inside FLN headquarters were at an all-time high. Habib Bourguiba, less than pleased to see his new republic turned into a base for 150,000 Algerians who were better armed than the newly formed Tunisian army and who had a tendency to flaunt the laws of the land as well, had to intervene.[2]

No sooner had Abbane and Ben Khedda reached the safety of the brother country than they found themselves targeted by the colonels of the various *Wilayas* who were convened in Tunis for a meeting.[3] The most notorious ones were Lakhdar Bentobbal who had taken over the command of *Wilaya* 2 after Youssef Zighout's death and Abdelhafid Boussouf who had replaced Ben M'Hidi in the Oran region. Both men were adamant in their demands for an overhaul of the CCE and the appointment of a new leadership. Added to this was the mounting political tension, official claims of solidarity notwithstanding, between the Algerians and their Tunisian hosts. The Tunisians were eager to safeguard their recently acquired independence and had little patience for Algerians with a tendency to behave like conquerors in a conquered land.

Fanon arrived in Tunis to find Ben Khedda sidelined and Abbane engaged in a heated debate with the colonels. Abbane, who was persuaded that the political wing outweighed the military one, had managed to repeatedly offend the military leadership with his Robespierre airs. "You have created a power that is based on military might, but politics are another matter and cannot be conducted by illiterates and ignoramuses." We naively attributed his impossible temper to his ill heath; he did, in fact, suffer from a painful gastric ulcer, and later, he developed a goiter. Nonetheless, the colonels were his true bane. He was disturbed by their indiscriminate assumption of absolute power. "They are oriental potentates in the making," he reportedly told Ferhat Abbas, who had been the most prominent figure in the UMDA and had recently become a member of the exiled FLN.

They think they have life and death powers over the people in their command. They embody the exact opposite of the freedom and democracy we want for an independent Algeria. If they stand for the future, then I cannot collaborate with such a future. You can count me out of your precious future. Algeria is not the Orient where absolute potentates can rule unchallenged. We shall protect our freedom come hell or high water. Even if we must die in the process.[4]

Tensions were running high.

Abbane immediately appointed Fanon to the press office that was working out of Tunisia and Morocco and was still at an embryonic stage. Mahiedine Moussaoui and Rheda Malek were heading the small Moroccan team; the Tunisian office fell under the aegis of the Base and answered directly to Commandant Kaci. The two Algerian attorneys Bouzida and Chentouf were doing what they could to ensure the continued publication of *Résistance algérienne*. *El Moudjahid* was still on the backburner.

Fanon also started part-time work as a psychiatrist at the Manouba Hospital. Ahmad Ben Salah, the minister of health in the new postindependence Tunisian government, supported the Algerian cause and had intervened on Fanon's behalf as he would for a great number of exiled Algerian medical professionals. Located just outside the city limits, Manouba was a large psychiatric facility, the Tunisian corollary of Blida-Joinville. It has been claimed that Fanon was hired under a pseudonym, as Farès. In fact, everyone knew him as Fanon, and the Farès identity may have been used only for inconsequential administrative forms. Later on, however, he did travel under this name to Africa and Europe; after 1959, he signed himself as Farès in all his correspondence with François Maspero. Skilled and educated Algerians, especially those in health-related fields, were offered paid part-time positions in the public sector by the newly independent Tunisian State. They were, however, barred from working in the private sector, both by the host nation and by the statutes of the FLN. At any rate, nothing could have been further from Fanon's mind, and in this he was not unusual; the prospect of a private practice held no appeal whatsoever for the tuberculosis specialist Chaulet, or the surgeon Michel Martini, or the gynecologist J. Belkhodja, or many other physicians belonging to the exiled medical community. They did, however, welcome the opportunity to make a living, no matter how modest, wanting not to become a financial burden to the FLN. In his capacity as a staff psychiatrist, Fanon qualified for a lodging at Manouba's Razi Hospital. Josie and Olivier had arrived in Tunis shortly after Fanon, and the family soon found itself settled in new quarters. Josie, who had no official affiliation to the FLN, worked for a literary program on Tunisian Radio before joining the staff of *Action*, the Tunisian magazine that had been launched by Béchir Ben Yahmed and that would later become *Jeune Afrique*.

Until March 1960, when Fanon started his African travels as an itinerant ambassador for the Algerian cause, his psychiatric and political work as well as his work as an intellectual and writer continued to be tightly enmeshed.

Fanon, who had officially joined the FLN when he received his appointment to the press office, wasted no time producing a pair of articles for the somewhat flagging publication known as *Résistance algérienne*. The first article appeared in late March and discussed the urban militias that France had implemented in Algeria; the second, published in May, discussed the role of Algerian women in the fight for independence. In those early, anonymous articles, Fanon's language was clearly recognizable behind the militant discourse; his uncanny ability of moving from flesh to word and showing how "bodily tensions" evolve into "consciousness" was clearly at work. "These planned and orchestrated murders," he wrote in his article on the militias, "only increase the force with which the Algerian nation contracts its muscle, renews its commitment to the struggle and hones its political awareness."

During a short trip to Tetouan, a town on Morocco's Mediterranean coast, Fanon took part in discussions on how best to restructure the movement's press and information office. Jean Daniel remembers meeting him on this occasion. He had approached Fanon in his capacity as a politically committed and informed journalist wanting to know more about the "Algerian revolution." "Fanon," he recalls, "was attentive and gentle. He weighed his answers carefully. He was especially interested in getting to know me, in asking me questions, but he ended the encounter by emphatically stating his radical break from the world he assumed I stood for." After he became an official member of the FLN, Fanon confronted all French interlocutors, including the most progressive ones, with similar claims about his clean break with the French intelligentsia and its political agendas. He had, in this way, already offended Jeanson, whom he loved. When the Communist filmmaker René Vautier approached the FLN about making a documentary about the Algerian *maquis*, Fanon was even more intransigent than Abbane, insisting that all the images had to pass the review of the ALN and the information services and claiming that it was preposterous to "contemplate that the leadership of the FLN would allow a French Communist to roam freely inside the Algerian *maquis* and film footage which he would then be able to diffuse without the FLN's seal of approval. In revolutionary times," he added, "we cannot take the risk of trusting an individual who does not belong to our ranks."[5]

In early June 1957, Fanon was catapulted into the role of spokesman for the FLN. This development coincided with the uncovering of the Melouza Massacre. On May 31, the *gouvernement générale* announced that it had stumbled, quite by chance, on the bodies of 300 men who had been killed in a *mechta* in Melouza, a rural area in southern Kabylia. Robert Lacoste alerted the French and foreign press, impressing on them the urgency of bringing the massacre to worldwide attention. The news spread quickly. Algerian communities in Cairo and New York were deeply perturbed, the latter managing to save face by demanding an investigation.[6] Fanon, in the company of Mohamed Ben Smaïl, the editor-in-chief of *Afrique-action*, Commandant Kaci, and two military men in sunglasses, put all his eloquent brio into a statement to the Tunisian press in which he held the French army responsible for the massacre. This would not turn out to be the case. The wholesale slaughter had been carried out on orders from Amirouche, the military commander of *Wilaya* 3. It has recently surfaced that Fanon and Ben Smaïl based their accusations on a secret report from *Wilaya* 3 that reached Tunis through an "internal" channel. This report allegedly cleared the ALN of all suspicion. Fanon and his colleagues at the press office were relatively cut off from alternate sources of information, and they had no real reason to doubt the veracity of the intelligence that had been delivered to them in complete secrecy directly from the *maquis*. The report, it turned out, had been concocted by the same individuals who had carried out the massacre.

Fanon, who had been deceived and exposed, would never again refer to the incident. It was the first trial of his life as a militant; others would follow. But he believed that "the people are always right"; he also believed that regardless of what one may think of them in private, one does not undermine one's representatives in times of battle. Fanon's adherence to Resistance culture did not mean he had either the taste or the aptitude for political manipulation. He was frequently outspoken with Abbane, who happened to share a similarly dim view of some of the leadership, and even flippant, referring to some of the commanding officers as goatherds. Fanon felt a special connection to Abbane during this period; he admired his intransigent side and saw him as a true revolutionary leader of the new Algeria. He also got along with Ben Khedda, who was, at the time, one of the most progressive members of the political leadership and whose reemergence from the shadows, after having been sidelined for some time, coincided with the constitution of the third GPRA.[7] Fanon had a passable relationship to Krim Belkacem, a man who had a sixth-grade French education and had joined the *maquis* before 1954. Fanon considered Krim a man of the people and respected him accordingly. Boussouf and Bentobbal, however, were men he claimed to have nothing in common with, and he disliked the pair of them intensely. In private, he faulted them for "failing to envisage anything beyond independence and for constantly vying for power. Ask them what this future Algeria will look like, and they don't have a clue. The idea of a secular state or of socialism, the idea of man for that matter, these are things that are entirely alien to them." This purported lack of vision was confirmed in the unpublished memoir of Lakhdar Bentobbal with Gilbert Meynier: "We would be looking in vain if we expected this text to provide a detailed program for the revolution that he had fought for. The leitmotif is one and the same throughout: giving power to the people by arming them; and the one overriding conviction is—if it is not a simple truth, then it must be suspect."[8] Safia Bazi, the high school student who went into the mountains and joined the *maquis* in 1956, also corroborates the man's inadequacies. "Many of our leaders," she says, "couldn't see beyond independence. Most of the young volunteers couldn't either. Abbane and Ben M'Hidi were different. Ben M'Hidi had a very human side. He would talk to us, some of us were still high school students, wanting to know more about our motivations, our ideas for the future of our country. Abbane was more radical. One night, he told us this is going to be a long struggle; many of you will not live to see the end of it. And independence, when it comes, will be only the beginning. I remembered those words I heard as a seventeen-year-old for a long time. Even then, it was clear that the volunteers of *Wilaya* 4 were not all motivated by the same things: some wished only for independence and didn't concern themselves with political change, some wanted to create a new society, and some simply wanted to defend Islam."[9]

Fanon's loathing of the two *B*'s became even greater after Abbane's disappearance. In Fanon's eyes, Abbane was Algeria's true and designated leader,[10] and the reasons behind his disappearance, a settling of personal scores, struck him as beneath contempt. Fanon was deeply marked by the loss of Abbane, a man to whom he had been close both personally and ideologically. After Fanon's death, Josie came across an empty black binder that had belonged to Abbane; Fanon had kept it stashed away with Sartre's letters. Fanon always spoke with sadness about Abbane's death. Fanon had not only lost a dear friend, but this death had also exposed the erosion of the revolutionary mandate of the war of liberation. Abbane, like Fanon, believed in the possibility of a new form of human interaction, a new society that could be achieved only through a revolutionary dismantling of the colonial state, and both men held out hope that Algerian Jews as well as Algerians of European descent would become part of the new Algerian nation. Fanon, in fact, never contemplated the possibility of a new Algerian state that did not include some proportion, even if small, of this non-Muslim population. This principle of inclusion had a special significance for Fanon because it was intimately linked to the idea, still very much at the forefront of his mind, that every new step toward liberation would transform whites as well as blacks, colonizers as well as colonized. The circumstances surrounding Abbane's death had been kept under wraps but not from Fanon, who was more or less in the know; this episode was the second trial, an especially harrowing one, in Fanon's life as a militant. But Fanon endured and continued to share his political concerns and disappointments only with a select few. He never publicly disassociated himself from the struggle to which he was deeply committed. Consequently, in his writings and public statements he was always emphatic about the unity of the Algerian nation, placing it front and center and above the machinations and the divisiveness; he praised the FLN and denied the internecine struggle that plagued the ALN inside the country proper, even though he knew the opposite to be the case; and he rejected the theories that attributed the Algerian struggle to external factors that had parachuted in from Egypt or the Communist bloc. By this point, the injunctions that ruled Fanon's public life were quite clear-cut: to be a disciplined militant for the cause he upheld and to look to the leadership, despite its many missteps, for the revolutionary virtues with which he would increasingly try to identify. He never managed to be totally successful and had a tendency to lose his bearings when his life was inordinately dominated by action. He needed to write.

Before his death, Abbane had been more than a political referent for Fanon; he had also paved the way for him to become a writer for *El Moudjahid*. In June 1957, the CCE was in the midst of complete restructuring. In a meeting that took place in Cairo a month later, Abbane's mishandling of the military command, which is to say of the very people he routinely dismissed as ignorant illiterates, had resulted in a hands-down victory of the military wing.[11] The newly formed internal council was now much smaller and included all the colonels and only one civilian, namely Abbane. His duties included overseeing the press and information bureau, and he immediately undertook a major overhaul of these services. He brought in Rheda Malek and Mahiedine Moussaoui, both of whom had been stationed in Morocco, and with their help managed to restructure the bureau's various branches; he also laid the groundwork for the launching of *El Moudjahid* as the official organ of the FLN. Fanon was appointed to the paper's editorial staff and became a pivotal force in the writing room. Fanon stayed on at the paper even after Abbane had died. His work at *El Moudjahid* continued uninterrupted until 1960. His steady stream of contributions was hardly disrupted by his occasional missions abroad (Morocco, Cairo, Ghana, and the Congrès des Écrivains et Artistes noirs that was held in Rome in 1959). The issues to which Fanon did not contribute in some way can be counted on the fingers of one hand. Under the direction of Ahmed Boumendjel,[12] the editorial "committee" was made up of Rheda Malek, Brahim Mezhoudi, Mohammed El Mili, Abdallah Cheriet, and Mahiedine Moussaoui. In December 1957 and on Abbane's recommendation, Pierre Chaulet also came on board shortly after arriving in Tunis. The team met at least twice a week at Rue Mokhtar Attia (the former Rue de Corse) in one of those bleak locales one had come to associate with the FLN organization. The mood was generally good, relaxed, at least among the members of the core group who enjoyed each other's company and liked working together. If the atmosphere got testy, as when Fanon, for example, tried Cheriet's patience by pushing an argument to an aggravating extreme, the latter would remove his jacket. Fanon, on his part, used to signal his discontent by removing his watch. "There wasn't a single journalist in the bunch," Pierre Chaulet remembers. "We had all agreed to the rule of group work and anonymous publication [. . .] Throughout those two years, Fanon was a living lesson in discipline and modesty; there he was, a brilliant intellectual, skilled at defusing situations and at persuading through seduction, who had agreed to work anonymously for the common good and to submit to the constraints without glory that are the hallmark of activist journalism."[13]

The team held meetings in which they discussed developing events as well as other related issues. There were two editions of the paper, one in Arabic, the other in French; these were not translated versions of the same paper, but the stories they treated and their approach to these stories were essentially similar. Fanon wrote for the French edition, and his submissions, like everyone else's, were reviewed by the entire team. This policy also meant that some of the articles in Arabic were permeated by Fanon's ideas. The pieces were never signed and often represented a group effort. The group as a whole, therefore, had a hand in editing the articles that were subsequently attributed to Fanon and posthumously published in *Pour la révolution africaine*. These writings, it should also be noted, were written in the name of the FLN and represented the organization's official position. Furthermore, the book is both incomplete and inaccurate: it fails to include a number of the short pieces Fanon wrote during this period, while falsely attributing certain other pieces to him—the article on the Antilles, for example. But these questions of authorship are neither here nor there.[14]

This was a relatively young team of writers; most of them were on the youngish side of thirty. They had made a practice of exchanging and discussing books all of them were discovering for the first time. Rheda Malek, who had been a philosophy student until 1955, introduced Fanon to Engels's *The Role of Violence in History* and *Anti-Dühring*. Fanon's reaction was not all that enthusiastic. He thought the works were too removed from the individual's qualitative experience of violence. The pieces written by Rheda Malek, however, made frequent reference to Richard Wright—no doubt an outcome of his conversations with Fanon. But when the paper decided to publish a review of Wright's *Listen, White Man* in August 1959, Fanon's critique of the author whom he had admired so greatly only six years prior turned out to be a harsh one. He faulted Wright for writing only about an elite, about the tragedy of a Westernized black consciousness, "no doubt painful, but nothing to kill a man," especially in light of the life and death crisis faced by most of Africa. "Trois ans après Bandoung," "Conflit algérien et l'anticolonialisme africain,"[15] and "Rendez-vous d'Accra,"[16] however, are more difficult to attribute to Fanon. The same incertitude applies to the interviews with Félix Moumié and Dica Akwa, who were representatives of L'Union des populations du Cameroun in 1958,[17] and to the interview with Pecar, the Yugoslav journalist who had spent considerable time in the Algerian *maquis* and had published a lengthy feature in *El Moudjahid*. The only claim that can be made with any certainty is that Fanon and Pecar knew each other, as the photograph in which they appear in the company of Rheda Malek attests.

El Moudjahid also published excerpts of the papers Fanon delivered in Accra at the 1958 Conférence des peuples africains that he attended, together with Boumendjel and Mostefai, as a member of the Algerian delegation;[18] Fanon's contributions at the Congrès des Écrivains et Artistes noirs, held in Rome in April 1959,[19] were also excerpted. At the time of the Rome conference, extensive quotes from "Culture nationale et guerre de libération" were printed under the following heading: "At the Conference of Black Artists and Writers that was recently held in Rome, embattled Algeria was present in the person of Dr. Fanon who, strengthened by his experience of the Algerian revolution, spoke with authority on national culture and its relationship to the war of liberation."[20] Fanon had approved the heading. We will return in more detail to this work, which occupies a position in the development of Fanon's thought that falls midway between "Racisme et culture" and *L'An V de la révolution algérienne*, the latter still in gestation at the time. The sections dealing with black American jazz and with ideas surrounding the evolution from a national to a universal culture were struck—for lack of space?—from the official organ of the FLN.

In November 1959, *El Moudjahid* published a selection from a forthcoming work by Fanon, which at the time was still entitled "Réalités algériennes, révolutions algériennes, l'an V"; the excerpted passage discussed how father/son relationships in the Algerian family had changed in the aftermath of November 1954.[21] Again citing lack of space, the editors decided to cut the long passages that discussed Algerian women. Finally, shortly after Fanon's death and the publication of *Damnés de la terre*, several pages were set aside for extensive selections from the book in two separate commemorative issues.[22]

During the years of his tenure at *El Moudjahid*, Fanon's main areas of inquiry included the French reaction and developments in France, life inside Algeria proper, and the political future of the African continent. In group meetings, Fanon clearly refrained from voicing an opinion on Pan-Arabism and the idea of an Arab nation, and in 1958, he did not pronounce himself on the Antilles. He had not authored the article on the Antilles that was published in *El Moudjahid*, and later, attributed to him in *Révolution africaine*; in fact, he had refused the assignment. Today we know that Pierre Chaulet anonymously authored the piece. Fanon was nonetheless very attentive to the Antillean independence movement, and in January 1960, he published "Le Sang coule aux Antilles sous domination française" in *El Moudjahid*. He dedicated *L'An V* to Bertène Juminer, his Antillean friend who was working as a biologist in Tunis at the time;[23] he also supported a number of Antillean draft dodgers and deserters, some of whom had joined the ALN and who, at Independence, would stay on in Algiers for a couple of years. In 1961, Fanon sent a telegram of support and congratulations to the founders of the Front indépendantiste antillo-guyanais.

In his early days at the paper, he was primarily interested in the conflict between colonizer and colonized and in how the response in France escalated or diffused the way this confrontation played itself out on the ground. Between December 1957 and January 1958, he drafted a long piece addressed to French intellectuals and liberals, which, for reasons having to do with layout, was printed as three separate foldouts. This series was the logical outcome of two previous articles; the first, written in September 1957, discussed the use of torture in Algeria,[24] and the second, written in November of the same year, "A propos d'un plaidoyer," was a brief but powerful piece about the case of Djamila Bouhired. Even in these early writings, Fanon had argued that torture is inextricably linked to colonial law. "All French people in Algeria are perforce torturers. The Algerian people realize full well that the colonial structure must of necessity rest on torture, murder and rape. The French are only concerned for the French," he admonished. At Blida-Joinville, his patients had included a number of French police officers, and he was very aware of the ravages torture can visit on the torturer. He had witnessed its toll on the mental health of these officers who suffered from ills that ranged from suicidal fantasies to sadistic behaviors toward their own family members. He reproached the French for their failure to envision the suffering of the Algerian people and for their inability to identify with that suffering. He was, in essence, wishing for the impossible circumstance in which the overwhelming majority of French people would identify with the struggle of the Algerian people. This in a nutshell, he explained, was the wish of the colonized. And this wish intersected in large part with the aims of the FLN, the unions, the students, and, probably even those of the Messalists—all laboring in the name of the "communal interest of the working classes of the colonial country and of the entire population of the conquered and dominated country."

The three later pieces in *El Moudjahid* that Fanon addressed to France's intellectuals and liberals did not stray from this line of thought. He did, however, step up his argument by calling on the working class, the intelligentsia, and the liberals to do their duty and demand that "their government respect the right of nations to self-government." The Left had failed to carry out its duty. It had not supported the right of colonized people to self-determination, which beyond serving the common interest of the working class and upholding the right of nations to self-rule would have also lent support to "the defense of an idea of man that is contested in Western nations" and a "refusal of institutional participation in the degradation of values."[25] While there was doubtless a solidarity between a number of Algerian leaders and French liberals, the latter were entrapped in a logic that made it impossible for them to support the colonized nation without opposing the national agenda, thereby making the struggle against colonialism one and the same as the struggle against the home nation; they had been paralyzed by the specter of treason. This was how the Left had failed. The Liberals had allowed themselves to be trapped by the faulty logic of national betrayal and it was high time they removed their blinders.[26]

It was at this point in his argument that he introduced a new twist. Algeria's friends, he wrote, had offered advice and criticism; they had called us to task about the future of Algeria and demanded we condemn acts that they have described as "barbarian," for example the ambush of Sakomody in which ten French civilians died as well as other incidents that qualify as "acts of terror." But colonialism, he countered, is far worse than a tally of individual violent events; it is an entire system that sustains itself by oppression, repression, and torture. Yet, while he privately deplored the summary executions of young Algerians, many of them students who had left their homes in the cities to join the *maquis* and had been accused of treason by the leaders of their *Wilayas*, he did not speak out, as others did, against the urban guerilla campaign. He only went so far as to wonder if the bombings in Algiers would achieve any long-term gains.[27] For Fanon, as he had pointed out with respect to Djamila Bouhired, the individual was the expression of the entire nation.

The third segment of the series was an appeal to French intellectuals and liberals. He was not asking them to join the armed struggle as such—even though he did pay a special tribute to draft dodgers and deserters—but to wage battle inside French society. The leftist French press felt it had been unfairly targeted in the first two segments of the piece and published a strong rebuttal in *France-Observateur.* Gilles Martinet, the paper's editor-in-chief at the time, immediately arranged for a trip to Tunis. The job of calling the French intelligentsia to task had been entrusted to Fanon on the assumption that he was more familiar with their world than the other members of the team, and the piece that was published in the end reflected a disappointment in and a disapproval of the French Left that they, to a man, shared with Fanon.

Fanon was deeply interested in the lives Algerians, civilians and combatants both, were leading inside the country. The conditions of this existence became a subject of his writing, and he attached a special value to the stories that were filtering out of Algeria. Later, even when he played a much smaller part in the publication of *El Moudjahid,* he remained very interested in accounts of daily life on the inside and carefully read all the articles on this topic.[28] In a conversation that took place on Rue des Entrepreneurs in late 1959, he recommended that a historical and national archive be created for the systematic compilation of testimonials and first-person accounts.[29]

A serious investigation of Arab-Muslim ideology and of Qu'ranic teachings did not really factor into Fanon's relationship to Algerian society. While his political views never lost sight of the relationship between politics and culture, these were deeply rooted in atheism and the relationship between religion and politics never entered into them. He firmly believed that a culture under colonial domination became fossilized and that the struggle for liberation ensured the emergence of new and different forms that would be radically different from the tradition-hardened, obsolete, and deadly ones that had preceded them. His efforts to increase his knowledge of local custom, cultural institutions, and culturally sanctioned expressions of the imaginary were just as great in Tunis as they had been in Algeria, but this interest did not extend to the ways in which the religious and the political intersect, and he did not subscribe to the Arab-Muslim discourse that had been espoused by certain factions of the FLN and had reached as far as Tunis. At *El Moudjahid,* this discourse was kept to a minimum, obscured perhaps, by a more overtly socialist stance. Fanon was, in actuality, more closely aligned with the position of the CCE, at least while it was still based in Algiers, until its forced withdrawal in February 1957. He was unable to grasp the full implications of the divisions in the leadership; in part, this was a result of his sketchy understanding of the nationalist movement prior to

1954, namely, his unfamiliarity with the valiant efforts of the MTLD in 1949 and 1952 and with the historical antagonism between the *udmistes* (affiliated to the movement led by Ferhat Abbas) and the centrists (MTLD). When he started working with Boumendjel, who was a member of the old UDMA, he came to appreciate him in much the same way he had appreciated Ben Khedda, a centrist.

Fanon, even during this period, refrained from writing about the Maghreb and the mutual relationships of the three countries it comprised. He broke his silence only once—after the incident at Sakiet, a border town inside Tunisia proper where several civilians were killed during a bomb attack by the French army. He was much more inclined to write about sub-Saharan Africa and his hopes for its liberation.

The years 1957 and 1958 did not bode well politically. Fanon did not delude himself about the conditions facing combatants inside Algeria, although his support for them never flagged, or about the military abilities of the frontier army, claiming that "we will never be in a position to commandeer large battalions, and without large battalions, victory is impossible." Nor did he have any great illusions about the political substance of the revolutionary leadership. He continued to view the triumvirate of Krim-Boussouf-Bentobbal as lacking any vision for the future of independent Algeria. "They want to have power in this new Algeria," he would say, "but to what end? They, themselves, don't know. An incantation to the people, meaning what exactly? They think that anything that is not a simple truth is dangerous to the revolution." He was angered by this. The ideas that he prized so highly—revolution, socialism, and secularism—did not seem to concern them in the least. Independence could not be won militarily, but military men were ultimately waging the political battle. Great though these concerns about strategy and these political disappointments may have been, they did not weaken his ties to the Algerian struggle to which he remained and would continue to remain all the more steadfast. If he strayed at all, in the face of such bleak prospects, it was by widening his field of action to include sub-Saharan Africa.

For the time being, Fanon remained in Tunis where he continued to devote much of his time to psychiatry. This was work for which he had a deep love, and it would not have crossed his mind to shirk his duties at the Razi Hospital in Manouba where he had been posted shortly after he arrived in Tunis. Maréchal, the French psychiatrist who had been the asylum's head physician, left a few months prior to Independence. Ben Soltane, his long-time assistant, had replaced him as the hospital's new director. Ben Soltane, a classically trained psychiatrist, was a harried man who had learned next to nothing from his mentor. Sleim Ammar, younger but better trained, was a recent addition to the Manouba team. The two psychiatrist who rounded out the team, Doctors Koskas and Lévy came from different professional backgrounds but shared a number of things in common: they were both Jewish, Tunisian, and Communist, and both had been involved in Tunisia's fight for independence. The two of them had recently returned from France to work in their newly independent nation.

Fanon reacted to his new setting in the same way he had to Blida. He wanted to change everything, implement institutional therapy, recruit and train the medical staff. His training and experience were far superior to those of his fellow psychiatrists. His Tunisian colleagues, especially the newly appointed director, were less than pleased by this peculiar Algerian who, to top it all off, was a black man. Fanon thought even less of them and their unbridled anti-Semitism toward their Jewish colleagues who had shown such flawless patriotism in the struggle for Tunisia's independence. Latent anti-Semitism, national mistrust, mandarin sensibilities—the place was a minefield and Fanon's welcome was growing more strained by the day. Add to this the fact that Fanon's psychiatric methods were met with the same disquiet they had triggered at Blida; the director felt that both his authority and his cavalier approach were being challenged. The atmosphere was fast becoming suffocating. Fanon's bitter complaints in private about the racism and anti-Semitism of his Muslim colleagues did not get in the way of his work, however, and in public, he remained impassive. He organized working sessions with his Tunisian Jewish colleagues and brought Pierre Chaulet on board as an interim tuberculosis specialist, a move that was long overdue and would benefit the patients greatly, and he obtained Ben Salah's permission to admit us, as soon as we turned up, as interns under his supervision.[30] There was plenty of work to go around, but there were also too many foreigners at the hospital. The already dreadful atmosphere at the hospital was made even worse by our arrival: more peculiar Algerian intruders and not one real Arab or Muslim in the lot. Fanon stood his ground. Throughout it all, our duties to the Algerian front were far from negligible. Beyond the strictly political responsibilities, there was an increasing need for medical personnel. The number of Algerians, fighters as well as refugees, who needed mental and physical attention, was rapidly growing. Combatants who had been wounded or had fallen ill were taken to a farm in the region of Kef, a town in the Tunisian heartland. A convoy of specialists—surgeons, ophthalmologists, lung specialists, and psychiatrists—made their way to the site on a weekly basis to care for the sick and share a meal of sorghum porridge. Those who needed further attention were relocated to hospitals throughout Tunisia. During the first year, only male physicians were included in these missions. Fanon was responsible for the mental health of the entire Algerian population in Tunis and some of his patients were members of the leadership.

Until the Bizerte Massacre of 1961,[31] Tunis was a lively and pleasant cosmopolitan city. There was swimming at the beach in Gammart; outings to the modest restaurants in La Goulette that served fish and chips topped off with a fried egg[32] and washed down with a swig of *boukha* (fig brandy) or Bokhobza wine; the countless establishments where one could sample local specialties, ranging from Tunisian-style sandwiches that could be had for a pittance to more sophisticated fare, affordable even on a modest budget: *meloukhia* (a slow cooking stew of lamb and leaves that have been especially dried and pounded to a powdery consistency), or *akoud* (a dish made with "white kidneys," a euphemism for sheep testicles). Excellent films were screened at the La Rotonde cinema. Theater companies, though uneven in quality, produced plays on a regular basis. There were two or three good bookstores, one that specialized in the humanities, with new and sometimes secondhand books on offer. Fanon enjoyed it all and felt entirely in his element. He liked the movies, where he always sat in the front row because of his myopia, and he did not dislike the beach, even though he usually remained fully clothed, he enjoyed sharing a meal with friends in La Goulette, he regularly dropped in on Mr. Lévy at the bookstore for a spot of book-burrowing. In this cosmopolitan city, there were Tunisians, Jews, and Muslims; French and Italian families who had resided in Tunisia for generations and who chose to remain in the country even after it had ceased being French; young men and women, French for the most part, who were completing their tour of duty in the civil service; a large contingent of Algerians, militants as well as others who had come to sit out the troubles, members of the FLN support networks in France and Algeria, draft dodgers, and deserters. And then there were the people who were just passing through, journalists from everywhere in the world, militants associated with other revolutionary movements, and "agents" of various kinds—in short, people who had come to see this "Algerian revolution," purportedly unlike any other, up close. In this great mix, Fanon was called on to work or simply meet with a great variety of people.

The pleasures that Tunis had to offer did little, however, to ease the tensions at Manouba. These had, in fact, reached a breaking point when Fanon and his interns were accused of taking part in a Zionist plot and of using their cover as doctors to torture the fighters who had been entrusted to their care. Doctor Ahmed Nani Bouderba, a senior medical official in the Algerian organization, heard the charge; he listened politely to the recriminations and promised to make an example of the guilty parties and sentence them to death. He then proceeded to say that the Algerian security services would conduct an investigation, and if the charges turned out to be fabricated, the same punishment would be meted out to the slanderers. The accusation was immediately withdrawn. To cut this sad story short, Fanon and his team were transferred, on Ben Salah's recommendation, to Charles-Nicolle, the major general hospital in Tunis, where Fanon became the director of one of the psychiatric services. Charles-Nicole and Manouba could not have been more different. Charles-Nicole was a friendly and more cosmopolitan institution: Tunisian and French physicians worked side-by-side without any apparent friction; the presence of the Algerians was fairly well accepted; the dormitories were home to Tunisians of all faiths and to a wide spectrum of foreigners. The foreigners included those who had come for political reasons: Algerians, Cameroonians, Union des Populations du Cameroun (UPC) activists, Haitians fleeing from Papa Doc, and others who had been drawn to the loveliness of the place: Turks, Armenians, Germans, Iranians, as well as Frenchmen. This diversity also extended to the paramedical staff; Tunisians side-by-side not only with Algerians but also with French, Maltese, and Sicilian co-workers.

A new psychiatric opportunity had availed itself to Fanon. Cheered by the warmer welcome and the manageable size of the service, he decided to explore a new approach: the one-day stay. With the support of an intelligent director and backed by an enthusiastic team made up of Tunisians and Algerians, he launched the Neuropsychiatry Day Clinic, which soon became known as the CNPJ. Fanon oversaw the running of the clinic with the help of his extremely motivated team that now also counted Marie-Jeanne Manuellan, a social worker, among its members. This is how, against a background of political struggle, psychiatric investigation, and the complicities of friendship, Marie-Jeanne became Fanon's writing assistant, thereby making it possible for him to write *L'An V de la révolution algérienne*, in addition to countless articles and conference papers.

Marie-Jeanne Manuellan was French and had come to Tunis with her husband, who was completing his civil service there. She was a social worker by training and had been hired by the Tunisian Ministry of Health a short time after she had arrived in the country in 1957. In 1956, in light of events in Budapest more so than those in Algeria, Marie-Jeanne decided to leave the Communist Party she had joined in the immediate aftermath of the War. She came from the Corréze region and was a Corrézienne to the core; the rural traditions of grandparents who migrated North in the winters had been deeply instilled in her, and her memories of her life in an area of France that had protected the Jews in the 1940s were still very much with her.[33] In her first job in Tunis, she had assisted Pierre Chaulet in his work with tubercular patients and had worked in a facility that was located in

Djebbal Ammar, an exceptionally poor neighborhood. "I liked my Djebbal Ammar," she later told us, "and when I heard I was being moved to CNJP, I wasn't especially pleased. I didn't want to leave Djebbal Ammar behind, and I had never heard about this Doctor Fanon." In fact, during her first months at CNJP, she barely left her office—a closet, really, that didn't even have a door. Finally, she was approached by Fanon who wanted to know if she was interested in learning. She was, and he sent her off to Mr. Lévy with instructions to purchase every book by Freud she could lay her hands on. "I didn't even know about the unconscious," she recalls. "I had been a member of the Communist Party at a time when psychoanalysis was considered a bourgeois science. This was in the day of the journal *La Raison*,[34] when one could be turned into a laughingstock even for reading something by Maryse Choisy, the Director of the *Revue internationale des sciences de l'homme et de psychanalyse*, who had just written a book about raising her child. My second assignment was when Fanon sent me out to buy some play dough and a couple of dolls and put me to work with a couple of little girls. I was instructed to just let them play at first, to not intervene, but I was supposed to write everything down. I was such a novice that for the longest time I neglected to mention that one of the girls had repeatedly mentioned a bird that had kissed her hard, and I was quite taken aback when Fanon lit into me about the omission. 'You know perfectly well that this little girl's mother is pregnant!' he told me."

Write everything down. That would become Marie-Jeanne Manuellan's mantra. By early 1959, she had become Fanon's right-hand woman, his other writing self—a job that had fallen to this author until she became the beneficiary of grants and scholarships awarded by nations "friendly to the Algerian revolution" and started traveling to distant places to pursue her studies. Fanon used to dictate everything: articles for *El Moudjahid*, psychotherapy reports, patient interviews, including those with Algerian fighters who were reluctant to speak frankly in front of a third party. Dictation, taken by Marie-Jeanne, was Fanon's method of choice when he wrote the two books that would be his last, *L'An V* and *Les Damnés*.

From the beginning, Fanon was immensely invested in the CNJP and in the experiment it entailed. Fanon had been given a free hand to practice the kind of psychiatry he believed in, and he was now in a position to implement a novel approach, unfamiliar even in Europe, in a developing country and to indulge his delight of sharing this knowledge with others. Aside from Tunisian patients, the facility was used by the Algerian military and political leadership and was a place of special solace for the young officers working in the signals corps, "the Boussouf Boys," whose needs were particularly well-suited to the day clinic model, as they were required to report to camp at nightfall for security reasons.

Fanon's main base of operations for the duration of his stay in Tunis, despite his many other political, scholarly, and social obligations, was the CNJP. He arrived early in the morning, pulled on a fresh smock to which he always fastened a pin he would use in the neurological examination he performed on every patient who was admitted to the hospital; a protocol that made absolute sense when one stops to consider the setting and the patients' general inability to distinguish psychiatric problems from neurological ones. The pin was dragged across the bottom of the foot to test for the sign neurologists refer to as the Babinski reflex. Fanon could never resist a bit of fun at Babinski's expense, even when he had to undergo the test himself. But he wasn't always in a joking mood. One day, the mother-in-law of an Algerian minister turned up at the hospital. She started screaming from the moment the pin grazed the sole of her foot. Fanon was livid and asked the nurse to translate: "Tell her I have no time to waste on the mothers-in-law of ministers. I'm here to take care of the poor." It just so happened that the lady in question spoke excellent French, and the nurse couldn't have been more mortified by Fanon's request.

But Fanon had an immense respect for the sick. He not only did not fear the mentally ill, but he was always ready to engage with madness, and he had a profound regard for psychological suffering. Instances of conversion hysteria were not an unusual occurrence at the hospital, and we would often see young women in the grip of the kind of alarming fits that must have been witnessed by Charcot. Fanon, who could be so impatient and demanding, also knew how to be compassionate and wait things out, to bide his time and address the patient when the right moment presented itself. His manner impressed the Tunisian and Algerian staff immensely; they had, more often than not, been inclined to call in the exorcists. Fanon was not quite so patient, however, when it came to negligence on the part of the nursing staff, and he was perfectly capable, as he proved one day, of firing people on the spot. He had an idealized and demanding expectation of what a human being should be and was always terribly shaken when people shirked their responsibilities. But, he was averse to solitude. "I'm moving too fast," he would worry, "and I am afraid I'm going to end up all alone." This may have been one of the reasons why he always wanted someone along, as a scribe or simply to keep him company. He was the only neuropsychiatrist at Charles-Nicolle and was often called away for consultations, or to attend conferences on neurology, or to participate in studies on psychiatric cases, and he usually asked an intern, or his assistant Marie-Jeanne, to accompany him.

The psychiatry department was running quite smoothly, and Fanon began to devote more and more time to one-on-one therapies that drew heavily on psychoanalysis. It was around this time that he expressed his intention, in private of course, that "when all of this is over (this being the Algerian revolution) I'd like to have the time to go into analysis." In addition to Freud and Reich, whom he had already read, he discovered the translated works, few and difficult to find at the time, of Sándor Ferenczi. He was captivated by Ferenczi's discussion of the neuroses of war and by his ideas on trauma. He was on the lookout for people who could translate Ferenczi's other works. Fanon, who had a very poor command of other languages, was often on the lookout for people who could translate from English, German, or Spanish; but nothing had changed since Blida, once he had the manuscript in hand, he was disappointed and found fault with every translation that was turned in to him.

Some accounts of the experimental Charles-Nicolle Day Clinic have survived. Fanon and Charles Géronimi co-authored a piece that was included in a longer article about the hospital and published toward the end of 1959 in *La Tunisie médicale*. The piece reads like Fanon's will and testament to psychiatry. He rushed to finish writing it, he was not dictating it this time, before his trip to Africa and his break—a temporary one he insisted—from the "vocation" he loved so passionately. The article does a fine job of capturing the daily round at the CNJP; sadly, the quality of the facility went into a downward spiral after Fanon's departure. The CNJP was groundbreaking in many ways, especially given its Third World setting; in fact, it would have been groundbreaking in France. The guiding principle at the clinic was the breakdown of barriers that are traditionally associated with psychiatric wards. It was modeled on an open-door policy that was already being practiced in the English-speaking world. At the time, the experiment had not yet been attempted in France.

The first section of the article bears only Fanon's name, and in it, he summarized the Day Clinic guidelines: it did not force the patient to break with his/her habitual environment; it did not rely on the magical cessation of conflicts—a practice usually resulting in institutionalization and in the repression, calcification even, of said conflicts, and rarely, if ever, in their resolution. "The patient is not separated from the familial environment, and, in some cases, may even continue to participate in his professional environment, and the psychiatric symptomology is not artificially suffocated by confinement." The conflictive elements, he explained, persist in all facets of life. The setup of the Day Clinic allowed for these conflicts to be engaged in an open therapy in which they did not become "objectified" and for the doctor/patient relationship to unfold in a realm of mutual freedom. At the end of this first section, Fanon asks himself two questions that seem, at surface, to belong to two completely different registers, but that, in fact, correspond directly to his central, twofold preoccupation: the future of underdeveloped countries and his tireless examination of folly. First, he wants to know if a day clinic can operate successfully in a poorly industrialized nation. Two years had elapsed since the clinic had opened its doors, and the track record spoke for itself. Clearly, this was a question that could be answered in the affirmative. The model, he concluded, is efficient and economical, even in an underdeveloped nation. He also wonders if "it would be possible to set up a night service in the same site that houses the Day Clinic? This strategy is now common practice in Europe, but it is still a rarity in Africa, alas." In fact, Fanon had already presented the plan to health officials in Tunisia, who had responded favorably and were seriously considering his proposed restructuring. Fanon had a similar plan in the works for post-Independence Algeria.

The second question had to do with the limitations of the day clinic. Could the model handle the entire range of psychiatric afflictions? He concluded that the model was not appropriate to certain types of acute psychoses, to deliriums that could result in dangerous aggressive behaviors, and to legal medicine cases. It was, however, extremely well suited to everything else, including the so-called chronic illnesses that, paradoxically, seemed to be aggravated by the enclosed setting of an asylum. After this introductory summation of the clinic's guiding principles and the conclusions that the experiment had yielded to date, Fanon gives a detailed account of the daily protocols. The clinic was situated in a wing of a larger, general hospital. It was equipped with eighty-six beds: forty for male patients, an equal number for female patients, and six that were reserved for children. Except for Sunday, it was open every day of the week, between the hours of 7 a.m. and 6 p.m. Every nurse was assigned no fewer than six and no more than eight patients whose care she or he oversaw for the entire duration of treatment. Nurses had to perform a daily round of practical duties, and, more important, they were expected to engage patients, encouraging them to talk about the things they had done during their time away from the hospital and drawing them out on their relationship to their environment outside the hospital as well as asking them about their thoughts, their dreams and nightmares. The nurses had to be on the lookout for any sign of preoccupying or anxious behaviors and to signal these immediately. Fanon would frequently say: "Give me any ten nurses who haven't fallen into the habit of viewing patients as the bane of the staff's peace of mind, and I will turn them into full-fledged healers." A typical day at the CNJP was filled with a variety of therapeutic activities: support psychotherapies and psychoanalytically inspired therapies were the most common and always handled by Fanon, who turned over the better part of his mornings to this work. The morning was also reserved for the biological treatments that were prescribed at the time of the patient's initial pre-admission consultation, and these included sleep and rest cures, insulin therapy, and, on very rare occasions, sismotherapy. Afternoons were devoted to group activities: group therapies, or, more precisely, exercises in psychodrama that, interestingly, had little to do with ideas of psychodrama that were popular at the time and were closer to ideas that are in currency today. Psychodrama at the CNJP did not rely on the enactment of fictional scenes inscribed in the imaginary or the acting out of fantasies. Rather, a patient would be asked to address the gathering and speak about his or her life story. The patient, whose presentation elicited reactions from the listeners, was in a position to "demonstrate, analyze, and take charge" of his or her responses to conflicts. Additional therapeutic activities included craft workshops for the men, and for the women, apprenticeships in which they were taught simple skills, such as knitting, sewing, and child care. All of it may strike us as banal today, given the present-day proliferation of similar kinds of programs, but things then were not what they are now. In the second part of the text, signed by both Fanon and his intern, there is an insistence, paradoxical to those who knew and worked with the man, that this kind of institution be attached to a larger, general hospital. To what end, one may ask? In the eventuality of the discovery of new biological treatments? Or, so that the psychiatrist could "appear as a doctor like any other in the patient's eyes and in his own . . . and shed the fantastical and troubling aura of the psychiatrist locked up with his lunatics?" Perhaps. But while Fanon never called traditional medicine into question and was quite disinterested in challenging the ruling medical ideology, he did not really think of himself and never aspired to be "a doctor like any other." Whenever he returned from the lectures or presentations on patient cases he made to other doctors and interns in other departments at Charles-Nicolle, he could be heard thinking out loud: "They think I'm making up accounts of fantastic cases; they cannot, for a moment, imagine that these stories are told to us by our patients, and all we do is relay them."

In the car that was taking Fanon to the airport on the occasion of his trip to Accra, he entrusted Marie-Jeanne with a voluminous typewritten manuscript that also documents his activities at the time. The document was the detailed report of an extremely significant case study. It reveals a little known side of Fanon—his command of psychoanalytic theory and his understanding of the workings of the unconscious as well as his acute intuition. The report describes the case of a young, twenty-seven-year old patient who underwent one-hour sessions five times a week, very much in the fashion of Freud's early therapies. The case is surprisingly reminiscent of Freud's famous "Rat Man" and owes much to certain findings of Ferenczi, whom Fanon often spoke of at the time. The report reveals that Fanon had both an extremely attuned ear as well as considerable theoretical grounding. He hears not only the desired and negated homosexuality but is equally attentive to the repetitive pattern of signifiers. In the manner of classical analysts, he pays close attention to the denials and the lapses. But the idea of transference makes him extremely uncomfortable—here, just as in other therapeutic approaches, he finds the idea of his centrality burdensome. His discomfort does not stop transference from occurring, however; it is imposed by the patient who exploits the strategy to its utmost in his associations and in his accounts of dreams; later in the treatment, the patient relates the kind of transference dreams that contemporary psychoanalysts can only dream of. At first, Fanon did his best to sidestep the patient by encouraging him to focus on early childhood memories, but he eventually had to give in and "make do." In the fullness of time, he stops responding to the patient's wish—"I would have liked you to be my father," by saying, "I cannot be your father, I am your doctor." The young man in question made incredible progress. As did Fanon. There have been many who have taken remarks of uneven importance that were made by Fanon in different registers as evidence that Fanon was not a psychoanalyst. (Several of these criticisms point to the section in *Black Skin, White Masks* in which he argues against the existence of the Oedipus complex and of homosexuality in Antillean society.)[35] And, it is quite clear, that in 1952, he was not a psychoanalyst. His position in 1958, however, was much more nuanced, and in practice, he did not contest the universality of the Oedipal triangulation. He shied away from the idea of a collective unconscious and preferred to think of the unconscious as the repository of the trace effects of a specific culture and history—psychoanalysis, at the time, had a tendency to dismiss such particularities. He continued to argue that the Antillean tradition of the *commère* (granny) that allowed men to dress up as women was not necessarily a sign of homosexuality (not untrue). He continued to be greatly preoccupied with matters beyond the Oedipal configuration and with the psychic wounds that are inscribed in the evolving self; the preoccupation was central to Fanon's own personal experience, and in his own search for answers, he found his way to Freud by way of Ferenczi. He also had the great insight of using language to invoke the great tyrannical figures so that, through the intervention of a third voice, these figures could be made to retreat or take on another aspect. Though he may have often successfully helped others, he was never quite able to help himself.

Fanon came for work at the CNJP until the last day before he departed for Accra. His claim that he was leaving psychiatry behind with much regret was met with skepticism by some of his friends. Martini was one such friend who had difficulty believing that Fanon was sorry to leave—he remembers the energy Fanon had expended to be posted to sub-Saharan Africa by the GPRA.[36] There is no doubt that Fanon, at the time, was confident in his political abilities. He believed that the work he would carry out in sub-Saharan Africa could be very important for the future of the African continent, where independence was beckoning and just around the corner for many countries. Still, the career he left behind had meant much to him, not least of all the experience of touching the lives of suffering individuals.

The hasty creation of the CNJP, early in September 1958, coincided with the September 9th creation of the first Provisional Government of the Algerian Republic. M'hammed Yazid was named Minister of Information. Of Blidaen descent, he had studied at the Lycée Duverrier and was at home in both French and Algerian culture. As someone who had spent time in Paris, he was predisposed to being seduced by Fanon and quite capable of seducing him in return: the two men shared a love of language. Yazid was a diplomat, however, both in letter and in spirit, a fine strategist who took great care to treat his interlocutors tactfully. Fanon, at least where politics were concerned, was utterly lacking in these skills. It soon became apparent that the two men did not really see eye to eye, and Fanon found himself increasingly excluded from developments at the Rue des Entrepreneurs and the office of Information Services. Journalists from everywhere in the world began flocking to Tunis to become part of what was being referred to as the "Maghreb circus."[37] The GPRA made it known, through its spokesman on the scene, the minister of information, that it no longer wished to be represented by Fanon in its interactions with the media. Furthermore, Yazid styled himself as a "European-style revolutionary."[38] He valued his relationship to the European Left and his priorities did not include viewing Algeria as a nation that had been entrusted with an international mission or the Third World as the harbinger of a new age. Though Fanon had not articulated these vanguard ideas quite yet, his growing interest in the liberation of the African continent as a whole and his impatience with positions of nationalism at any cost give one a fair idea of the direction he was about to take.

All the same, Fanon continued to write for *El Moudjahid*, which had been granted full autonomy by Yazid. The newspaper's office had been relocated to the headquarters of the Algerian Ministry of Information; this new arrangement meant that the two men were destined to cross paths often. Fanon was also expected to comply with additional political duties. In the summer of 1959, he joined Ben Yahia, Omar Oussedik, Abderrazak Chentouf, Lamine Khène, and Messaoud Aït Chaâlal as a member of the commission that was in charge of developing the program that was slotted to be presented at the end-of-year CNRA.[39] Fanon was increasingly involved in fostering relationships between the Algerian Revolution and the liberation movements of a number of African states that were on the brink of independence. The FLN officially acknowledged him in this liaison role.

Fanon's political concerns did not abate, and late in 1958 as well as throughout 1959, after de Gaulle had acceded to power in France and the GPRA had been formed, he continued to find the situation worrisome. Events had reached a standstill. The GPRA did score a number of diplomatic victories, but the relationship with the ALN, in exile and great chaos, was strained and difficult. The electric fences that France had erected on the frontier between Algeria and Morocco (the Challe line) and between Algeria and Tunisia (the Morice line) were seriously obstructing the passage of people, weapons, and ammunition into Algeria. One effort to breach the fence en masse ended up costing 2,000 men their lives. Krim Belkacem, the GPRA Minister of the Armies, had attempted the organization of a military operational command (COM) on two fronts: the one in the west under the leadership of Boumedienne, who had replaced Boussouf as Colonel of *Wilaya* 5, and of Commandant Saddek (Slimane Dehiles); the eastern front was under the command of Mohammedi Saïd—alias Colonel Nacer.[40] Nacer's men rebelled, and the resulting conspiracy went so far as to set its sights on toppling the GPRA. Participants in the coup were judged by a military tribunal presided by Boumedienne and Saddek. Lamouri, the man who had led the rebellion, was sentenced to death and executed, but corruption and demoralization continued to plague the frontier army. In an effort to stave this deterioration, the CNRA, after seemingly unending talks, decided to name Boumedienne as the sole Chief Commanding Officer, and in January 1960, he was entrusted with the job of restructuring the army.

Inside Algeria, the situation was just as dire. The reports that were trickling out from the *Wilayas* were not encouraging. The Challe Plan, that involved infiltrating the *Djebel* by posting French troops in mountain areas, was taking its toll on the resistance. Threats, punishment, recruitment of informers, and especially the forced relocation of civilians had resulted in an almost total breakdown of communication between the *maquis* and the inhabitants of the surrounding villages.

The purges known as the *bleuite* were another terrible and debilitating factor. The pursuit and exposure of traitors, or alleged traitors, resulted in the deaths of numerous leaders. Captain Léger's, and later Colonel Godard's, methods of psychological intoxication proved successful. They forced

Algerian militants to bear false witness against fellow members of the *maquis;* the accused were subsequently sentenced to death by their leaders. This scourge caused ravages in 1958 and 1959. The deadly purges that were carried out in Amirouche's *Wilaya* 3 as well as in *Wilaya* 4, despite its purported openness and relative safety, targeted intellectuals and students who had joined the *maquis.* Fanon did not know everything; still, he was better informed than most because of his ties to Omar Oussedik and to Colonel Saddek—ties that were nurtured by all concerned and that would endure until the end of Fanon's life. Fanon was deeply affected by the reports, and he did not like any of it, not the Challe Plan, or the *bleuite,* or the discord among the higher echelons. Many years later, Ferhat Abbas would recall a conversation he had with Fanon about the rivalry among the colonels and the latter's remark that "One day, Colonel Boumedienne, will settle all their scores. His taste for power and authority borders on the pathological."[41] Fanon worried about the shape of the new society that would emerge in post-Independence Algeria; the prospects were dim—a new bourgeoisie ready to pick up where the others had left off, or a power struggle between different clans, or a religious movement that would succeed in determining the nature of the State.

The likelihood of military victory was out of the question. De Gaulle, for his part, was waffling—caught between the idea of French Algeria and Algeria for the Algerians. On reading one of de Gaulle's 1959 speeches that raised the prospect of self-determination, Fanon, contrary to expectation, was ready to consider the possibility of negotiation.[42] He was, for the first time, in agreement with Bourguiba, the Tunisian president, and his position was no longer in line with the much more circumspect position espoused by the GPRA.

Sékou Touré[43] of Guinea flatly turned down de Gaulle's plan. Touré's refusal gladdened Fanon immensely. It was around this time that members of open as well as clandestine movements of African liberation began to pour into Tunis. Fanon met them all, striking up a friendship with Félix Moumié who was quite taken aback by the unfriendliness of the Algerians. When Fanon informed Malek that the Africans were not finding the Algerians particularly hospitable, the latter, without a trace of irony, responded: "But I bought him a cup of tea!"

Very quickly and with the GPRA's support, Fanon became the key intermediary for the African community. More and more, he was put in charge of missions in Africa, and in December 1958, he attended the conference in Accra as a member of the Algerian delegation. He presented a paper that drew heavily on his publications in *El Moudjahid* and that caught the attention of many who were discovering him for the first time. His presence and participation reflected well on Algeria, and Fanon, despite his political reservations, did not begrudge Algeria the privilege.

While still in Tunis and despite his taxing work schedule as a psychiatrist and political activist, Fanon began to look for a way to fit in more creative pursuits. He once confided to Marie-Jeanne Manuellan that during his student days, one of his professors had told him in jest: "You will not live to comb gray hairs. You want to do too many things." At the time, he was busy preparing the paper he would deliver shortly thereafter in Rome at the Congrès des Écrivains et Artistes noirs. But this did not stand in the way of his accepting a teaching position that was extended to him by Granai, a professor of sociology at the university. Fanon agreed to the position straightaway, and he embarked on a series of lectures that were mainly about Chester Himes.[44] At the time, the topic was quite exotic—especially for an Algerian audience that expected a more traditionally academic approach and a subject matter that would be more in line with the pressing issues at hand. Some came away with the feeling that Fanon lacked gravitas. He made a far better impression, however, in cosmopolitan Tunisian circles.

In truth, Fanon needed to breathe, to meet people. On one particular Christmas Eve Fanon spent with his friends dancing, drinking, singing *béguines*, and exchanging confidences, he spoke to one of his dance partners about his birthplace and what it meant to him, about the home we all leave but never leave behind. Fanon was the very embodiment of someone who had separated from his origins but had never refuted them. When all is said and done, his most intimate relationships were generally with others who were in the same bind. Even though he was a disciplined militant working for a cause whose greatness would eclipse his, and even though he tried to use political action as a means to the kind of revolutionary virtues he admired in Abbane and would later celebrate in Moumié, his mentality was always that of a minority and an outsider. Even though Fanon may have been heard to say in passing, "I am a very important person in the FLN and cannot fraternize with French people," the truth remains that the only people with whom he was truly at ease and with whom he struck up countless friendships belonged to Tunis's cosmopolitan circles—Tunisian Jews, French volunteer workers, French people who had decided to remain in independent Tunisia, Europeans who worked with the FLN. These were the people with whom he went to the beach and to the movies, with whom he listened to music and conversed. It was in their homes that he sang and danced the night away on New Year's Eve. He loved those gatherings and had never felt free enough to dance around any of his Algerian comrades, at least not in Tunis. He was very comfortable in the company of Tunisian Jews, who formed a kind of militant bourgeoisie that numbered a great many Communists or ex-Communists. He developed profound ties to the Taïebs, who would remain loyal friends for the rest of his life. In addition to Marie-Jeanne, he was also friends with her husband Gilbert Manuellan, an Armenian who had been born and raised in Tunis and had been preparing his entrance exams to attend engineering school in Algeria when World War II broke out. Manuellan, who was barred from taking the exam as a result of losing his status as an Armenian refugee, joined the African army in which Fanon had also served and had taken part in many of the same military campaigns. Understandably, this shared experience provided an additional affinity between the two men. The Manuellans, like the Taïebs, supported the Algerian cause but were not directly involved in the movement; they, too, were ex-Communists, people who were proud of national origins with which they no longer necessarily identified. In both these homes, Fanon could posture and joke about issues of identity, or simply talk about music. Yoyo Taïeb was a pianist. Gilbert Manuellan, whose expertise was in agronomy, was also an excellent musician and jazz connoisseur. He would talk to Fanon, who was thinking a lot about black creativity, about black jazzmen and the musical revolution they had brought about. In this instance, Fanon did not feel the need to retort, as he had on other occasions, by saying, "Not bad for a black man." Some Sundays, Fanon would relax by playing cards, especially during the last period of his life. He preferred simple games like *rami* or *belote*, and card playing was the single leisure activity he shared with his Algerian comrades, Omar Oussedik and Si Saddek, formerly of *Wilaya* 4, as well as with his friends who were at a greater remove from the Algerian struggle.

Fanon also met a great number of academics who were passing through Tunis. It was in this context that he had an opportunity to cross swords with Raymond Aron whom he would sum up as "an intelligent and erudite man who doesn't want to know anything about alienation, not even his own." Through Granai, he also met Jacques Berque of whom he had been unaware previously and whose books he had not read. Before his meeting with Berque, which took place toward the end of 1959, he called on all his friends as well as on his trusty book vendor, Mr. Lèvy, in a last-ditch effort to get his hands on something by Berque. I am not sure he succeeded, but he and Berque got along famously all the same. Fanon was delighted by this European who was so profoundly familiar with Algeria and with the Arab and Muslim world as a whole; he admired Berque for the subtlety of his analysis, the depth of his commitment, and the measured and lucid manner in which he expressed his ideas. In the obituary he would later write, Berque would remember Fanon's anger, his reasoning powers, and his goodness. This was the impression Fanon had made on this sensitive, thoughtful, and extremely cultured man. The encounter made a lasting impact on Berque, and he referred to it at least twice in his writings, once in his *Mémoires* and again in *Présence Africaine*. In *Mémoires des deux rives*, Berque writes,

In that same city, I attended a dinner at the home of the anthropologist Granai and spent the entire evening talking with Dr. Fanon, a psychiatrist with fine powers of clinical observation. His work, tragically cut short soon thereafter, would have been a rich contribution to the Marxist theory of alienation that he had expanded to include depersonalization, split personality, simulation, etc. But, like almost all French supporters of the FLN, he failed to grasp the Arab and Islamic identity of the latter. On the day that followed the presentations at the Algiers Forum, he was surprised to hear me claim that the past century of colonial rule had contributed to making the veil of Muslim women a thicker rather than a lighter one.[45]

In "Une cause jamais perdue," a piece he published in *Présence Africaine*, Berque wrote at some length about the aforementioned encounter with Fanon:

I am not likely to forget the evening I spent with Fanon in Tunis. His book *L'An V de la révolution algérienne* had just come out. We discussed it in serene scholarly terms. Even though my own involvement was not of the same kind as the author's, we were, in essence, of one mind and agreed on the importance of how the idea of freedom would evolve in the Maghreb and on the responsibility of intellectuals to that evolution. The book, while being the work of a militant, did not, for all its anger, eclipse the positive. While talking to Fanon about his experience as a physician and a psychologist, I admired his power of observations. Few have managed, given the Islamic-Mediterranean's susceptibility to the double trance of history and atemporality, to gather such valuable materials and penetrating analyses. For the benefit of my interlocutor, I listed the handful of psychoanalysts practicing between Morocco and Baghdad, and together we discussed areas of study that could be pursued at some later date.[46]

Fanon was given to imagining this "later date." He had already envisioned a mental health program for the new Algeria, and he liked to envisage how the handful of Algerians who happened to be studying psychiatry in the various corners of the globe would come home and be trained by him to take part in the new psychiatric project he planned to implement; he was always ready to look to the future, never pausing to even contemplate the more than likely probability of apathy and inertia.

It was also in Tunis, some months later, that he met Giovanni Pirelli. The infatuation was absolute and mutual. Giovanni Pirelli was the scion of the powerful Milanese Pirelli tire dynasty. His life had been defined largely by the War and by a deep attachment to his great industrialist father, a man of exceptional moral and intellectual stature. By 1948, however, Giovanni would make a clean break with his past. While pursuing a degree in history in Lombardy, he participated in the unambiguously leftist cultural burgeoning associated with the Casa de la Cultura and the Einaudi publishing house. He distanced himself from his family's Christian humanism and began to write for publishers such as Moviemiento Operaio and Avanti, as well as for a number of newspapers and journals. This writer, journalist, and great benefactor was responsible for compiling and publishing the letters of Italian Resistance fighters who had been captured and sentenced to death. In a second book, he expanded the project to include all of Europe. He was the patron of a number of contemporary composers, including Luigi Nono. Nono remembers Pirelli's remarkable openness, his nondogmatic political intelligence, and his great talent as a good listener. "He had this incredible ability to resist synthesis. He wasn't driven by a need to unify things. He preferred to identify the possibilities. He also knew how to bring people together whom, on the face of it, seemed to have nothing in common. He was always in motion and knew how to pull others into this motion."[47]

In 1955, Pirelli became interested in wars of liberation. In 1959 he was sent to North Africa as an elected representative of the Helsinki Peace Committee; by 1960, he had arrived in Tunis. While in Tunis, Pirelli wanted to collect the letters of soldiers and members of the Algerian resistance who had been victims of repression. The book he had in mind was similar to his earlier compilations with their emphasis on firsthand accounts, depictions of the day-to-day, the uncensored writings of individuals speaking out of their subjective experience. In the course of his work, he met up with people in the small expatriate community and ended up at the Algerian Ministry of Information, where he would eventually meet Fanon. In addition to seeing eye to eye on the question of African liberation, Fanon and Pirelli were both drawn to the role that individual change played in the gradual transformation of the collective. Fanon was initially reluctant, questioning the relevance of Pirelli's project. But he was so affected by the power of the letters that Pirelli showed to him that he quickly changed his mind and agreed to support the project. In 1961, when Pirelli collaborated with Jacques Charby[48] on a book project about the writings and drawings of Algerian war orphans, Fanon again supported the project, offering advice on how best to conduct the interviews and on the selection of drawings. The affection, and especially the respect, between Fanon and Pirelli was completely mutual.

Fanon admired Pirelli for his immense erudition, his gift for being a good listener, and his generosity. Pirelli was likewise very taken by Fanon's generosity and by his intelligence. After Fanon's death, Pirelli spent a great many years translating and introducing Fanon's work to Italian readers. He also created the Frantz Fanon Center, a short-lived institution that ceased to exist after Pirelli's death in 1972.

These were the circumstances of Fanon's life when he wrote *L'An V.* On a spring day in 1959, he approached Marie-Jeanne Manuellan and asked her: "Can you type?" She answered, "No, but I can learn." And the dictation of the manuscript of *L'An V* began shortly thereafter.

Fanon arrived at the CNJP at seven sharp and began his days pacing back and forth in his office while dictating perfectly crafted sentences to a thoroughly inexperienced typist who had somehow managed to lay her hands on an old Chapy typewriter with quite a few badly damaged keys. Fanon almost never faltered and rarely revised his phrasing. Every evening, Marie-Jeanne would take the typed pages home, correct them, and bring them on the following morning so Fanon could read through them and make his handful of corrections. But the typing was not going as quickly as he would have wished; he waited a few days and then shared his concern with Marie-Jeanne. She reminded him that she had told him from the start she was just a beginner. To which he responded: "But I was hoping you would be a fast learner." Their collaboration came to an end at this point, but after a week had elapsed, Fanon called her in again having come up with the following solution: he would dictate and she would transcribe everything by hand, and then at night, she could take her sweet time typing it on the old machine in the peace and quiet of her own home and to her husband's great displeasure. The system worked like a dream, and the book was completed very quickly, in a matter of two or three months. The manuscript was almost finished when Fanon went to Morocco and was involved in a car accident that was rumored to be the handiwork of the Main Rouge.[49]

In mid-June 1959, Fanon was sent on an official mission to Morocco. When Fanon announced his trip, he did not expand on the reasons for this mission. If one were to speculate as to the purpose of this trip, it could have involved any number of things from a reorganization of the medical system to providing training to fighters on the frontier to meeting with representatives from sub-Saharan Africa. The trip, we were told, would be a short one. A few days later, the news reached us in Tunis that the car in which he had been traveling had crashed into a ditch. There were conflicting reports about what had caused the accident—some claimed that it had simply been an accident, while others spoke of sabotage and a mined roadway. No one knew for sure. But whatever the cause, Fanon's injuries were serious; he had sustained a trauma to the vertebrae and suffered a temporary paralysis, and before receiving reassurances that there had been no further internal damage, we were all deeply upset. There was even a rumor in Tunis, dispelled after a few long hours, that he had died. He received immediate attention at a Moroccan hospital, and soon after Josie reached his bedside, a decision was taken to transfer him to a clinic in Rome. His passage through Rome was also punctuated by a number of alarming incidents. The car, driven by the Algerian delegate Taïeb Boulharouf, that was supposed to pick Fanon and Josie up at the airport had been rigged with explosives. The timer on the bomb went off too early, causing a number of casualties, all of them Italian. The ambulance that was transporting Fanon, who was still incapacitated, Josie, and an Algerian official to the hospital was forcibly detoured by police and taken to a police station. The passengers were detained before being allowed to proceed to the hospital. Later that night, Josie and the Algerian official were again called in for questioning. Their interrogation focused on the identity of the patient they were accompanying who was traveling on a Moroccan passport and under an assumed name. On the following day, Fanon learned that the Roman papers were full of news about the Algerian leader who had been transported to a local hospital; one of the papers divulged the name of the hospital and the room number![50] At Fanon's request, the hospital, working in the utmost secrecy, arranged for his transfer to another floor. Pirelli reports that two armed individuals broke into the clinic on the following night and entered the room that had been previously occupied by Fanon. On discovering that the room was unoccupied, they escaped.

When Fanon had completed his course of physical therapy in Rome, he returned to Tunis and moved in with the Taïebs, who had a house on the outskirts of Tunis. Again, Fanon, in true fashion, made light of the events that had befallen him: "It took me a while to walk again, and I still have to go through another Babinski. This is all highly suspicious, what is my cortex up to?" To no one's surprise, we never did get the whole story. Fanon refused to elaborate on what had caused the accident in the first place and said little about what had happened in Rome except to confirm that he had requested a room change. That being said, Fanon did not joke about his fears of being attacked by the secret service. The assumption that Main Rouge may have had a hand in the accident was not at all unlikely, but it is also true that Fanon had an indiscriminate tendency to suspect espionage. This tendency would at times cloud the way he viewed French deserters, especially Communists; this was not just a case of sharing the FLN's openly suspicious posture toward Communists; it was also a personal trait.

As soon as he returned to Tunis, he got in touch with Marie-Jeanne, wanting to "wrap up" his book, especially the introduction, which was completed in July 1959.

Despite these setbacks and difficulties, the writing of *L'An V* was a happy period in Fanon's life. He felt that his ideas were falling into place and that this work was addressed to all concerned—to French as well as Algerian readers. Because he took his responsibilities as a disciplined militant very seriously, he arranged to meet with Ferhat Abbas, the president of the GPRA, and asked for permission to have the book published by Maspero. Abbas also reports that in the course of that meeting Fanon asked him to write the preface and that he declined.[51] But after that meeting, he and Fanon, whom he perceived as a "true Marxist," fell into the habit of conversing about "everything and nothing." Fanon, whose request for a presidential preface had been turned down, had to write his own introduction and was quite pleased with the results, but for reasons that even Maspero cannot recall, the introduction does not appear in the first edition.

What François Maspero does remember are the circumstances that surrounded the genesis and publication of this book.[52] How was it that Fanon, who was living in Tunis as a member of the FLN and tacitly barred from setting foot in France, came to be the author of a book that was published by a French press?[53] Maspero remembers that

in 1957–58, I was intent on publishing books about Algeria, and I made it known to those around me. I had already spoken about it to Robert Barrat and Jean Daniel, without any tangible results. I was aware of the Jeanson network, even though I wasn't part of it yet, that came later with the Curiel relay, but the network didn't move manuscripts. Mario de Andrade, the Angolan writer whom I had met through a group of young Portuguese anticolonial militants, was the first one who spoke to me about Frantz Fanon. I wrote to him right away, in the spring of 1959. Then things started to move very quickly, and by late November, the book was published. The longest thing was waiting for a preface. In my naivete as a neophyte publisher, I had approached Césaire, whose work I admired. By asking him, I had plunged him into a great panic, and it took him two months to inform me that he just couldn't do it. Albert Memmi bowed out on the spot; what is more, he advised me to proceed with the greatest caution: "keep your distance," he said.

And Maspero did think it judicious, at least for the first edition, to distance himself from the text, even though he felt no reticence about the content and thought the writing revealed a kindred spirit who was familiar and unfamiliar in equal measure. In lieu of a preface, the first edition appeared with a publisher's foreword that was, by and large, laudatory and that characterized the work as "a generous analysis of a nation that has been pushed to the edge by a suffering that we must all, regardless of party affiliation, acknowledge, and whose dignity, won at such a high price, we must accept. Frantz Fanon's work," the foreword went on to say, "moves us toward that bringing together of all beings on which the future depends." Maspero, who never met Fanon—he had caught a glimpse of him at the 1956 Congrès des Écrivains noirs at the Sorbonne, but their paths would never cross again[54]— was, like Jeanson had been a few years prior, gripped by the writing itself and succumbed to its power, above and beyond the validity of its arguments, as only a "brother in writing" would.

Was the book seized shortly after its publication? It appears to have been, at least that is what one gathers from consulting the Maspero archive. Seized on grounds of posing a threat to internal security. In late February, early March 1960, the book was again seized, and it is this second time that Maspero remembers in greater detail, recalling, for example, that the book was part of a shipment that also included *Le Refus* by Maurice Maschino (also published by Maspero) and *Le Déserteur* by Maurienne (Lindon). In addition to posing a threat to internal security, the publishers were also charged with inciting the military to insubordination and desertion. Later that year there was yet another seizure and yet another count of indictment against Maspero, this time for injurious actions toward the military. But these seizures did not significantly impair the book's circulation; hundreds of issues, most of them free, were distributed by attorneys and social workers in the prisons, and a dozen or so bookstores in France defiantly displayed the book. Safia Bazi was in prison when she received her copy of the book. She and Fanon had never met in Blida, and it was through this book that she came to know him. "It was the first time I had come across a book that offered a perspective on the conditions that my society and I had to face," she says.[55]

According to a passing hint dropped by Maspero, by the end of the Algerian War, the tills at the press were empty. The book was nonetheless reprinted after each seizure. This involved finding a reliable printer; the fallout of having a book seized at the printer's was far more serious. Maspero's foreword and the introduction that Fanon had held so dear and that had been cut from the first edition were both included in the second edition. Did Fanon fail to submit it on schedule the first time around or had Césaire's and Memmi's response warned Maspero off publishing it? Maspero cannot recall the exact circumstances surrounding this editorial decision. He does, however, remember that his dealings with the author were easygoing in the extreme. When Maspero showed Fanon the second foreword, Fanon treated this situation in the same way he had treated the previous one with Jeanson during the publication of *Black Skin, White Masks*. He simply left it up to Maspero, telling him "whatever you decide will be fine." Fanon was above all else interested in getting his work published, and he never gave his publishers any trouble, especially during this period. He was otherwise engaged, knee-deep in the Algerian War and the problems of the African continent; the preoccupations and difficulties of French intellectual circles that supported Algeria were not foremost on his mind. Also, he trusted this publisher, who had embraced his work. Fanon, who generally impressed people as a person who was deeply aware of his own self-worth, needed to feel accepted, and, perhaps more importantly, chosen. From this point on, his famously suspicious nature began to give way. Only his sensitivity to antiblack racism had rivaled it. He was scrupulously attentive to the banal, nonaggressive, but nonetheless real racism that cut across the Tunisian circles he frequented and could tell plenty of anecdotes to illustrate it. In some instances, he would joke about the situation. For example, he fell into the habit of giving his identity card to Youssef, an Algerian nurse with the ALN who was also black, and asking him to go pick up registered mail and parcels at the post office. "Go on," he would say, before sending him off, "these Tunisian post office employees can't tell one black man from the next."

Later, when Maspero changed the title of *L'An V* to *Sociologie d'une révolution*, Fanon was not as accommodating. He did not like the title, and he was not convinced by Maspero's observation that year *V* had passed and it was now year "*VII.*" Despite his displeasure, he did not stand his ground for very long. Fanon was particularly resistant to the idea of having the sociological label attached to his approach. At the outset, Fanon had toyed with the idea of entitling the book *Réalité d'une nation*, but even this title had been too abstract for his taste; it evoked the intruder's gaze and was too general for a book about changing life in war-torn Algeria. Fanon had expressly left the Algerian leadership out of this work, in which he makes no mention of official positions, charters, or pronouncements. This was not a book about the elites but a record of the daily trials and tribulations of common men and women. Fanon drew heavily on his experience in Blida, on his encounters with patients and their families, with nurses and militants, as well as on the time spent in Tunis, where he met so many Algerian refugees, not all of them patients. It is the stories of these people who came from every part of Algeria, the cities and the countryside, that this book tried to tell.

It is Fanon's view that the personal lives of colonized Algerians were shattered by the war of liberation and that radical mutations ensued in the process. The relationship between colonizer and colonized, he argues, is structurally "perverse." The defiant behaviors of the colonized must be seen as a consequence of the colonial structure and not as an immutable feature of the "base personality." A ruling colonial society, regardless of the diversity of its makeup, draws its strength from the lie of its domination. To reinforce its own power, it will appropriate the technological and cultural advances of the colonial subject and turn them to its own advantage. The uneducated colonial subject will, for his part, have difficulty separating the positive contributions made by a ruling colonial society from the lie it simultaneously propagates. These contributions will be viewed as suspicious or rejected outright, even though the existence of "technologies of progress" is an undisputed fact.

There is no such thing as a meeting of minds in a colonial system that pits those who lie against those who reject the lie. This rejection is expressed by the colonial subject's refusal to deal with the colonizer in a truthful way. "The motivations of the colonial subject's reactions constantly elude the colonizer," and those reactions become opaque and intractable.[56] It is unfortunate that the rejection that dictates interactions between colonizers and colonized is so frequently misunderstood as treachery.

In the course of the war of liberation, this rigid rejection of all things associated with or conveyed by colonial power begins to lessen, and the nation begins to reappropriate technologies, to embrace radio and medicine "when it realizes that these are things that will permit it to take charge of its own destiny." There are also profound transformations inside the home, affecting the behaviors and relationships associated with the traditional family. In the book's first chapter, entitled "L'Algérie se dévoile," Fanon attempts to historicize the wearing of the veil. Initially, the veil functions as an expression of rejection, and to wear it is to counter its active suppression by a colonial power.[57] Later, it is taken off by women combatants who want to move freely and not call attention to themselves in areas frequented by Europeans. In the case of these women, there has been a change in the relationship of the body to space, bringing about a shift in the inner perception of the body. At the height of combat, the veil makes yet another comeback as a cloak of anonymity that leaves the hands free and conceals not the body but the weapons that are strapped to it.

The rise and fall of the veil is dictated by a symbolism and circumstances that are in a continuous flux. Radio, too, would have its ups and downs. Viewed as the voice box of the colonial power, radio is initially rejected; later, when the news spreads through the countryside that the waves transmit the voice of the FLN, its fortune changes and it is a coveted by all. Demand is so high that the French army forbids the sale of radios. The ban gives rise to a wave of extraordinary electronic feats and to the fabrication of what Algerian children during World War II had mistakenly referred to as "crystal sets." Transistors and batteries become a precious commodity given the number of villages where there is no electricity.

The way in which medicine and physicians are perceived by the multitude also changes. The suspicion toward medical visits, the tale full of lies that patients tell physicians (even native ones are not exempt from being viewed as in league with colonial power), the resistance to medications and surgical procedures, the fear of betraying the traditional healer who is one of their own become things of the past. Knowledge spreads; one realizes that a person with an injured abdomen should not be given liquids, understands the importance of antitetanus serum, or the fact of a European doctor who, at great risk to himself, takes care of the wound and supplies medication, and in the process, negative attitudes toward modernity begin to change. Fanon keeps the examples coming. The historian Ageron had it all wrong when he read the chapter on the radio and concluded that the radio creates awareness, when, in fact, it is awareness that brings about a change in behaviors.[58] As Fanon's chapter shows, the actual message of the voice on the radio, often faint and indistinct and usually speaking a language that the rural dweller does not understand, is of little importance. It is the voice that matters, its presence and ability to connect the listener to a collectivity that is dreaming the same dream and forging the same new path.

Formidable transformations are also occurring inside the home, changing the old dynamic between husbands and wives. Husbands whose wives are leaving on a mission know that they cannot be privy to the plan, and fathers whose daughters decide to join the *maquis* have no choice but to acquiesce. Every aspect of life is politicized and everyone, down to the last person, is politicized. It is these politics of everyday life in the lives of simple people that interest Fanon. Shifts in mentality are as important as any artistic expression in the definition of a national culture. Revolution is understood not simply as a political phenomenon, in the strict sense of the term, but as a wider upheaval of a society that is redefined by the demands of the fight it is fighting.

The last chapter of *L'An V* (entire sections from this chapter were later excerpted in *Les Temps modernes*) focuses on the European minority. On this subject, Fanon's views overlap with those of the FLN and of the Soummam Valley charter, but he did not write *L'An V* as a spokesperson or a propagandist for the FLN, and these views also happen to be very much his own. In a nutshell, these views hold that individuals who constitute European society should not be mistaken for the colonial structure. Europeans, he goes on to say, do not form a monolithic bloc. Democratic Europeans live a hard life in Algeria. They have to live in a world the principles of which they reject and condemn. They are forced to keep all their interactions, not to mention their solidarity, with Algerians clandestine. The myth that colonial settlers form a united front in support of colonial domination must also be debunked. Here, Fanon provides countless examples of colonial farmers who turned down the protection of the French army, some of whom went so far as to help the FLN by offering shelter and provisions to its fighters. In conclusion, Fanon remembers the many Europeans who were detained or tortured for their support of the Revolution.

He devotes a section to Algerian Jews and reminds us that they are an integral part of Algeria and have also been subject to racism. One need only consider their meager participation in "French Algerian ultra groups." Fanon again calls attention, as he did earlier with respect to the Europeans, to the many Jews who have taken part in the struggle for liberation. "The Jewish lawyers and doctors who in the camps and prison share the fate of millions of Algerians attest to the multiracial reality of the Algerian Nation."[59] In fact, as Fanon knows full well, their number is very small, but he wants to place the emphasis on a kind of political conduct, not the politics of majorities and minorities. He concludes by saying, "Everyone is Algerian in the City that is being erected by the FLN. What this means is that any person who lives in Algeria is Algerian. In the free Algeria of tomorrow, it will be left up to every individual to choose Algerian citizenship or to forego it in favor of another."

Fanon had asked Ferhat Abbas for his seal of approval before publishing this book. The book, on the face of it, seems addressed to France, to the French Left and French intellectuals who supported peace in Algeria but who knew little about the country and were troubled by the actions of the FLN. The introduction Fanon wrote in 1959 would confirm that the book had been written with this audience in mind. The text is written in a sober language that does not reflect Fanon's customary style, and it attempts to deliver an accurate account of the historical moment. Fanon is, in effect, taking stock of the situation. The account he produces is an accurate representation of realities on the ground. Even though he was writing from Tunis, he was well positioned to have access to the best available information about developments in the *maquis* and about the prevailing mood inside the country.

Fanon begins by citing the atrocities that were committed by the FLN and by condemning them. He draws a parallel to World War II and to the shameful, criminal, and often fratricidal, atrocities carried out by the members of its *maquis* who appointed themselves as judges in order to mete out punishment and settle personal scores. But he also reminds us of the countless others, such as the militants who respect the rules of war and the French prisoners in their custody. He also cites cases of torture and murder and condemns them. He cites the French Army's unspeakable practice of murdering parents before the eyes of their children. We must, of course, "condemn . . . those brothers who have flung themselves into revolutionary action with the almost physiological brutality that centuries of oppression give rise to and feed."[60]

Why has this war become an unending one, he asks. The movement toward independence is irreversible—the transformations that have taken place in the Algerian nation are explicit in the existence of a newly found national consciousness that has been forged out of conflict. France, on the other hand, claims that it will not leave a million sons behind . . . not to mention the oil-rich Sahara. Why not negotiate and bring an end to this cruel war? The main opposition to negotiations comes from European fiefdoms inside Algeria and a sector of the army. They want to hold on to their image of the Algerian as inferior, as self-destructive, in keeping with the familiar refrain of the colonial structure and its infernal marriage of rejection and lies. They want to have us believe that the rebellion will be "quashed." Every commanding general in every colonial war has said the same thing. How can they possibly fail to understand that rebellions are never put down. Even though they can be derailed from their objective: "They tried to vanquish the U.P.C., but did not the Cameroons win their independence? The only difference is that colonialism, before it left, sowed half-treasons, prevarications, rancors in profusion among the Cameroonian people. As a result, the future of the Cameroons is jeopardized for several years to come by an evil and outwardly subtle policy."[61]

But a new Algerian man is coming into being. The paramount thing here is that when colonialism dies it takes both the colonizer and the colonized with it. "We want a democratic and renewed Algeria, free and open to all." This is a statement which Fanon believes profoundly. He is fully aware of the position held by most Europeans in Algeria, but he thinks—and in 1959, he is not alone—that the majority will want to remain. Tunisia, already three years into its independence, had not yet experienced its massive and devastating exodus of Tunisian Jews and Europeans. Fanon wants the colonial mentality to disappear, not the people. He is opposed to the idea of a theocratic Algeria, of an Algeria mired in anachronistic traditions.

This book is, furthermore, really addressed to the Algerian leadership in Tunis, namely to those who have not stopped to imagine a post-Independence Algeria and who lack a clear sense of the nation's future. He wants to make them aware of the rupture that has taken place and of the momentum that should not come to a halt at Independence. The social public arena, which is largely determined by political and economic factors, cannot entirely exclude the mutations that are taking place in the personal sphere. There should not be a disproportionate divide between the individual and the collective, the abyss cannot be too wide. For Fanon, these considerations were neither opportunistic nor contingent but paramount, and he had heard enough of the behind-the-scenes views of certain members of the Algerian leadership in Tunis to be concerned.

The sequence of themes that is sketched out in this early work will become a mainstay of Fanon's later work. First, there is rupture, a necessary precursor of change, and the break with the colonial order as well as the fossilized order of tradition. This is followed by renewal, the continuous rebirth of a culture and a nation in constant motion and inventing itself time and again in the face of new situations. This idea is spelled out more clearly here than in *The Wretched of the Earth*, where it loses some of its force; by then, Fanon had already witnessed the effects of neocolonialism and the unfortunate trajectories taken by newly independent governments in Africa. Finally, he writes that while violence may be the only way for a subjected nation to emerge from under the devastation—as total as that of any individual under the menace of subjective annihilation—the nation has suffered at colonial hands, and while it may be necessary to turn colonial violence on the colonial state, violence is not the be all and end all. Violence is the preamble to the true work out of which a new nation will emerge, and it should correspond to the deepest need of a people and not to dictates and decrees. Nor should it be restricted to the battlefield. The readiness of a society to embrace change, to be reborn and emerge as a new nation is also violence, albeit of a political kind.

Fanon was not a prophet, and many of his aspirations have been laid to waste by the present-day realities of postcolonial, independent Africa, and nowhere more so than in Algeria. Yet, even in the case of Algeria, are not these the jolts, accompanied by violence and sudden breaks, of a nation that is willing itself into being and refuses to give up?

L'An V, especially after 1960, is the work that is the least often cited by Fanon scholars. Is this because it is too dated? Have developments in Africa, and especially in Algeria, so belied the paths delineated in this book that they can only be revisited with discomfort? Are the discussions on minorities and on the changing status of women, in relationship to themselves, their families, and society, misguided? Could Fanon have been mistaken? The answer would have to be yes if we read the book as evidence of a society that existed at a specific historical juncture. But is this the best way to read it? Should we not read it instead as an expression of the things that would have to change if a nation is to achieve true liberation and renewal? The transformations that Fanon discusses were born through a struggle in which he, himself, was a participant. He chose to interpret them in the best possible light. His analysis is optimistic so as to instill optimism, magnanimity, and anticipation. He wished for the changes he had witnessed firsthand to become generalized and imperative. Had he idealized the situation? Was this yet another of his montages—half-real, half-imagined? It was a utopian wish to be sure. Not an ideological utopia, not the *good place* where human ties and diversities are nullified, but a dreamer's utopia motivated by the desire for a future in which relationships among human beings are of a different kind. Fanon believed in humankind in a way that itself defied belief. It was not a faith in progress as much as in desire, in the victory of life over death, the same death that he had dared so often. The accident in Morocco took place around the time he was working on this book, and he confessed later that he had wanted to join the *maquis* and had been ready to risk his life doing so. In *L'An V*, Fanon avows his faith in life's supremacy over death:

> The colonized, like all the people in underdeveloped countries and all the dispossessed everywhere, do not see life as blossoming and fruition but as a permanent struggle against *atmospheric* death. This death, this *mort à bout touchant*, manifests itself as endemic famine, unemployment, the high death rate, the feeling of inferiority, and the absence of future prospects.

Fanon had no wish to succumb to this endless chain of death, which must have had a faint but real resonance for a descendant of Antillean blacks with a long history of slavery and proximity to death.

Fanon's analysis transcends its historical moment. The subjected people's rigid refusal to accept the technologies and values of its oppressors, the oppressors' inability to interpret this resistance as anything other than insubordinate or incomprehensible, and the imperative necessity of having one's destiny in hand before embracing these values and technologies are notions that remain pertinent in Africa as well as Europe to this day.

Fanon and Africa

Sub-Saharan Africa awakens. Fanon envisions a united states of Africa. He speaks at the Second Congress of Black Writers and Artists in Rome and becomes war-torn Algeria's roving ambassador to Africa. He emerges as the self-appointed bard of African solidarity. The idea of a Trans-Saharan Southern front takes hold and Fanon works on the project to the point of exhaustion. The year 1960 proves to be the tumultuous "year of independence" and a political turning point at the heart of the "Algerian Revolution." Fanon distances himself from events in France.

Fanon's interest in the politics of sub-Saharan Africa took on a new life in the autumn of 1958. De Gaulle's September 1958 referendum project for African territories under French rule made Fanon extremely uneasy; the referendum allowed for internal autonomy while granting France jurisdiction over international policy. Fanon worried about the outcome of the vote. Would the countries accept the referendum and thus set back the prospect of independence? It did not surprise him that Félix Houphouët-Boigny of Côte d'Ivoire, whom he despised, had agreed to the referendum.[1] But Léopold Senghor of Senegal, his old friend at *Présence africaine*, was an entirely different and disappointing matter. He was overjoyed, on the other hand, when the Guinean Sékou Touré opposed the referendum and set himself apart by pressing for immediate independence.[2]

Fanon was better informed about African nations than his Algerian comrades. He had a fairly good grasp of African geopolitics and knew the history of slavery, colonialism, and the Cold War years. His knowledge was incomplete and he did not like to talk about its lacunae, but he was simultaneously and singularly aware of the significance of Africa's complex ethnic makeup, multiple languages, and its juxtaposition and syncretism of animism and monotheistic religions. He had met a great many black Africans during his student years, and as early as 1947, he had participated in the debates that had brought *Présence africaine* into being under the direction of Alioune Diop. He was aware of Senghor's family background and knew that his mother was a Muslim who had converted to Roman Catholicism at the request of her husband, a landowner from the savanna.

The strategic importance of creating a bond with sub-Saharan Africa, a region about which the Maghreb understood next to nothing at the time, was not lost on the Algerian leadership. Fanon was not only an Algerian militant, he was also a black intellectual who knew other black intellectuals and had ties, dating back to his student days in France, to the Fédération des étudiants d'Afrique noire.

In December 1958, on the occasion of the First Conference of the Union of African Nations, held in Accra, Ghana, Fanon was part of the Algerian delegation that also included Ahmed Boumendjel and Chawki Mostefaï.[3] The stated goal of the Conference, which had been organized by Kwame N'Krumah, the president of newly independent Ghana,[4] was the formulation of a Pan-African policy. The Algerian delegates had been sent to report on the status of the Algerian Revolution and secure the support of other African nations. Boumendjel's and Mostefaï's papers presented Algeria as the vanguard of the anticolonial struggle and hence worthy of support. Fanon also highlighted the importance of the Algerian struggle. He pointed out—as it was widely acknowledged later—that the Algerian War was responsible for accelerating the sociopolitical autonomy of other French African nations: de Gaulle's proposed referendum had been a way of staving off the emergence of armed resistance in other territories under French rule. Fanon placed a special emphasis on the unified struggle and solidarity of all Africans: "Every African must feel directly engaged and ready to answer the call of any and all territories and report in person . . . It is important that we not separate the national struggle from the African struggle." He continued by adding that an "Algerian cannot be a true Algerian, if he does not feel in his core the indescribable tragedy that is unfolding in the two Rhodesias or in Angola."[5] Fanon's statement was, in fact, slightly different from the ones that had been presented by the other members of the Algerian delegation. Even though Boumendjel and Mostefaï had vowed solidarity to Pan-Africanism, they were, like M'hammed Yazid, profoundly politicized and "Western." They were ready to applaud the Algerian struggle as exemplary and to claim its pivotal role in the struggle against colonialism; they had also expected to lobby for diplomatic support; but the idea that an Algerian could only be a true Algerian if he identified with an Angolan was not an ideology they could really sustain. They were, as Jean Daniel put it, "European-style revolutionaries, with ties to the European left," and their main point of reference in the anticolonial struggle was the Vietnam War.[6] They wanted to promote African solidarity, but they also wanted to establish ties with Asia, especially with Beijing, where a great number of Algerian delegations traveled shortly thereafter. But they were not really believers in a Third Worldism that would herald a new age, and their knowledge of sub-Saharan Africa was extremely limited. They knew the Maghreb and the limits of Maghrebi solidarity that never put national interests to the test, the conflicts over the Sahara being the most flagrant example.

Fanon stayed behind in Ghana, where he spent at least another twelve days meeting political leaders, all of them for the first time. In addition to N'Krumah, Sékou Touré, and several African delegates, he also met Félix Moumié, the leader of the UPC (People's Union of Cameroon), Thomas Joseph Mboya, a union leader who was also heading the Kenyan Independence Movement, and Julius Nyerere, the wise and strong-minded future president of Tanzania. He also spent time with Roberto Holden, the soon-to-be director of the Angolan UPA, and especially with Patrice Lumumba who, with Diomi Etnagula, was one of the representatives of the MNC (National Congolese Movement) and who was also attending a Pan-African forum for the first time. In the course of those twelve days, Fanon, who did not neglect his responsibilities as an Algerian delegate and continued to promote the exemplarity of the revolution, also had an opportunity to get a closer look at the pressing issues facing Africa. His interest did not stop at the Francophone countries, and he came away with a better understanding of the disparities that separated one country from another. He took note of the newly independent countries: Egypt, Tunisia, Ethiopia, and, most recently, Guinea. He discovered the similarities that characterize settler colonies—Angola, South Africa, the two Rhodesias, Algeria—the citadels of colonialism where "European settlements are fiercely defended" and where armed struggle is the inevitable outcome. He was especially preoccupied by those countries that, even at such an early stage in the game, would be independent in name only: Congo and Cameroon, for example. There the national bourgeoisies already were poised to take over where colonial power left off and colonial ties would be maintained, thus allowing alienating economic and devastating cultural structures to remain in place.

Fanon returned to Tunis with a whole new world on which to reflect and in which to act. He had liked N'Krumah's vision of a united states of Africa, even though he had his private doubts about the success of such an undertaking. The prospect seemed unlikely as long as countries were led by the likes of Senghor or Houphouët or by stand-ins for colonial power as in the case of Cameroon. Senegal, Côte d'Ivoire, and Cameroon were the countries that cropped up most frequently in his private conversations; he viewed their break with French culture and with French colonial interests as failed and incomplete. Of all sub-Saharan countries, these were the three he knew best; he was historically linked to them by colonialism as well as by language, friendships dating back to his student days, and World War II. He oscillated between high and low hopes. Even though he tried to stay away from the conflicts that cropped up among the North African "brother nations"—as we recall, he only intervened when the French Army bombed the Tunisian village of Sakiet—every day brought him new proof that a united Maghreb was not imminent. But his skepticism did not stop him from plunging headlong in pursuit of Pan-African unity.

It was after this first and fundamental encounter with sub-Saharan Africa that Fanon attended the March 1959 Deuxième Congrès des Écrivains et Artistes noirs in Rome.[7] The conference, which Richard Wright had refused to attend on grounds that the Vatican had funded it, opened on March 26 and went on for a week. Fanon was scheduled to speak on the first day. Great lengths were taken to keep him from the podium.[8] France had exerted enormous pressure on the Italians, who were underwriting the event, to ban him from attending. Important black writers intervened, coming up with the following compromise: someone else would read Fanon's paper. But when the arrangement became public, it created an uproar among the less important but more determined younger writers who were in attendance. They wanted Fanon, who was there in person, after all, to step up to the podium. Fanon, in his usual fashion, would later speak about the experience only in the vaguest of terms. All that mattered to him was the paper he had written on the reciprocity between national cultures and wars of liberation. As he had in 1956, he started by citing the harm inflicted on the culture of a colonized society, but he had considerably sharpened the tone. Culture, he argued, cannot exist in the context of colonial domination, which only allows for two possibilities: the fossilization of ancestral culture into stereotyped traditions of little use or the "forced appropriation of the occupier's culture." Only the emergence of national consciousness can restore a new inventiveness to all cultural forms. The struggle for national survival frees culture and opens it up to creativity. The attainment of national consciousness, which should not be confused with nationalism, is the finest expression of that creativity. The ideas are much the same as in *L'An V,* but Fanon had widened the scope to include all of Africa. The African intellectual who wants to advance his culture must take part in building his nation, a process that is by definition linked to the uncovering and furthering of universalizing values. In an even more radical turn, Fanon criticized value systems such as negritude and even went so far as to attack "Muslim-Arabism" for its failure to consider the evolution and differentiation of the peoples who build a nation. The problems facing black Americans were not the same as those facing black Angolans, and Algeria was not the Middle East. In an increasingly clear-cut way, Fanon was privileging the emergence of historical identity over cultural perpetuity (by which he also meant ethnic, even though the word had not yet entered his vocabulary). Here, he was in agreement with his contemporary the anthropologist Georges Balandier, who viewed ethnic arguments with suspicion. Fanon would refer to this category for the first time shortly before his trip to sub-Saharan Africa.[9] Like Balandier, Fanon believed that Africa, divided in such a cavalier manner into ethnic groups by 1950s ethnography, was caught in a colonial structure that functioned as the "main production site" of the African society of the day. Fanon did not cite Balandier in *L'An V* or in his Rome presentation, but he agreed with Balandier that the recourse—to religious syncretism in Balandier's case and to fossilized traditions in Fanon's—was, in point of fact, a form of resistance to colonial domination. He also agreed that colonial policy showed no reticence in promoting ethnic divides that it could exploit to its own ends. Both Fanon the Algerian and Fanon the African agreed on one thing, however: culture was not the fixed expression of an abstract and immutable symbolic realm; culture was action, political action. Neither Fanon disavowed the young man who had written *Black Skin, White Masks*, demonstrating to Mannoni that the ethnicized and culturally static Malagasy no longer exists.[10] In 1967–68, when Francis Jeanson, who recently had been named to found the Maison de la Culture of Chalon-sur-Saône, found himself pondering the question of culture in action, he settled on a contiguous approach. Culture, he concluded, is a thing in the making, "wherein every cultural act translates into a political one,"[11] reuniting a community to its voice and regenerating the fabric of socialization in the process. Jeanson's dynamic definition of culture relies, in part, on the one that had been advanced by Fanon.

Jeanson and Fanon, as was mentioned beforehand, were only able to meet in person three times: at Éditions du Seuil in 1952, in a secret location in 1957, and at the Madrid airport in 1959. Jeanson, who was left with a lasting impression of being poorly treated by Fanon, recalls the meetings as generally unpleasant. Fanon's deep respect for Jeanson was never at stake, however. The two men were philosophically matched, both were close readers and followers of Sartre, and they both differed with him in the same way, believing, as they did, in the concrete application of theoretical positions and in the importance of the intellectual's commitment to action.

Who am I if I do not try to give meaning to my life? I think it is possible to understand fellow human beings and to fight them on occasion, to labor in the service of a more humane world and to feel a decent amount of happiness in the here and now. But if I am happy just to think it, then it is just opinion, a pointless awareness, a phantom thought, pure fantasy. But if I set myself the task of living by it, then it is a "wager" on which I shall stake the meaning of my life.

This passage from Jeanson's *La Foi d'un incroyant* (Paris: Seuil, 1963) captures the nature of the decision Fanon had to face in Rome.

Fanon "wagered" by choosing to take the podium. His presentation on that first day received a lukewarm response. His insistence on linking cultural survival and national liberation was cause for shock and disagreement. But a growing interest unexpectedly followed this mixed reception, as Fanon found himself very much sought after in the days that followed. Curiously, this two-pronged response, consternation followed by attentiveness, prefigured the reception of *Les Damnés de la terre*.

The physical experience of going to sub-Saharan Africa had a profound effect on Fanon. He was transformed by seeing this new world firsthand, a transformation that was made all the more powerful by its timing at the height of the tumult of its break with colonial power. Furthermore, Africa was a study in half measures, in every possible compromise that could be passed off as "Independence." Fanon learned a great deal from the journey and from the leaders, both official and unofficial. Just as he had in Lyon and Blida and Tunis, Fanon sought out the truth of the situation before him and tried to respond in kind.

After this point, Fanon enjoyed a special status, most often in his capacity as an Algerian representative, with delegates representing provisional African governments as well as with the representatives of national liberation movements, some more clandestine than others. In November 1959, he made a short trip to Ghana, but most of these meetings took place in Tunis, which had become the destination of choice for all kinds of delegations and where the Second Congress of African Nations was held in January 1960. Fanon maintained his other responsibilities during this busy time and started to work in earnest on the paper he planned to present and that the GPRA implicitly expected him to deliver. He had reached the point, precipitated by the time spent with the African delegations, of wanting his political and personal choices to reflect a greater clarity. He knew he had an affinity with the Ghanaian N'Krumah, the Malian Modibo Keita, and almost everyone who was associated with the UPC in Cameroon, a movement that was still underground and opposed the terms on which Cameroon had been granted its independence. He also was focused on the brutal battle that was unfolding in the Portuguese colony of Angola and in the Belgian Congo. He had not made up his mind with respect to Angola and had yet to weigh in either on the side of Amilcar Cabral, of the MPLA, or of Roberto Holden, of the UPA.[12] He considered Lumumba, whom the young Olivier referred to as "daddy's friend," a friend and ally. The same went for Félix Moumié, and when Moumié was assassinated, he described him as "the most concrete, the most alive, the most impetuous man. . . . Aggressive, violent, full of anger, in love with his country, hating cowards and maneuvers. Austere, hard, incorruptible."[13] He possessed the same "revolutionary virtues" Fanon had admired so unreservedly in Abbane. Fanon's own efforts to appear austere and hard never came to much; he never could keep up the pose for any length of time. He was much too fond of love and friendship and too sensitive to human suffering. When he ran into Jacques Charby,[14] who had recently arrived in Tunis and whom he met quite by chance at the Algerian Ministry of Information, he immediately wanted to know: "How is Francis [Jeanson]?" When Charby revealed that Jeanson was not at all well, Fanon did not miss a beat: "Tell him to take care of himself. Nothing is more important." That was in 1960; Fanon was still unaware of the illness that was about to afflict him.

In January 1960, as the Second Conference of African Peoples opened its doors, we find Fanon and Tunis in full swing. The city, with its newly acquired cosmopolitan mantle, is in a state of effervescence and festivity. Fanon, for his part, seems to be everywhere one turns. He has been assigned the task of drawing up the balance sheet of all the changes that have occurred since the Accra conference. He speaks of his wish for the creation of a massive African front that will come to the aid of an Algeria he describes as the "beacon" for all of Africa. He wants, among other things, the formation of an international African volunteer corps, a kind of African Legion, that will assist Algeria and be trained in guerilla warfare in the process.

From this point on, Fanon became very invested in the idea of a united African military force as well as in the idea of a continent-wide African workers union. He approached union leaders, who managed, despite some opposition, mainly Tunisian, to convene a meeting in which they agreed to form a centralized African syndicate that would work toward "the social and economic revolution that would follow political independence."

This is where things stood when Fanon, three months later, was officially named the GPRA ambassador to Africa. He was based in Ghana. On previous occasions he had accompanied the GPRA's Minister of Foreign Affairs, Krim Belkacem at the time, to Cairo in order to do archival research and meet with "commanding officers" about African policy. That trip would be the first of many: April 7–10, Conference on Peace and Security in Africa, Accra; April 12–15, Afro-Asian Conference, Conakry; on to Liberia to solicit recognition of the GPRA; July-August, Conference of African Youth, Accra; by late August, early September, he was in Leopoldville. In April, he delivered a paper entitled "Why Have We Chosen Violence?"[15] that caused quite a stir and drew remarks from abroad. He again underscored the importance of the Algerian struggle to the liberation of the entire African continent. "France's new policies in African nations have come about under the pressure of the Algerian War, the proposed Commonwealth of States is a preventive measure to avoid the emergence of new armed fronts in other territories under French occupation." One cannot, he insists, "separate the Algerian War from the African War," because "one cannot practice selective politics with colonialist forces." African nations must unite; "imperialism is consolidating its positions, coming up with new forms, new strategies for ensuring its permanence." Fanon's discourse was political and its ultimate goal was mobilization. Even so, he was the only one—in an event ruled by enthusiastic encounters and self-congratulation—to raise a double alarm, warning against the noncombative stance of African anticolonialism and against new, camouflaged forms of colonial domination. Anticolonialism for an African, even one who belonged to an independent nation, had to be militant anticolonialism that should never become "a sector of ethnic consciousness." Fanon's warning was twofold: he wanted to alert his audience to the dangers of ethnic identification, and he wanted them to remain vigilant and hold their new leaders accountable for their actions.

Despite the success, and the charisma, that held considerable sway over many of the African delegates, despite the numerous and greatly remarked upon speeches and presentations, and despite the atmosphere that did not frown on fun, Fanon suffered immensely in Africa. Social isolation certainly was not the problem, and he made many new friends there. Some of them were Algerian, Boualem Oussedik who was the GPRA's representative in Conakry, and Omar Oussedik, the Algerian delegate to Bamako and Fanon's frequent travel companion. The two would share many experiences, not all of them having to do with politics, as they moved from one tumultuous area to the next. This good companionship notwithstanding, Fanon often felt helpless as he witnessed the very things he had intuited and feared unfold before his eyes: "postcolonialism," the instatement of compromise governments, the power struggles, corruption. It was in this context that he began to think of the rural, peasant masses as an active, revolutionary force. Houphouët-Boigny was no better than a puppet king, he thought, a stand-in for the old Metropolis in Côte d'Ivoire. The Mali Confederation that was created on June 21, 1960, between Léopold Senghor's Senegal and Modibo Keita's Sudan lasted a mere three months, at the end of which it included only Sudan. The Cameroon, whose longstanding clandestine liberation movements Fanon still supported, had agreed to prejudicial terms and a so-called independence that safeguarded settler interests. His friend Félix Moumié had been assassinated. Finally, there was the Belgian Congo that, despite its June 30, 1960, independence, was spiraling into disaster. Its Prime Minister Patrice Lumumba, who was Fanon's political ally and dear friend, was increasingly marginalized; after being dismissed as prime minister, he was imprisoned and executed shortly thereafter by the Belgian-supported secessionist regime in the rich mining region of Katanga de Tschombé with the collusion of President Kasavubu and Colonel Mobutu. Fanon was also of two minds about the Angolan struggle; even though he was closer to Mario de Andrade and Amilcar Cabral, in the end, he threw in his lot with Roberto Holden, whose movement was reported to have a wide rural base. Fanon was fighting an uphill battle. He had hoped that the Algerian War would be a magnet for the African continent, and the desire that had taken hold in 1959 for a united Africa grew to the point of becoming a desperate need. The more facts flew in the face of this idea, the more determined he was to seeing it through. He advanced his project of unity as a way of combating the rise in tribal and regional rivalries. With local "compradores" bourgeoisies on the ascendant and the unions, whose members, when all was said and done, represented a minority that pertained to a culture that was more or less imported, in a powerless state, Fanon began to look to the rural, peasant classes, perhaps the most important sector of this decidedly nonindustrial part of the world, as the true spark of the revolutionary mandate.

One should not conclude from this, as Josie Fanon explained many years later in a conversation with Maspero, that Fanon was a standard-bearer for the Comintern or for Maoism. These labels that more than anything else reflect the doxa of the times should not be attributed after the fact to a man who never considered aligning himself with the positions they represent. Fanon worked toward an African revolution, and his writings on the subject, posthumously published by Maspero, attest to this. Fanon kept his own counsel and his ideas were not ideology-bound; they were guided by his interpretation of power relations, the victory he longed for, and the failure he foresaw. The situation on the ground, not a desire to emulate China, steered him to the rural, peasant masses. He had simply had the foresight to see where Africa was headed and was doing everything in his power to fend off the vision.

The months Fanon had spent in Africa, caught in endless contradictions, were taking their toll. He was commuting to Tunis on a regular basis to be with his family. Josie and Olivier had joined him at first, but soon after their arrival, Josie caught malaria, a condition that would nag her for the rest of her life, and the two returned to Tunis. Olivier remembers his father's fluctuating moods on those visits home, enthusiastic at times and tense at others.

"We should all go to the Congo." This was all Fanon had to say about Africa to his small circle of friends in Tunis. His work there, he kept to himself. There were those who thought that the African Fanon, who had been forced into tough political choices, had been too quick to choose and had done so blindly. This was the opinion of Serge Michel, a Frenchman who was a longstanding supporter of the Algerian cause and who, while in Tunis and out of the blue, suddenly found himself appointed as Lumumba's press attaché. The relationship between Michel and Fanon had always been problematic; Michel was extremely critical on the entire subject of Fanon in Africa; he accused him of having a "quick temper and of carrying on like a prosecutor," but he especially faulted him for allowing himself to become fascinated by "imposters, a fascination that had led to rigid theories founded on nothing more than appearances and distorted accounts."[16] Serge Michel was an extremely intelligent and politically intuitive man to whom the Algerian cause was greatly indebted for countless selfless acts; he was also completely unpredictable and at times quite quick-tempered himself, but he had charm and a knack for making the most of any situation, he lived by the "what is mine is yours" mantra, and, in his case, there was nothing affected about it at all. Yet I can only smile when I think of how those two must have gotten on each other's nerves.

There is no doubt that during this period, Fanon, who was fighting exhaustion, often came across as irritable, intransigent, and even as lacking "political realism." But Fanon had never been a realist. All those who knew him, and not only his detractors, agree that he was quick to idealize. Though he tended to think of himself as arrogant and suspicious, he was ready to put his faith in anyone with a project, never once stopping to question the person's abilities or intentions. It soon became clear that Fanon needed time to reflect, he needed to return to his solitary, nocturnal regimen of reading and writing. There had been no time for that in the political whirlwind that was Africa in 1960, "the year of independence." That was what was missing, and that same year he wrote to Maspero with a book proposal. The book he had in mind would be called *Alger-Le Cap* and contain seven chapters: 1. "The Maghreb War and the Liberation of Africa."

2. "Notes on courage in Algeria." 3. "Morality and Revolution in Algeria." 4. "Notes on the Psychiatry of War." 5. "Violence in Africa." 6. "History and Psychology." 7. "Negritude and Black-African Civilization, an Illusion." This project, which he had to abandon, was not quite *The Wretched of the Earth*, even though it broached similar themes. It does, however, bear the imprint of his difficult African experience that will serve, especially after his falling out in Tunis with Algerian liberation thinkers and his impatience with their contradictory and limited views, as the basis of the political vision that he would present in *The Wretched of the Earth*.

The period in Africa also marked a political turning point in Fanon's relationship to the Algerian Revolution. In the course of that year, the GPRA, plagued by factionalism and infighting, had been engaged in negotiations with de Gaulle and with the newly restructured frontier army. The GPRA, in short, was in the grip of the same kinds of power struggles and divisions that characterized African independence movements. Throughout it all, Fanon had been mostly preoccupied by sub-Saharan Africa. The ins and outs of diplomacy did not speak to his imagination or desires; he was far more interested in the strategies and logistics that would bring about Africa's liberation. To this end, he conceived of the idea of a Trans-Saharan front. He had been in discussions with President Modibo Keita of Mali, a country that borders the Sahara. In Bamako, Fanon started to set the project afoot; both Guinea and Mali had signed on to serve as bases of operations for the projected Southern front. The movement of men and arms had been sharply curtailed, had, in fact, become suicidal, since France had built electrified fences, known as Challe and Morice, along the Algerian border with both Tunisia and Morocco. A Southern front would have made it possible to move arms and munitions via Bamako into the Sahara, thereby creating a new arms route to the *Wilayas*, perhaps even as far north as Algiers, and including remote desert communities in the process. The project, which received the seal of approval of the GPRA, involved a number of men from the military leadership, namely Boumedienne, who was their incontestable leader. Abdelazziz Bouteflika, who was one of the leaders of the Oujda PC in Morocco, was entrusted with establishing a third military base in the Sahara. It was at the time of these operations that people began to refer to him as "Abdelkader Mali." Fanon was taken with the project, and it inspired some of his finest writing on Africa and the importance of this front.[17] He was a member of the reconnaissance mission that took place in November 1960 and about which he wrote in "L'Afrique à venir."[18] "There were eight of us: a commando, the Army, transmission, political commissars, the sanitary corps. Each of the pairs is to prospect the working possibilities in respect to his own field" (TAR, 181). This expedition proved full of setbacks, but there were also meaningful encounters—with the other men, with the desert, with books. During a rest stop, Fanon delves into his books about the history of Sudan:

> I relive, with the intensity that circumstances and the place confer upon them, the old empires of Ghana, of Mali, of Gao, and the impressive Odyssey of the Moroccan troops with the famous Djouder. Things are not simple. Here Algeria at war comes to solicit aid from Mali. And during this time Morocco is demanding Mauritania and a part of Mali. (TAR, 186)

Leave it to Fanon to choose the middle of a dangerous mission as a time to lose himself in his books and use them as an excuse for reverie and reflection. It was during this mission that the relationship between the young "Boutouf," yet another one of the monikers of Abdelazziz Bouteflika, and Fanon developed. According to Claudine Chaulet, Bouteflika was one of the many, most of them less famous, scribe/typists of *The Wretched of the Earth*. The mission in the desert had come to nothing. Fanon had fallen ill. One wonders if this highly symbolic project could have been implemented without him. Pirelli contends that Fanon had been both its inspiration and its embodiment.

It was this contact with the armed faction and, paradoxically, the connection to ex-UMDA militants such as Ahmed Boumendjel, who frequently traveled to Africa as a representative of the Ministry of Information, that Fanon met Houari Boumedienne, whose real name was Mohammed Boukharouba, in 1961. But we are still in 1960, with the armed struggle at an all-time high and preparations for future negotiations between GPRA emissaries and those of General de Gaulle on a steady course. In Tunis, Algerians are pondering their options: five more years of warfare or the possibility of being home by spring. Fanon is doing the same.

Fanon's time in Africa also had the effect of greatly diminishing the importance he had formerly attached to the French position. With very rare exceptions, after January 1960, he stopped attending editorial meetings at *El Moudjahid* and almost stopped writing for the paper altogether. That same month, he wrote the short piece "Blood Flows in the Antilles under French Domination" in response to the uprising in the Antilles; in it, he applauds the Guyanan-Antillean rebellion and expresses his hope for a united Caribbean; but that was the end of it, and from this point on, Fanon had little to say about anything unrelated to the topic of African solidarity. He stopped making public statements about French internal politics and the situation in Algeria. Whenever we met in private during his visits to Tunis, he no longer seemed to want to tackle these issues with his old gusto. He only wanted to relay his experience in Africa or tease his Algerian friends about the differences between Algerian and African Islam: "Muslim men in Africa don't lock up their women at home. The women are free to walk around, often wearing next to nothing."

And yet, 1960 had been a year of intense political activity in Algeria as well as France. The FLN was having its own problems; Algerians abroad were divided, forming "hard" and "soft" camps, with hard-liners arguing against what they saw as a premature independence that could derail the revolutionary process. The conflict between the GPRA and a military command opposed to negotiations was at an all-time high by the end of 1959. The colonels, led by Boumedienne, faulted the diplomats for placing far too much value on talks and negotiations and of losing sight of the armed struggle in the process, of letting themselves go soft from all the luxury that was on offer in the big cities. Discord over the direction in which policy was heading had already triggered a colonels' rebellion (Lamouri), which resulted in a military tribunal presided over by Boumedienne. After the long and stormy debates at the CNRA in Tripoli, Boumedienne was entrusted with the restructuring of the central military command in January 1960. He established his headquarters in Ghardimaou, leaving the West PC of the ALN in Oujda in the hands of the young captains, namely "Si Abdelkader," or, if one prefers, Abdelaziz Bouteflika.

Fanon, who had been for negotiations in 1959, did not make his views public, but he was gravitating toward the military's position and quietly distancing himself from the GPRA.

Fanon remained laconic, even in private, through the many heady events of that period. Fanon was still in Tunis, when the "ultras," with the support of General Challe, organized a weeklong protest (Barricades Week) by a French Algerian army of those willing to put pressure on de Gaulle. This episode did not seem to affect Fanon half as much as a similar demonstration organized by the same group in 1958. In late January, in the immediate aftermath of the Barricades, Ferhat Abbas, who had survived the CNRA in Tripoli and was in his second term as president of the GPRA, addressed the Europeans of Algeria: "Algeria for Algerians of all origins." Fanon nodded his approval but that was all.

Fanon followed events in France, many of them in line with the changes he had wished for in 1956–57, from a great distance. While de Gaulle was facing down the "ultras" and finding ways to open the talks that would lead to the June meeting in Melun,[19] many of the people associated with the Jeanson network were arrested. A profound public debate ensued as a result of these arrests. Again, Fanon remained detached from a polemic which a few years prior would have engulfed him. When Jeanson went on trial in September 1960, Fanon showed next to no interest. He was not even swayed by the fact that even Sartre, whom he still admired immensely and who was in Brazil at the time of the arrest, had sent a telegram and a letter[20] in support of Jeanson. His only comment with respect to Sartre was "he should have been there."

Antiwar demonstrations in France were closely followed by the Algerians in Tunis, who were thankful that the French Left was mobilizing at last—"they've finally stirred," people were overheard to say in the hallways of the Algerian Ministry of Information. Fanon perceived these events as belonging to a far-off place from which he had ceased to expect anything. Even the *Manifeste des 121*, published the day after Jeanson's trial began, did not seem to affect him even though this text formulated a position he had expressly wanted French intellectuals to espouse in early 1957. He had overtly solicited it in the appeal he had addressed to French democrats and intellectuals that year. As far as he was concerned, the manifesto had come too late. He continued to deplore the fact that support of the networks that supported the French Federation of the FLN was limited and had failed at mobilizing a broad popular and international anticolonialist front. Barring exceptional circumstances, he had no dealings with the people who had worked in these networks and who, in 1960, were fleeing to Tunis in great numbers. This was how he came to meet and like Jacques Charby, who had been part of this exodus and who had, with Pirelli's help, collected the drawings and firsthand accounts of Algerian war orphans. Fanon would advise him on how to best interview the children. On the other hand, he found Annette Roger exasperating, invasive, and incompetent.[21]

Even the growing signs of a Franco-Algerian understanding had little effect on Fanon. He appeared almost oblivious to the landmark June 1960 meeting between the UGEMA and the UNEF[22] in Lausanne. This was the meeting, after all, that brought about the motion of the 49th Congress of the UNEF, cosigned by the Fédération des étudiants d'Afrique noire en France and North African and Antillean student groups, demanding negotiations with the FLN. Throughout this time, he was completely immersed in Africa and especially concerned by events in the Belgian Congo. The momentous meeting at Melun, at which de Gaulle for the first time acknowledged the GPRA as a legitimate negotiating partner, seemed to strike Fanon as just another event in a long chain of events. He did not even seem to care that his friend Boumendjel, who was summoned from Leopoldville where he happened to be with Fanon at the time, had been selected along with one other person to represent the FLN at the meeting. The proceedings did not directly involve Fanon and that seemed to suit him just fine. His focus and effort as a member of the commission at the 1959 meeting of the CNRA in Tripoli are difficult to reconcile with his lack of involvement in the elaborate negotiations that were set in motion by the end of 1960. This time around, he did not put in an appearance—not as an éminence grise or even as a "compiler of documents," a job that was generally relegated to the support staff of the Algerian revolution. As far as I have been able to determine and as many of my sources have confirmed, Fanon was simply not invited to the table.

It is difficult to ascertain, however, that Fanon's exclusion was solely the product of his increased political distance from the GPRA. It was around this time, three months before the negotiations at Evian that, at least in theory, resulted in a declaration of peace in Algeria, that he was diagnosed with the illness that would end his life a year later.

The Last Year of Fanon's Life

Fanon is ill, diagnosed with myeloid leukemia, a fatal disease at the time. His Algerian comrades arrange for treatment in Moscow, the prognosis is not good and his days are numbered. He continues to work and write as before. He steps up his ties to the Frontier Army and conducts classes attended by ALN officers. He writes his last book, The Wretched of the Earth. *He agrees to travel to the United States for a new course of treatment. He dies in Washington, D.C., and is buried in Algerian territory.*

At the end of December 1960, Fanon returned to Tunis to spend the New Year holidays with his family. He was extremely tired and had a lost a considerable amount of weight. Thinking he should look into it, he went to the laboratory of his friend and colleague, the biologist Charles Zerah, where he requested a routine blood test, a very routine blood test. Later, he returned to pick up the results. Eighteen thousand white blood cells—as a physician, he needed no one to tell him that he had leukemia. Downtown Tunis in those days was not the large and bustling place it is now. He had barely stepped outside the lab and was still holding the results in his hand when he ran into his friends—Charles Géronimi and the Chaulets—to whom he immediately broke the news. That same evening, he invited himself and Olivier to dinner at the Maneullan's, insisting that they cook him a good meal. When the children went off to play, he turned to his hosts and announced, "Have I got one for you!" and then proceeded to tell them about his illness. He dismissed their dismay, "I don't want to see those faces. You're going to have to help Josie. And I'm going to fight this one with my cortex." Later, when his eye fell on an unappealing apple sitting in a fruit bowl, he joked about "that sorry looking apple, probably has leukemia." With that, he dropped the subject. As he was leaving, he turned to Marie-Jeanne and said, "I'm going to need you . . . for a new book."

Further tests revealed that Fanon had myeloid leukemia, a very serious form of the disease. The news spread, setting off a tide of emotion in Tunis, especially inside the Algerian community. Whatever political and personal differences people may have had with Fanon fell by the wayside and the decision to make every effort to secure him the best care possible was unanimous; the important thing was to find a cure for him and prolong his life. Everyone rallied, but the situation was handled in a chaotic manner. Martini remembers that people were ready to send him to the moon if need be.[1] Ultimately, he went to Moscow. Why Moscow and not Great Britain, or Sweden, or Switzerland? "The choice was not really political or partial," Martini reports:

> At the time, Soviet preventive medicine was considered the best in the world, and we were all under the impression that medical treatment there would be good, on a par with other areas of Soviet excellence, the advances they had made in space exploration and so forth. We couldn't have been more mistaken; the Soviet Union did not view curative therapy as important to its development. At any rate, in those days, it didn't matter much where he went. The prognosis was hopeless regardless of which country he ended up in.

Fanon went to Moscow in mid-January 1961. He came back after a few weeks. He had put on a little weight, and his white cell count was significantly lower; the Soviet doctors had promised him a five-year reprieve. The most renowned European specialists concurred with their Soviet colleagues.[2] Martini remembers that Fanon came back expressing a great interest in the achievements of the Soviet Union. I remember him as being more circumspect, however, particularly where social problems were concerned. "The Russians and the Ukrainians," he said, "see the Chechnyans and even the Georgians as barbarians." He was disappointed that his meetings with Soviet psychiatrists had been so cursory and that the authorities, using his poor health as a pretext, had refused to authorize more substantial encounters. The only psychiatric establishment he had been permitted to visit did not meet his approval. "Their system relies primarily on confinement, and there are no open clinics," he protested.[3] Apart from these few observations, he really did not care to delve into a detailed analysis of the Soviet State.

There were other things on his mind. He was in a state of emergency and had much to do. Now his days were numbered, but he refused to alter his life in any way. He did, however, request permission to join the internal *maquis;* the idea of dying in combat instead of in the comfort of his bed appealed to him. He would have preferred to die with others and not alone. The Algerian leadership, including his friend Oussedik, paid no heed to this request. They were all moved, however, to do anything within their power to extend his life. Many of those who had accused Fanon of being intransigent and aggressive realized that he was, in fact, courageous, lucid, and attentive. Even his greatest detractors understood that the thing they had mistaken for a taste for power was a kind of determination—a refusal to allow an opportunity to shape the course of history pass him by, an "immeasurable" sense of responsibility.

Throughout 1961, with the exception of those periods in which he was too weakened by great bouts of hemorrhaging, Fanon continued to write and fulfill his political responsibilities. During this year, Fanon's ideas became even more exacting and their terms more stringent. The thing he wanted to avoid at all costs was a loss of momentum—he did not want to see "this Algerian Revolution," this African movement, "lose ground."

This was also the year in which Fanon became more closely allied to the Frontier Army and its leader, Houari Boumedienne. He regularly visited the army post, where he delivered lectures and conducted classes that were attended by the young officers. Fanon's relationship to Boumedienne has continued to puzzle Pierre Chaulet to this day. Chaulet believes that Fanon had allowed himself to be "taken in."

He, like many other members of the GPRA, must have dreaded seeming too bourgeois [. . .] He hadn't been included in the team that prepared the Evian accords. What's more, there were schisms between the political leadership and the old guard of the UDMA, people like Boumendjel, whom Fanon admired, were now being sidelined by the GPRA in favor of Ben Khedda and the MTLD.[4]

In a curious reversal of allegiances, Ferhat Abbas and Boumendjel, tagged as the "moderately bourgeois," were now seen as closer associates of Boumedienne. "The Frontier Army courted him," Chaulet explains. Fanon, as it so happens, had no quarrel with the decision to appoint Ben Khedda, dubbed the Chinaman, as the new President of the GPRA.[5] "Victory is certain," he would say, "but there will be many dead, entire towns on fire, bloodbaths." Was Fanon imagining a worst-case scenario or relating his premonition of things to come? In a sense, the answer is both; Fanon was given to speaking of the larger picture, especially during this period, and 1962 was indeed a year in which many people lost their lives and countless towns were devastated.

Boumedienne had restructured the army by organizing it into sectors: combat troops, liaison office, secretariat, political branch, literacy campaign. The highly trained battalions under his command adhered to a strict military hierarchy and had undergone a rudimentary political education. Their posts were signposted with slogans that read "independence is just a step, the final goal is revolution," or "the land belongs to the peasants, the factories to the workers, schools to the children, hospitals to the sick." Boumedienne, himself the son of a peasant, was not associated with any of the several pre-1954 nationalist movements; his political background was, by and large, a product of the time he had spent in Cairo. While his apparent goal was the preservation of unity, he reproached the GPRA for its failure to include a social and populist message in its independence program and for being too lenient in its dealings with France. Fanon had already met many of Boumedienne's most loyal lieutenants in the course of his earlier encounter with the Southern front. He was struck by the slogans—"land to the peasants, hospitals for the sick"—that he saw everywhere on his visits to the post, and his perception of the Frontier Army as the wellspring of renewed revolutionary zeal began to take hold. Was Fanon, in the last year of his life, swayed by a formula with greater Maoist overtones? He certainly never thought so. The simple truth of it was that the highly organized army impressed him and the large battalions he could only have imagined two years prior were now a standing reality. The army he saw before him was a far cry from what it had been in 1957. The young officers, with their elementary political ideas and self-acknowledged peasant backgrounds, seemed to resist the idea of settling for a fictitious independence of the neo-colonial sort. Fanon could not help but notice the effort that had gone into educating these young peasants turned soldiers. These young officers were a new hope, yet another point of departure to begin envisioning the new Algeria, and for a man who was troubled by illness and still feeling the sting of his African debacle, they were a solace. Did he really think that the Frontier Army had more revolutionary authenticity than the GPRA? He would have liked to think so.[6] Mostly, he was happy to feel that he and his passion were welcomed there and to be afforded one last opportunity to convey his ideas and teach them to others.

Fanon had met with Boumedienne's approval, "unlike other intellectuals, he did not take himself seriously. He was a modest man who wanted to learn and understand, but he didn't know the first thing about Algeria's peasants."

This description of Fanon as a modest man who did not take himself seriously begs for interpretation. There were plenty who saw him as the exact opposite—a man who took himself far too seriously and never second-guessed his self-worth. Fanon did, in fact, take his ideas and actions very seriously and believed in the importance of their impact. As for the claim that he knew next to nothing about Algerian peasants, it rests entirely on the invocation of an apparently timeless authority that equates expertise with native entitlement.[7] Clearly, Fanon was not an Algerian peasant or a French or Antillean one for that matter. Likewise, he was not familiar with Europe's great industrial centers and had never set foot in the factories of highly industrialized nations. Algeria's rural population, on the other hand, was not entirely unknown to him; many of the boarding patients at Blida were country people, and he would meet many more among the soldiers and Algerian refugees he would later treat, or simply meet, in Tunis. But Boumedienne's double gesture, his approval laced with dismissal, was lost on Fanon. He was too ill and in too much of a hurry to perceive the spurn. He truly believed that he had been fully accepted, which he was, by some of the younger officers on whom he would make a lasting impression. He felt he had found an attentive audience, that his lectures were being heard. In any case, Boumedienne's reservations were not exactly unreciprocated; Fanon's admiration for the organization that Boumedienne had put in place did not stop him from privately expressing his discomfort with the harsh discipline and lack of freedom of speech that were rife inside the army. Fanon-the-militant never succeeded in eclipsing Fanon-the-psychiatrist. His longstanding friendships also held firm; Fanon's closest ties inside the army continued to be with the members of the old guard of *Wilaya* 4: Commandant Azzedine, Colonel Saddek, and Omar Oussedik, who was rumored to be a crypto-communist and never denied it.

But Fanon had other urgent matters to attend to. His wish to die fighting in the *maquis* had not been granted, and now, he had a book to write. Day-to-day life was far from easy. He could no longer count on a steady income, and the complexities of transferring his royalties, disbursed to Josie's parents in France, to Tunis were apparently insurmountable. His friends the Taïebs and a few refugee bourgeois families from Blida took turns hosting the Fanons, until an apartment was assigned to them shortly before Fanon died. Their new quarters were in El Menzah, the brand new development where many apartments had been earmarked for the Algerians. The modern complex was an expression of the new Tunisia; this was the neighborhood and the site of the welcoming festivities that greeted the Algerian members of the French soccer team that had helped secure so many international wins for France, the place where the players were triumphantly paraded through the streets. In 1961, these same players joined the National Liberation Front in Tunis to great media attention.

As soon as he returned from Moscow, Fanon set about writing his book. Marie-Jeanne Manuellan was summoned. When she stopped by to pick up the pages she had expected to type, Fanon looked at her in surprise, "Pages! What pages? The book is all here!" he said, pointing to his head. In much the same way that he had written *L'An V,* Fanon dictated the text and barely glanced at the typed pages before entrusting them to Claude Lanzmann. Lanzmann and Marcel Péju had been sent by *Les Temps modernes* to attend a conference on colonialism that was being held in Tunis. It was under these circumstances that Lanzmann met a very enfeebled Fanon. Lanzmann knew Fanon's work, but as far as I have been able to determine, this was the first time the two men met in person. Fanon disliked talking about his illness: "let's talk about something else," he would say. He was much more interested in talking about Sartre and Sartre's philosophical writings.[8] Fanon was one of the few who had read Sartre's most recent work, *La Critique de la raison dialectique,* a book that was largely disregarded at the time of its publication. Lanzmann returned to Tunis to write a piece on the frontier ALN, visiting many of the places where Fanon had become so involved in recent months. Shortly thereafter, Lanzmann became the emissary between Fanon and Maspero, and, more significantly, between Fanon and Sartre.

In a letter to Maspero, dated April 7, 1961, Fanon conveyed his intention to write "something." This new book had nothing to do with *Alger-Le Cap;* that project, as we saw earlier, was the subject of numerous exchanges between Fanon and Maspero in 1960. When Fanon submitted the outline for the earlier project, he attributed the work to a certain Nadia Farès, "writing from Geneva." Fanon signed himself Farès, the pseudonym he had settled on in order to travel to Accra, in most of his exchanges with European contacts, and for the last two years of his life, in all his correspondence with Maspero. In that April letter, Fanon wrote about *Les Damnés,* a new book he wanted to write in lieu of the one he had proposed eight months prior, insisting that it was of the utmost importance that it be published as soon as possible. His failing health was not among the reasons he supplied to explain his great haste; he spoke, rather, of the urgent need for "a deliberation of this kind in Africa and Algeria." He also asked Maspero to approach Sartre about writing the foreword:

> Tell him that I never sit at my desk without thinking of him [. . .] he who has written so many important things for the future of us all and who cannot find readers at home who still know how to read, or here, on the out-

side, where they simply cannot read [. . .] Dear friend, I would like this book to come out in late June.

In this race against time, it soon became clear that one typist could not handle the job alone. Fanon asked two young French women who had secretarial training to join his writing team. They had come to Tunisia to accompany husbands whose beliefs and activities had made them undesirable in both Algeria and France. The two women agreed on the spot and worked free of charge on the book for which, if we are to believe Pierre and Claudine Chaulet, the typing skills of the young "Boutef" were also put to good use.

Addressing us from his bed, where he now spent much of his time, Fanon read the opening chapter on violence to the group of friends who had gathered around him. "Like a great classical hero who has been wounded in battle and calls his companions to his side to deliver his final words," is the way Claudine Chaulet remembers those evenings that were so thick with feeling and emotions.[9] Claudine Chaulet and I see eye to eye on most things that have to do with Fanon and his work but comparing Fanon to a great classical hero is not one of them. No, Fanon had nothing to with Moses or Ajax or even Antigone! He was much too human, put too much effort into trying to identify with others, and most of all, he could not bear being alone. He reproached friends who stayed away during periods when the episodes associated with his illness were especially acute. "You have to come," he would say laconically in a voice that had regained much of its strength.

Fanon knew that he had to use his time wisely if he was to finish the book. He did not have time for details, draft revisions, philosophical and literary flourishes, or to engage in debates. He wanted to pass the sum of his experience on to others. He worked at a furious pace but never referred to his own race against death in his correspondence with his publisher. He only admitted to pressure once, in a letter he wrote in late May, 1961, in which he speaks with regret about his wish for more time, and his fear that he may have been too vehement in his portrayals. "I thought that the stakes were in great jeopardy," he explains.[10] He also apologizes to Maspero for not meeting the agreed upon June deadline: "I hope you will forgive me for being the bearer of bad news. The manuscript will not be ready on the agreed upon date. I am sending you the third chapter and hope to have the fourth one, on national culture, shortly. We are back to our October publication deadline." On July 25, Fanon sent the completed manuscript with Lanzmann and pressed for a September publication date. "I am only compelled to insist because of concrete and important political considerations." In early August, by which time he had decided to call his book *Les Damnés de la terre*, Fanon again reiterated his request for a September publication date. "This book is being impatiently awaited in Third World political circles." He wanted the book to be widely available in Africa and Latin America and specifically asked for it to be distributed in the most efficient way. Sartre, to whom Lanzmann had already conveyed an early copy of the manuscript, had agreed to write the foreword. In fact, Lanzmann had arranged a meeting between Sartre and Fanon, and in April of that year, the two men finally met in Rome. Simone de Beauvoir devotes several pages in her memoirs to the time they spent with Fanon.[11]

In the days leading to Fanon's trip to Rome and especially after he returned, I had the opportunity to spend quite a bit of time with him. He was my neighbor. Shortly before his trip to Rome, the Fanons were moved into the El Menzah complex where I also had been assigned housing. Omar Oussedik was borrowing my car, "another old Pigeot," to take Fanon to and from the airport. Fanon, who was exhausted and feverish, spent the hours immediately before and after his journey recuperating in my house. I have a vivid memory of the day he returned from Rome. It was a typically Tunisian summer day: 40 degrees centigrade in the shade. Fanon was not at all well, shivering one minute, bathed in sweat the next. I must admit I was more concerned by his physical state than by the uninterrupted flow of words that was being directed at me. The book was "almost finished"; he would have liked to have more time to develop his ideas, to change the order of the chapters and also the tone; "it's too vehement at times, but things have come down to the wire. Who knows? It may even be too late." Too late politically as well as too late for him. "I don't know how much time I have left." And then he changed tacks, talking about a host of projects he planned to undertake. He was feverish, burning, just as Simone de Beauvoir would later describe him. What she did not know, aside from the fact that Fanon was fighting for his life, was how much he would have preferred to meet just with Sartre. "I met with Sartre. I wish I could have had a moment alone with him. But Simone was omnipresent, she never left us alone, and she is one of those people who save themselves up." Even before he became ill, Fanon often used the expression. One must not "save oneself up," and Fanon had no time for people who did. "But Sartre listened to me, anyway," he continued, "and agreed to write a foreword for my book." The thought that Sartre was going to write a foreword for his book was extremely important to him, mattering far more than the actual content of said foreword. "What will he write?" I dared ask, to Fanon's great surprise. It had not occurred to him to ask. The substance of the foreword was not the important thing here; what was far more important was that Sartre was putting his seal to Fanon's last book, a book that Fanon did not expect to be around to defend when the time came.[12] This was a final acknowledgment from a person who had entered Fanon's life when he was twenty and had profoundly influenced his intellectual trajectory ever since, and who, with the sole exception of Césaire, was the only French intellectual whose opinion he respected. What he had found in Sartre was a similar urgency and hope for an altogether different kind of human interaction. He also was delighted that Sartre and Simone de Beauvoir, neither of whom had met him beforehand, had not realized the extent of his illness and physical exhaustion. Simone de Beauvoir's account of the encounter is extremely interesting and, at times, amusingly off track. The interest follows, in part, from her ability to capture Fanon's excessive side. She accurately relates some of Fanon's characteristic traits: "with a sharp intelligence, intensely lively, darkly humorous, he explained, clowned about, interrupted, imitated, recounted. He had an ability to bring all the things he talked about come alive in the room." She also writes about his erudition, the speed and audacity of his mind. "He was an exceptional being." She also singles out certain personality traits, his sensitivity to remarks about the color of his skin, his propensity for exaggeration—what he knowingly called "pulling a Fanon." And then, there are the remarks we can only smile at, such as qualifying Fanon's need for only four hours of sleep as a common trait of Algerian revolutionaries. There were indeed young Algerians—most of them closer to twenty than thirty—trapped in this "messed up" revolution whose vigilance and doubt and desire for survival kept them up through the night. This was how they "partied," as young people call it today, gathered around an illicit bottle of wine and engaged in endless, nocturnal discussions. Their youth, in comparison with the majority of their European contemporaries, consisted almost entirely of the broken lives that were everywhere around them, the studies they had to cut short, the knowledge they had to forfeit, and the life experiences associated with early adulthood they would never have. Fanon, on the other hand, had never been one for sleep, even before he ever set foot in Algeria.

On a more important note, Simone de Beauvoir also claims to perceive a discomfort in Fanon for his failure to "fight in the country of his birth, and, furthermore, for not being of Algerian origin." There is little doubt that Fanon was infuriated when Krim Belkacem, who had meant only to honor and thank him, greeted him by saying "you who know all our secrets," casting him, in fact, as a mere "relation" of the Algerian struggle.[13] But the fact that he was not of Algerian origin did not trouble Fanon in the least, such a preoccupation would have been unthinkable to him—otherwise, he would not have been Fanon. Anyway, what did it mean to be of Algerian origin in the context of the Tunis-based Algerian leadership? Did it mean a Berber unionist who spoke no Arabic and claimed to be an atheist, an ex-Corporal who was both Arab and Muslim and had served in the French army, a graduate from the Zitouna seminary, or even a European or an Algerian Jew? There was almost no one in the leadership with whom Fanon could totally identify. At any rate, he had always had a tendency to gravitate toward a "minority mind cast" and being part of a majority consensus did not really sit well with him. If the term *bastardy* were not so archaic, it would accurately qualify Fanon's position in the intellectual ambit of the day.[14]

Fanon arranged to have the manuscript delivered to Maspero at the end of July. By August 10, he had made up his mind to call it *Les Damnés de la terre*, a title he chose entirely on his own—a first in his life as a writer. On October 3, Maspero informed him that he had received Sartre's foreword and that "it is beautiful, violent, useful, at least for those of us who are here in France." He also promised that the book would appear by the end of the month; actually, the book appeared later, due to printing delays. Servan-Schreiber, who had requested Maspero's permission to publish excerpts from the Sartre foreword in the November 16 issue of *L'Express*, was asked to hold off for another week: "The book will not be ready until then, and it is of the utmost importance that there be no copies of the book at the printers, because the risk of seizure is the same as with Fanon's previous book." The book was banned on publication. Leftist newspapers, among them *L'Humanité*, protested the ban. *Tribune socialiste* printed the letter Maspero had written to protest the baseless interdiction: "This book offers a global historical and sociological critique. How exactly does this constitute a threat to national security?" The government's measures did not stop news of the book from reaching the media, and newspaper reports on *Les Damnés de la terre* began to appear. The first was Jean Daniel's review in the November 30 issue of *L'Express*, followed by the December issue of *Jeune Afrique* that included a piece by Césaire as well as one by Anna Gréki, a writer and poet who had sought refuge in Tunis.[15] Whether it was praised, criticized, or violently dismissed, one thing was certain, this was not a book that left its readership indifferent. But Fanon was gone. He had died, under difficult circumstances, on Wednesday, December 6, in Bethesda's National Institute of Health, a government-run clinic not far from Washington, D.C.

In mid-October, Fanon, whose book was in press and whose health had taken a turn for the worse, allowed himself to be convinced to check into a hospital in the United States—"this clinic for American Marines," as he called it. M'Hammed Yazid offered to pay for the ticket and purchased a round-trip fare. Fanon reluctantly agreed; he did not want to go to the

United States, a place that was the embodiment of neocolonialism, the oppressive nation par excellence, responsible for the exploitation of Latin America, Africa, and its own American blacks. Despite his repugnance at the idea, he decided to go. En route, he stopped in Rome, where he and Sartre met for the last time; Sartre's last image would be one of Fanon contorted on his hotel bed; Boulharouf, the same Algerian representative who had accompanied him in Rome in 1959, was at his bedside. Fanon was spent, "embedded in his mattress," as he used to say, unable to speak, his body in a state of total rebellion. Matters in the United States did not proceed smoothly. His admission to the hospital was delayed, and he had to spend some ten days by himself in a hotel room.[16] In the letter he wrote to his wife, he recalls how they first met on the stairs outside the theater in Lyon. He also wrote a long letter to his friend Taïeb:

If I had left Tunis four days later, I would've been quite dead by now. All the doctors here have told me as much. Where do things stand now? I'm in a delicate stage of the illness. The big hemorrhaging episodes are behind me, but the leukemia is still active and on an all out assault—that's why they have me on a round-the-clock watch. What I want to say to you, Roger, is that death is always with us and the important thing is not to know how to avoid it but to make sure we do our utmost for the ideas we believe in. The thing that shocks me as I lie here in this bed, feeling the strength exiting my body, is not that I'm dying but that I'm dying of acute leukemia in Washington, D.C., when I could have died three months ago facing the enemy on a battlefield, when I already knew I had this disease. We are nothing on this earth if we do not first and foremost serve a cause, the cause of the people, the cause of freedom and justice. I want you to know that even when the doctors had lost all hope, I was still thinking, in a fog granted, but thinking, nonetheless, of the Algerian people, of the people of the Third World, and if I managed to hold on, it was because of them.

This letter, written in solitude, from the loneliness of a no-man's land, is the truest and most intimate expression of Fanon's state of mind as his life was ending.

Josie and Olivier, who was six at the time, joined him. Who financed the trip? No one who was around at the time remembers,[17] including Olivier. He does remember, however, being enrolled in a school, and the afternoons he spent in a hospital room watching his father pacing back and forth. Fanon needed total transfusions to "change the blood" in order to stimulate the bone marrow—a procedure he withstood very badly. He experienced the transfusions as an imaginary trauma. Was there an effort afoot to whiten him?

There were short periods of remission during which Fanon received visitors such as Abdel Kader Chanderli, the Algerian representative at the United Nations, as well as other African delegates. Roberto Holden came to see him as did Olie Iselin of the American State Department; Josie reports that Fanon warned the latter that the government of the United States would soon have to face the rebellion of black America and South American guerilla armies.[18] The confidences Fanon had shared in his letter to his friend Taïeb did not stop him from carrying on as though he planned to beat the illness; he talked about the books he planned on writing one day: *The Leukemia Patient and His Double* was the title of one of them, there was also one on jealousy, as well as a history of the ALN.

The periods of remission grew shorter. *Les Damnés de la terre* was published, and Fanon was able to see it. An Algerian friend managed to get it to him three days before he died. Josie read him the first reviews, namely, the article Jean Daniel had written for *L'Express*. Fanon listened to it, then said, "Yes, fine, but it won't give me back my bone marrow."[19] He died three days later of double bronchial pneumonia.

Fanon lived his death and fought it to the very end. He had not wished to die in the United States, a place he perceived as ideologically hostile—even though the references to it in *Les Damnés de la terre* are very sporadic—a place that was even more hostile than the Europe he had turned his back on in the last two years of his life to address himself exclusively to the Third World, primarily to Africa but also to Cuba and South America.

Fanon's wish to be buried in Algerian soil was granted. He was given a state funeral. The leaderships of the GPRA and of the ALN were in full agreement about this, even though there were two separate eulogies. Despite the distance that had installed itself between Fanon and the paper, the team at *El Moudjahid* thought of Fanon as their longtime and loyal colleague for whom they had the greatest affection and admiration, and they were adamant about covering the burial. If one overlooks the grandiloquent style that was part and parcel of the militant discourse associated with the publication, the paper gave an accurate and detailed account of the funeral proceedings.[20] A special airplane had been commandeered to fly Fanon's body to Tunis. In the early afternoon of December 11, 1961, the plane was met at the El Aouina airport, and Fanon's body was carried inside the airport's *Salon d'honneur*, where members of the GPRA gathered around the casket that had been draped in an Algerian flag. The crowd that had gathered at the airport to greet the body was so large that it was difficult to distinguish close friends from militants and observers from the merely curious. Some of Fanon's closest friends were in the front row, there to carry the casket; others tried to hide their pain by losing themselves in the anonymity of the crowd. Many who had gathered on the esplanade were overcome by emotion, and the gray December light made the whiteness of the hall seem drab. The emotion did not abate during the wake that was held at the headquarters of the Algerian Mission. Throughout the afternoon, an endless file of people passed through the room. Some simply signed the open register; others wrote heartfelt messages. "The signature of an Ambassador is next to that of the militant, the sympathy of the Cameroonais is expressed next to the testimony of the Algerian guerilla" (CS, 235).[21] Among those who had come to pay their respects were journalists and ex-colleagues from Charles-Nicolle, mainly nurses, who had come to say their good-byes, many of them intimidated by the proceedings. Fanon had expressly asked to be buried in Algerian territory. At nine o'clock the next morning, a brief ceremony marked the departure of the body. Close friends had stepped forward to carry the casket. The ceremony was simple: Vice-President Krim Belkacem gave a farewell address,[22] a summary of Fanon's itinerary that paid homage to his "patriotism, revolutionary fervor, and tireless dedication to the people's cause"; he did not neglect to mention Fanon's outstanding psychiatric work and his intellectual merit and courage. "Your example shall always live on, rest in peace, Algeria shall not forget you." It is difficult to know who wrote Krim's farewell address that points out, among other things, that Fanon's desire to pursue serious schooling did not stand in the way of his desire to be part of the anticolonial struggle. It is possible, therefore, to be both an intellectual and a revolutionary, the resistance fighter Krim concluded; also adding, without any ambiguity whatsoever, that for him, Fanon will always be part of the Algerian nation.

A convoy was formed to deliver Fanon's body to Ghardimaou, where he was to be buried in a plot of "liberated" Algerian soil. Roger Taïeb and Pierre Chaulet, two of Fanon's closest friends, accompanied the body, and it is largely thanks to them that we know about the journey in such great detail. The casket was transported in an ambulance that was accompanied by a cortege of twenty or so vehicles. People along the way stopped to salute its passage. In every village, there were refugees or Algerian ex-combatants standing at attention. At 12:30, the convoy arrived in Ghardimaou, where it stopped inside the courtyard of an ALN country hospital. This was the moment of leave-taking for those who had come from Tunis. They were not permitted to proceed beyond this point. The casket was entrusted to the ALN and placed on a litter of branches that was carried by fifteen soldiers; later, other soldiers took their place, as the march through the woods was a long one. The sky was luminous and the silence absolute. Canon fire could be heard somewhere to the north. The war was very near, but a remarkable calm had settled on this last march. Two hours later, the marchers reached the cemetery of the *chouhada* (martyrs who died in battle), situated in the recently liberated area of Aïn Kerma, a place geographers refer to as *Bec de Canard*. Many of the military men present knew Fanon. Ali Mendjli, a commander in the ALN, delivered the eulogy in Arabic. Unlike Krim's earlier address, this one did not dwell on biographical details and made no effort to link Fanon's psychiatric and political activities. It highlighted Fanon's militancy and spoke of him as "a living model of discipline and respect for principles, during the entire time that he was carrying out tasks given to him by the Algerian Revolution" (CS, 236). The commander also reported that Fanon had refused to obey orders to cease his revolutionary activity and devote himself to seeking out the care his illness required. Apparently, Fanon responded to the command by saying, "I shall not desist from my activities as long as Algeria is at war, and I will persist in my duties to my last living day." The eulogy began with "Our late brother Frantz Fanon" and ended with the promise "to build a free, independent, democratic and social Algeria, one in which human rights will be respected" (CS, 237). At the stroke of four, the ceremony was over. "It is finished," *El Moudjahid* reports. "The coffin rests on a bed of lentisk branches: above, branches of cork tree" (CS, 237). Later, I heard that the last part of this voyage, the crossing of the woods and burial of Fanon's body, had been imbued with a great serenity and a strange beauty.

The readiness of the GPRA and the ALN to grant Fanon's wish and bury him in state was a foregone conclusion. In light of the atmosphere of the times, political strategy did not come into play. Almost everyone in the leadership had known Fanon. Krim Belkacem, in a manner of speaking, owed him his life. We recall that Fanon, already ill at the time, had alerted the surgeons to Belkacem's symptoms after concluding that they were not related to anxiety about the impending Evian negotiations. Fanon had also recently spent time with the ALN. And Fanon left no one indifferent. Regardless of how people may have felt about him, the mere fact of his presence affected them. The power of his presence is a constant in any representation we may draw of the man, and it divides those who knew him in person from those who knew only his writing and judged him on the basis of his work. Those who encountered him, regardless of background or theoretical differences, invariably invoke the intensity of his presence, his outbursts of laughter, his aura and generosity. "It is impossible to have known and spent time with Fanon and remain impervious," Pierre Chaulet wrote in December 1987. "He is a call to consciousness, a call to vigilance. Not just a cortical vigilance that enables one to pay attention to others, but a muscular, permanent vigilance that prepares one for acts of solidarity."[23] The Algerian militants of 1961 saw Fanon in a similar way. Even Chanderli, the Algerian representative at the United Nations, who met Fanon in the last weeks of his life, spoke of the intensity of his gaze, the sharpness of his faculties even as he was dying, his gift for making all things come to life. The Algerians of the day, those he disturbed as well as those he attracted, those who loved him as well as those who despised him, meant it when they spoke of Fanon's demise as an "irremediable loss."

The news spread very quickly. Albert-Paul Lentin,[24] one of the most committed journalists of the "Maghreb circus" who had been born and raised in Constantine, announced Fanon's death in *Libération*. Fanon had been no stranger to him: "exemplary militant, generous friend, original and powerful thinker, profoundly revolutionary, Frantz Fanon leaves an irreversible void," he wrote. The December 11 issue of *Jeune Afrique* dedicated several pages to Fanon's death. Guy Sitbon writes about the friend he lost, describing his affection and esteem for a man who had never intended to be a pure person.[25] In the same issue, Césaire wrote a superb tribute to his former student, "the one who didn't allow you to close your eyes and doze off to the hum of a tranquil conscience."

Fanon's death was a public event, but strangely, neither mother wanted to inform her child. Mireille, his eldest who lived in France, came across the announcement and a photograph of her father in a *Paris Match* someone had left behind. Josie, despite our advice to the contrary, was determined to keep the news from Olivier, and he spent the next three or four years in what he describes as a total haze. His father had often been away from home toward the end, and he had become accustomed to seeing him come and go. For Olivier, the prolonged absence of a father who had become mythical required a homecoming to become substantive.

Tributes to Fanon kept appearing in the months that followed. *Présence africaine* published a special issue about Fanon that brought together friends like Bertène Juminer as well as figures such as Césaire, Maspero, Pierre Stibbe, Edgar Morin. Simultaneously and despite the ban, *Les Damnés de la terre* was enjoying a wide distribution and instant success. It was a controversial book, praised in some quarters, violently criticized in others, that left no reader indifferent.

The Wretched of the Earth

Fanon's last words are a message to the colonized, asking, "After decolonization, what?" He believes the success of decolonization depends on the liberation of psyche and body by the reversal of colonial violence. The rural, peasant masses acquire a voice of their own. Fanon expresses the imperative need for a political structure accountable to all and administered in a spirit of collegiality. Fanon speaks of wars of liberation that misfired in such a way as to provide a visionary warning. Fanon is involved with artists and intellectuals and is focused on the traumas of war. The Wretched of the Earth and its reception: Europe shocked, the Marxist reading, inaudible violence.

In his last book, unlike in *L'An V* which was still, in part, addressed to the French Left, Fanon spoke directly to the colonized. He wrote it with his Algerian and African comrades in mind. The book picks up where *L'An V* left off and multiplies its cautionary warnings against the implicit dangers associated with the national liberation movements that prevailed in Africa during those years. National movements with the sole aim of recuperation of national territory are doomed to failure and degeneration, he warned. Drawing on his own experience from recent years, Fanon was keen to impart the knowledge he acquired and the lessons learned in the process. The historical context is contemporaneous; he is speaking from the historical moment in which he is immersed; it is necessary for him to work through his experience. His inquiry draws on observations, discussions, contacts, friendships, and rivalries. Among the experiences that touched his life directly and left a terrible mark, he includes the assassination of Moumié, who died of thallium poisoning in Switzerland, and the betrayal and murder of Lumumba, a man who despised violence and put his faith in the power of language and died in conditions of extreme violence. For Fanon, who was incapable of killing another human being, these shameful deaths are an outcome of colonial violence.[1]

Fanon begins his book in much the same way he did *Black Skin, White Masks* and *Studies in a Dying Colonialism*, with a singular observation that then develops into a general point of view. This is a much less *written* book than his previous ones: the ideas are laid out, dispersed, and then repeated like the stanzas of a poem. Fanon did not have time to revise or edit. The style is unquestionably his, persuasive rather than illustrative, and the rhythm that characterizes all his writings is more rapid, choppy. As in *Black Skin, White Masks*, his writing is a bodily feat; in this case, the feat is literally and figuratively more precipitous than ever. It is this quality in the writing that sustains the five chapters of the book.

Taken as a whole, the book is an analysis of decolonization, an inquiry into the future of Third World nations, mainly in Africa but also with an eye to South America and Cuba in particular. Fanon is no longer content to summarize the colonial situation, the in-depth analysis he may have devoted to it in *Studies in a Dying Colonialism* notwithstanding. He turns his attention to the effects of decolonization on the individual; "decolonization," he argues, "must be the decolonization of the individual being." In light of the fact that the colonial enterprise is based on individual and collective violence, decolonization cannot be achieved without violent action. He outlines the conditions in which true decolonization is likely to occur and gives a lucid and unflinching description of the obstacles and impasses that are becoming realities in newly independent nations. This book is a distress signal, not a work that aspires to be an economic, sociological, or even political study; rather, it is a warning, written from the "inside," to alert African nations to the inherent problems of their relationship to the developed nations of Europe. It puts newly decolonized nations on guard about their future. Fanon ends his book on a rallying note addressed to those he calls "the wretched of the earth."

Come, then comrades; it would be as well to decide at once to change our ways. We must shake off the heavy darkness in which we are plunged, and leave it behind. The new day which is already at hand must find us firm, prudent and resolute. [. . .] Leave this Europe where they are never done talking of Man, yet murder men everywhere they find them, at the corner of every one of their own streets, in all the corners of the globe. [. . .] When I search for Man in the technique and the style of Europe, I see only a succession of negations of man, and an avalanche of murders. [. . .] Let us try to create the whole man, whom Europe has been incapable of bringing to triumphant birth. [. . .] Europe has done what she set out to do and on the whole she has done it well; let us stop blaming her, but let us say to her firmly that she should not make such a song and dance about it. [. . .] For Europe, for ourselves and for humanity, comrades, we must turn over a new leaf, we must work out new concepts, and try to set afoot a new man. (TWOE, 253).[2]

Fanon's *wretched* are not to be mistaken with the proletarian masses, the *arise ye wretched of the earth, ye slaves of hunger* of late nineteenth-century industrialized nations. By recycling the anthem, Fanon, in addition to tweaking the term, also shows up the racism of a European proletariat that is indifferent toward the colonies that have indirectly benefited it. Fanon's *wretched* are the dispossessed inhabitants of the poor nations—the ones to whom *earth really* matters . . . as does bread. In this book, it is their voice we hear.

The book's opening chapter, "Concerning Violence," sets out to answer two questions, the second one a corollary of the first. What are the necessary conditions for decolonization to succeed? At what point are conditions right for a national liberation movement to emerge, and who should constitute its vanguard? Fanon has to address the subject of violence if he is to answer these questions. This point is worth emphasizing because the chapter on violence, after Sartre's foreword, was the object of heated controversy in France. The work was instantly labeled an "apology for violence," and the label was extended to include Fanon's person. Many readers, including militants and intellectuals, were disturbed by the book. Jacques Azoulay, who had at one time been Fanon's student, didn't know what to make of it and was even personally upset by it: "I didn't understand him anymore. I became deeply estranged from him." The general perception was that Fanon had become an apologist for violence, an advocate for death and destruction. The irony was that Fanon was not and had never been a violent man. People who had known him invariably used words like love, generosity, and humanism to speak of him. In the tributes and obituaries that had been written by Césaire, Berque, and others there was only mention of his goodness, his attentiveness, his inability to abide injustice, and . . . his anger. Césaire had called him a secular Paraclete.[3] Even his anger was a kind of awareness of his own limits in the face of unjustified violence.

The book opens with a discussion of colonization that does not touch, at least in this first section, on diplomacy, economics, or politics. Decolonization, Fanon argues, is a process that occurs at the level of being. Decolonization, a "moment of complete disorder," gives rise to a new order and the emergence of a new society. The struggle for liberation allows the individual who has been objectified, demeaned, reduced to the status of an animal, and identified as "quintessentially evil" to regain his humanity. Fanon stood by this belief. He had reached it as a result of personal experience and of his understanding of the human psyche. His work with the mentally ill, those other wretched of the earth, that had served as a springboard for his theories on colonization had shown him as much. A similar argument had already been broached in *Studies in a Dying Colonialism*, but, here, he makes the point more forcefully and speaks about the impossible encounter between two structurally antagonistic forces, two worlds that are completely cut off from each other and kept apart by their reciprocal exclusion. This exclusion is, itself, an unmixed expression of violence. The native is purported to understand only the language of force, the colonizer's force, which is in fact the opposite of language and leaves the native with no other response but submissive paralysis or rebellion.

The sole interlocutor and intermediary that the dominant society assigns as its representative to the colonized world is the soldier or the policeman. In Western societies, on the other hand, compartmentalization is negotiated by an often mystifying but nonetheless present third player. "In capitalist societies the educational system, whether lay or clerical, the structure of moral reflexes handed down from father to son, the exemplary honesty of workers who are given a medal after fifty years of good and loyal service, and the affection which springs from harmonious relations and good behavior" constitute a buffer. "In the capitalist countries a multitude of moral teachers, counselors and 'bewilderers' separate the exploited from those in power" (TWOE, 31). The colonial structure includes no such buffer and relies entirely on the nonlanguage of repression, punishment, and domination. Manicheanism and the impossibility of genuine behaviors pertain to both worlds, however.

Fanon goes on to give a detailed account of the psychological state of a colonized individual. Guilt, as an internalized emotion, is not the primary response of a colonized person; rather, this person will feel a shame that is perceived as a curse. Having been made to feel inferior, the colonized individual fulfills the expectations of his accusers while remaining unconvinced of his inferiority. What are the available resources for the colonized individual to break out of this psychological state while still under power of colonial rule? Dreams, of course, are one, but also a state that Fanon describes as a continuous state of physical tension. It is perhaps not an accident that Fanon places such an emphasis on the afflicted body, capable of expressing itself only through muscular release. "The native's muscular tension finds outlet regularly in bloodthirsty explosions." He turns on another colonized individual, becomes an erratic killer, or resorts to the tribal feuding that only serves to "perpetuate old grudges buried deep in the memory" (TWOE, 43). Trance dances serve as another outlet for this accumulated and impotent violence; these ecstasies are "muscular orgies" that provide a temporary emotional relief. A culture's magical superstructures are yet another source of comfort, and cults that center on zombie worship, for example, can release the colonized psyche from its submissive status. As zombies are more terrifying than colonizers, fearing them becomes a way of deterring and insulating oneself from the terrors of colonial reality. But these are violent fantasies, activities without a real object that unfold in an imaginary world. They do little to further the process of decolonization. The time of "total disorder" is invariably attained through struggle. Violence is the means by which the reduced colonized individual is restored to his personhood and to the freedoms of possibility. What forces will step forward to direct this violence, to fill the shoes of the third player—political parties and intellectual elites who botch the job and whose actions fall short or by the wayside of expectations? Liberation can follow only from the creation of a space in which individual violence is mediated into collective struggle. Psychological and physical liberation are inextricably linked to the process of desubjugation. Violence is needed to undo the original violence that inflicted the alienation in the first place. At what point does the political leadership channel this individual violence into something other than the murder of fellow individuals or acts of self-destruction? Will they, in other words, find a way of harnessing it to secure a collective survival by means other than those that involve entrusting one's fate to a living god or withdrawing inside self-destructive tribalisms?

The following section, entitled "Spontaneity: Its Strength and Weakness," is a discussion of the *time lag* that separates the national parties from the largely rural populations they purport to represent. If Fanon places a special emphasis on the "rural masses," as he repeatedly refers to them, it is not to glorify the peasant classes, but because he accurately identifies them as a clearly demarcated insurrectional force of any process of decolonization and of the Algerian one in particular. They are the disinherited majority, and whether they have remained in the villages or migrated to the city slums, they constitute a desperate and ready lumpen proletariat. Their wholesale oppression—economic, social, and psychological—means they have little to lose. It is important, therefore, that they not be left on the side of the road. According to Fanon, the nationalist parties are out of step with the "rural masses." Frequently modeled on their European counterparts, the urban-based parties are suspicious of a peasantry they view as fixed in tradition and trapped in a feudal system. They treat the rebellion in the mountains and valleys as "a sort of manna fallen from heaven," but "they don't send leaders into the countryside to educate the people politically, or to increase their awareness, or put the struggle onto a higher level" (TWOE, 94). But when a fugitive and tracked *maquisard* seeks refuge in the mountains, "the peasant's cloak will wrap him around with a gentleness and firmness that he never suspected" (TWOE, 101).[4] A dialogue is initiated: the political man listens to the peasant and speaks to him. The political man realizes that only praxis, only the confrontation of immediate, daily problems, can bring political enlightenment and a discriminating awareness to the countryside and enable it to leave the Manichean night behind. Fanon, in effect, dwells on the point that while "the determination to fight for one's life which characterizes the native's reply to oppression" is reason enough to join the fight, "hatred and resentment—'a legitimate desire for revenge'—cannot sustain a war of liberation [. . .] hatred alone cannot draw up a programme" (TWOE, 111). While the disinherited constitute a subversive force, this force alone is unequal to the task of achieving a meaningful liberation. For this to happen there must be a sustained interaction with "revolutionary elements coming from the towns." Only then will the peasants acquire a sense of personal responsibility and "pass from total, undiscriminating nationalism to social and economic awareness" (TWOE, 115).

At the end of the third chapter, "The Pitfalls of National Consciousness," Fanon revisits this dialectic of how knowledge is shared by the popular masses, intellectuals, and the political leadership: "In an under-developed country, experience proves that the important thing is not that three hundred people form a plan and decide upon carrying it out, but that the whole people plan and decide even if it takes them twice or three times as long" (TWOE, 154). Time must be allotted, even if the changes are slower in coming and give rise to greater conflicts; this is all part and parcel of liberation—*enlarging the mind* so that it may become more nuanced, more human in order to emerge out of Manicheanism; the collective made all-inclusive and every last person impervious to influence and cured of credulity.

To achieve such a goal, Fanon writes, specific measures need to go into effect on the morrow of independence. He appeals to the party or parties without government affiliation, reminding them that it is not enough to exist in form only, as empty shells content to pass down instructions from the top and neglecting to convey the preoccupations and solutions of those at the bottom to the top. He recommends the total separation of political and administrative spheres: a party leader, regardless of rank, should not be given administrative regional authority. He argues for a total decentralization: the importance of the urban centers, especially the capital city, must give way to a move toward the interior. A professional army and career officers should become things of the past. Education of the young, even in sports, should not "cultivate the exceptional" or promote the cult of the hero or star (TWOE, 157). Fanon lays out the broad outline of a political structure that would be accountable to the collective and operate in a collegial fashion. When nationalism is not elucidated, when it does not evolve into social consciousness, it will lead to an impasse, he warns. Political education, he insists, must be rooted in a concrete and quotidian reality. "Now, political education means opening their (the masses) minds, awakening them, and allowing the birth of their intelligence: as Césaire said, it is 'to invent souls'" (TWOE, 157).

> If the building of a bridge does not enrich the awareness of those who work on it, then that bridge ought not to be built and the citizens can go on swimming across the river or going by boat. The bridge should not be "parachuted down" from above; it should not be imposed by a *deus ex machina* upon the social scene; on the contrary it should come from the muscles and the brains of the citizens. Certainly, there may well be need of engineers and architects, sometimes completely foreign engineers and architects; but the local party leaders should be always present, so that the new techniques can make their way into the cerebral desert of the citizen, so that the bridge in whole and in part can be taken up and conceived, and the responsibility for it assumed by the citizen. In this way, and this way only, everything is possible. (TWOE, 160)

Liberation can be achieved only through praxis, not with brass bands and national anthems, not with a flag and a few reforms at the top while faceless and "medieval" masses continue to stir down below.

This is also the chapter in which Fanon speaks of newly independent nations with a ferocity matched only by his despair, and the picture he paints is absolutely prophetic. National bourgeoisies are content to be intermediaries. Western bourgeoisies have had their creative period, their entrepreneurial and innovative economic strength enables them to institutionally sustain parliamentary regimes in which differences can be subsumed, and to hold, despite their fundamental racism, a humanist discourse that purports to be universal. African bourgeoisies, on the other hand, are exclusively dedicated to replicating the waning consumerist phase of Western bourgeoisies. They have nothing to show for themselves and have not introduced a single economic or industrial innovation nor have they succeeded in promoting a single new agricultural technology. They are happy to occupy the role of the intermediary and liberal sector, often pushing out the "whites" and taking over their positions, appropriating old homesteads and farms without a thought as to how these can be adapted to the needs of the population. They secure their position and protect their privilege by resorting to the most archaic means, fueling clan enmities, ethnic rivalries, and religious tensions. At the institutional level, an uncompromised parliamentary model becomes unthinkable under the circumstances. The implementation of a single party, that only transmits orders from the top down and whose members quickly turn into corrupt administrators, becomes the preferable way to go. To perpetuate this status quo, it will choose a popular figure, generally an old patriot with ties to the struggle for liberation, to head the country and to serve as its guarantor: he will ceaselessly remind the country of his heroism and use his prestigious past "to become the general president of that company of profiteers impatient for their returns" (TWOE, 134). In the end, the army and the police become the pillars of the regime. This lack of democracy can quickly develop, as witnessed in the countries of South America, into a "dictatorship of the national-socialist type" (TWOE, 138).

Compradore bourgeoisies, single-party bureaucratic states, regimes upheld by police and military forces, leaders made legitimate by hero cults, administrations paralyzed by clan rivalries, these are the pitfalls of newly independent nations as Fanon portrays them in 1961. It is hard to disagree with the accuracy of his vision. The bloody and brutally repressed rebellion that took place in Algiers in 1988 is a case in point; moreover, it took place in the country on which Fanon had pinned his highest hopes and whose leaders in both the GPRA and the ALN, if we are to believe the statements they made at his funeral, shared very similar hopes, at least on the eve of independence.

Chapter 4 revisits the talk that Fanon had delivered at the Rome Congress of Black Writers and Artists in 1959. In it, Fanon analyzes the relationship between national culture and liberation movements. The man of culture must participate in the evolution of the nation. The version of the essay that is reproduced here diverges from the original only in its reassertion of the role of the state. This passage, which appears toward the end of the essay, reminds artists and intellectuals of the necessity of shattering the "old strata of culture" so that these may be renewed in a universal dimension (TWOE, 197).

The book's final section, "Colonial Wars and Mental Disorders," is a series of psychiatric case studies. This casebook seems to have struck most readers as having no apparent relation to the preceding overtly political chapters; its dismissal has been so unanimous that, until this writing, it has been treated as incidental and its discussion relegated to the footnotes. Yet these reflections on psychiatric illness were central to Fanon's argument. They had, since 1956, been at the basis of his involvement. Fanon's original intention was to publish them in *Alger-Le Cap*. He often used to say that he had no wish to be a professional revolutionary, and it had been his express desire to improve his understanding of the mental illnesses associated with war. He deplored the fact that so little had been written on the subject. The cases are recorded without much in-depth analysis. Fanon was quite aware of this and would have liked to have had more time to develop these somewhat hasty reports. He anticipated the "psycho-affective disorders" that would persist for at least one generation and affect both the perpetrators and victims of so much rape, murder, and torture carried out in the name of war. "In other words, we are forever pursued by our actions. Their ordering, their circumstances and their motivation may perfectly well come to be profoundly modified a posteriori. This is merely one of the snares that history and its various influences sets for us" (TWOE, 207).

The case studies are arbitrarily divided into four categories: reactive disorders in response to single traumatic events or to life under conditions of total war, mental disorders appearing in the aftermath of torture, childhood abandonment among orphans and refugees, and psychosomatic pathologies. The Algerian studies are undoubtedly the most complete, and they describe European casualties as well as Algerian ones—Algerian militants whose wives have been raped or mothers murdered and European servicemen dealing with the torture they inflicted on others. Fanon explores psychological behavioral disorders, the effects of routine mistreatment, compulsive murders, as well as sexual impotence which was just then beginning to emerge as an identifiable symptom. The case of an Algerian militant whose mother had been killed and sisters sequestered by the French army and who then compulsively murders a woman against whom he harbored no particular ill will is particularly powerful. After reconstructing the chain of events, Fanon provides a very subtle analysis of how this act triggers an extreme state of depersonalization during which the young man is haunted, for an extended period of time, by two women figures. Fanon's catalogue of the disorders associated with the aftereffect of torture is also noteworthy, especially when one considers the date of its publication. It is an early antecedent to the steady stream of reports that have spanned the intervening decades, starting with Argentina in the 1970s and ending with Bosnia, that have exposed the psychological consequences of torture, murder, and rape. Post-traumatic psychological syndromes are widely acknowledged today, and in the rich and advanced nations of Europe, there is a whole spectrum of centers specializing in every kind of trauma. But in the 1960s and for many years thereafter, the psychological consequences of the trauma incurred by the generations who had suffered or inflicted the acts of terrible violence associated with the Algerian War was buried in an absolute silence. As psychiatrists, this damage was our daily fare, and no one was more aware of it than Fanon. It was of the utmost importance to him to include this dimension of the war, even in an unpolished form, in this his last book and final statement.

The censor-defying *Les Damnés de la Terre*, appearing around the time of Fanon's death, caused quite a stir. Its reception in France ran the gamut; it was praised in some quarters and vehemently criticized by, among others, the leftist media. The critics, in addition to pointing out that the book lacked an economic plan, reproached Fanon for his attack on Europe, for embracing a peasant model, for his violence and his humanist idealism. The response the book was eliciting was also viewed as disturbing. The French press applauded Fanon's exposure of the failures of the national bourgeoisie as remarkable, but it responded with great reticence, and in some cases virulence, to what it viewed as his espousal of the peasantry, to the important role he attributed to violence, and to his antagonistic stance toward Europe. Newspapers of the Right described the book as a call for hate. Gilbert Comte, writing in *La Nation française*, spoke of a "Mein Kampf de la décolonisation."[5] Leftist publications included the total endorsement of Fanon's views by *Les Temps modernes* as well as the much less enthusiastic response written by Jean-Marie Domenach for the journal *Esprit*.[6] Domenach, while conceding his admiration for Fanon, pointed out that Europeans were simply the last in a long line of colonizers and that, when all was said and done, the colonized had learned a lot from Europe. Had not Europe elevated universalism as the highest standard and was it not responsible for the idea of a free humanity? He wrote, furthermore, that he found it difficult to subscribe to the idea of decolonization as a time of total *disorder*. He admitted that violence may be at times a necessary tool of resistance, but, in the end, it could only backfire on itself. The true tools of liberation, he concludes, were work and language.[7] Jean Lacouture, who contributed to the tribute to Fanon published in *Présence africaine*, wrote an indignant review in *Le Monde*. He expressed a profound disagreement with positions that espouse peasant revolts, red *Chouan* rebellions, a return to the land, an attempt to found a civilization based on violence and race, a disdainful attitude toward the history of a people for whom colonization by the West is, after all, just a stage: "Sooner or later, the new nations will have to reverse the various phases of their history—primitivism, feudalism, imperialism, dissociation, regrouping and finally colonization—instead of furiously fixating on this latest phase and casting the responsibility for all their ills on their most recent foreign invaders."[8] Jean Daniel also expressed reservations. Like Memmi and Fanon, and unlike Jean Lacouture, he had firsthand knowledge of the colonial situation, and his review in *L'Express* was, on the face of it, full of praise. He saluted Fanon's magnanimity and humanism, but he disagreed with Fanon's position with respect to Europe and with what he described as his "theory of violence." He faulted him for transposing a psychological model of violence, which he conceded had some applicability, onto a political canvas. There can be no possible transposition from one domain to the other, he writes.[9] Nghe N'Guyen, a Vietnamese Communist writing in *La Pensée*, would have similar objections and criticize Fanon for entertaining a residual existentialist and subjectivist vision. He reproached Fanon for moving, without any sign of transition, from the political and historical sphere to the individual one, when, in fact, the violence of class struggle was pragmatic and structural, not existential. N'Guyen, expanding on this Marxist view, pointed out that while the solidarity and importance of the rural masses to the armed struggle could not be underestimated, the peasantry did not automatically qualify as a revolutionary force. Their "political and ideological education" needed to be ongoing if they were to retain an active political role in the aftermath of the armed struggle. Without the guidance of the working class, the rural masses "are sure to succumb to the influence of the bourgeoisie," or what's worse, "supply troops to feudal leaders, through the intervention of religious sects." N'Guyen was even more disapproving of Fanon's denunciation of Europe. Europe, after all, had been responsible for the invention of democracy and socialism and for the creation of new technologies, he wrote, taking Fanon to task. To reject its values and technologies is to risk "playing the game of those who brandish traditional values in order to obfuscate a political system that is reactionary through and through."[10] N'Guyen's criticisms, drawn from an actual knowledge of the colonial situation, armed struggle, and the aftermath of independence in Vietnam, would have been very relevant to Fanon, if he had, in fact, written the things he was being accused of writing.

Fanon had never called the achievements of modernity into question. What's more, his book was not addressed to Europe. While Europe is admittedly not absent from the work—difficult to imagine how it could have been—Fanon's quarrel was not with an idealized Europe; he had no interest in changing Europeans. He was not making a case for the Third World as the wellspring of revolution in the West, as many European Third World sympathizers had done in the sixties. Even Francis Jeanson believed that the Algerian Revolution would bring about socialism in France. Fanon was never a Third World supporter in this sense. Even when he urged his fellow

Africans to work toward the creation of a New Man who would not take the dehumanizing technical spirit of Europe as his own, the idea that Europe's revolution would come from the South never entered his mind. If this problem had ever interested him, it certainly had stopped doing so by this point.

As to his purported espousal of the peasants—it must be remembered that Fanon was writing from his direct experience on the ground. The efforts at decolonization of urban-based Algerian nationalist parties organized according to the metropolitan model had repeatedly failed. These parties, furthermore, were plagued by schisms and rivalries. The bourgeois, petit bourgeois, and emerging proletariat that constituted Algeria's urban minority were generally more ambivalent toward the colonial enterprise than their counterparts in the countryside. Despite the fact that these urban classes were constantly being stripped of their rights and dignity, deprived of their culture and language, consigned to a subaltern status, they were also generally accommodated by the system, and the colonial administration was able to integrate them at different levels of its organization and assign them to emblematic positions. This was the case of the *Bachagas* on whom the colonial administration depended. The Algerian peasants, conversely, did not stand a chance of being integrated into a colonial world whose identity depended on their exclusion. At the height of the crisis inside the national parties, breakaway sectors that reached out to the peasantry quickly realized that these neglected *fellahs* were ready to revolt. The conditions for launching, if not a revolution, at least a war of liberation appeared to be in place. Fanon was less interested in glorifying the rural masses than in relating a historical account of the facts. The dynamism of the peasantry and the lumpen proletariat, he wrote in "Spontaneity: Its Strength and Weakness," can ally itself with "revolutionary as well antirevolutionary" aims.

People also took exception to Fanon's discussion of violence. Even readers such as Azoulay responded with shock to the book. Azoulay spoke of the great distance he suddenly felt toward Fanon, his mentor and teacher, the one he had so loved and admired. This condemnation of the book was due, in part, to the foreword that had been written by Sartre. When Fanon read the foreword in late October, he reportedly did not say a word.[11] In 1967, Josie playing the part of the difficult widow to the hilt, insisted, for the wrong reasons, that the foreword be dropped.[12] Beautiful and violent as it may have been, Sartre's foreword had, in a sense, betrayed Fanon. After stipulating that the book was addressed to the Third World, Sartre proceeded to write mostly about Europe. More significantly, he justified violence whereas Fanon had analyzed it and not promoted it as an end in itself but as a necessary phase. Sartre, who had wanted to please his friend, in fact, wrote a foreword that distorted Fanon's tone and intention. Writing in powerfully imagistic prose, Sartre depicted colonial violence as well as its inevitable reversal that "is neither sound and fury, nor the resurrection of savage instincts, nor even the effect of resentment: it is man re-creating himself" (TWOE, 18). This assertion of what this violence is *not* smacks of denial. Is Sartre speaking to his own doubt? In the early years of the Algerian War, he had effectively distanced himself from the increasingly violent direction the Algerian insurrection was taking. He also qualified Fanon's relationship to violence: "Moreover, you need not think that hotheadedness or an unhappy childhood have given him some uncommon taste for violence; he acts as the interpreter of the situation, that is all" (TWOE, 13). Here again the impulse is to deny, as though Sartre at some moment in time had indeed attributed these personality traits to Fanon. Furthermore, sentences like "read Fanon: you will learn how, in the period of their helplessness, their mad impulse to murder is the expression of the natives' collective unconscious" (TWOE, 16) diminish the scope of Fanon's ideas because they seem to argue not for violence but for murder pure and simple. We are, here, in the realm of criminality, and the focus has shifted away from violence as a means of human reassertion for human beings whose humanity has been denied. These departures, in all likelihood, reveal something about Sartre's own relationship to violence; writing from a safe haven, sheltered from extreme circumstances, Sartre displaces the conflict onto another register, namely, language. By his own admission, he allows himself to be swept by a torrent of words. Fanon, however, is speaking of an altogether different kind of violence. Those who fault him for applying existential considerations to political scenarios forget that the violence he describes is the violence leveled by societies at individuals, barring them from being and stripping them of the possibility of becoming themselves. This violence is a commonplace of the powerless everywhere. Even at birth, the outcome of this primal violence depends on the receptivity of the environment. The newborn's sudden death or anorexia, attributed to ill health and mourned in our democratic societies, also pertain to this order of violence, a violence that is experienced and withstood within the self and determines who will live and who will not. Violence is an appeal, a desire for change awaiting a response. Few today would argue with the idea that the foundational violence of a society extends to individuals within that society and that the refusal to admit this legacy can result in even greater violence. There is little doubt that it is far more manageable to consider this violence as it manifests itself in individuals, to concur that a child who has been mistreated and violated may grow up to subject others to the same violence; societal violence, even in societies that are not officially at war, poses a far greater challenge. How does a violent society respond to those who, as a result of its violence, have lost all sense of self and whose only resource to affect a change is violence? Are we not guilty, even now, of singling out the allegedly symmetrical violence of the Albanians against the Serbs as inhuman and an affront to civilization while we overlook the violence of Serbian militias who have yet to acknowledge or be held accountable for their criminal actions?

Fanon's interpretation of violence refers first and foremost to a specific societal and colonial context in which manifest violence operated on many fronts: aside from economic oppression and exclusion from the agora, it targeted the collective and the individual to deny them their history and language, going so far as to deny them the right to language by refusing them admission to the space of language; allowing purported negotiations only so as to improve its abilities to repress and infiltrate; eradicating the spaces of language and leaving no other recourse but violence as the sole means of defending against and putting an end to violence. Fanon extended the interpretation to include any society that deprives its members—especially the dispossessed—of their authentic voice as a society whose violence drives those it excludes to violently reclaim their self-expression. To attribute this violence to an individual temperament is to miss the point entirely.

Fanon may not explicitly refer to the writings of Freud—*Totem and Taboo, Moses and Monotheism, Why War?*—but he does concur, in his own way, that the one who possesses power, women, and wealth does not step down of his own accord. He has to be put to death if the society of equals that Freud would have qualified as democratic is to occur.

We can speak, therefore, of a liberating violence but not of the purifying violence that has been attributed to Fanon by many of his interpreters. What is at stake here is not purity but humanity, the possibility of coming up with a new way of being. Purity was never one of the goals of violence as Fanon understood it; the category, itself, would have been alien to him. The words purity and purification rarely appear in his writings and are not part of his habitual terminology. The revolutionary moralist he sought to advance was light-years away from the notion of purification. Those who knew him, including myself, never heard him speak of purity, not even "revolutionary purity." He did not consider violence as a purifying or even cathartic force. Even in strictly psychiatric terms, Fanon had his doubts about the value of catharsis. "It may be a release, but it does not confer freedom," he would say. Was this not precisely his point in his discussion of the shortcomings of the muscular orgies associated with trance states? The significant thing for him consisted in confronting the violence that impedes being, appropriating it in an act of desubjugation, and turning it against the oppressor, especially when the historical conditions were such that the space of language had been obliterated. He did not see violence as the endpoint but as the engine of liberation, a mechanism whereby the self could be freed from the colonizer and all those who appoint themselves as living gods.

The place from which Fanon chose to write his book and the prose of *Les Damnés de la Terre*, qualified as "impossible to classify" by some and as "lyrical" by others, have not been an overriding or overt object of criticism. I would remind those who fault Fanon for not writing in a demonstrative mode and for sacrificing objectivity and efficiency in the interest of an unconventional style that he introduces a language that arises out of the body in motion, out of intentionality. The human being is judged not only by the efficacy but also by the motivation of his acts. The remark, "witness the results" follows from the same logic; it is the mirror image of the "one need only" that he lambastes in *Les Damnés de la Terre*. To accuse Fanon of voluntarism and reproach him for enunciating what should be, what could be, as, in fact, being, is to betray an inability to accede to a certain mode of thinking and to align oneself entirely on the side of realism, efficiency, and objectivity. For Fanon, the intention behind the act, the movement toward the act was as valuable as the outcome in the subject's evolution toward freedom.

This book, which was the object of a rather negative reception in France and a markedly better one in Africa and black America, was written as a warning to the nations of the Third World. It also raised the alarm about a world that was becoming increasingly technological and unequal, a fact to which we can attest today. Does the privilege of hindsight suggest the obsolescence of its vision? Did it not reveal the methods as flawed and as unequal to preventing the renewed rise of barbarism?

After

While Algeria forgets, and Fanon is relegated to a difficult past, France represses; decolonization and Third World solidarity become things of the past and take Fanon with them. Third World interest remains undiminished: Fanon's work is turned to advantage. A positive response in the United States: Fanon finds a following in black America. Fanon makes a comeback in the Antilles in the 1980s.

From July 1962 until June 1965, Fanon's presence continued to be felt in Algeria under Ben Bella's leadership. These were the years during which Algeria opened its doors to African, Haitian, and African American political dissidents. These were also the years of *Révolution africaine*, the journal where Josie Fanon worked. An atmosphere of political effervescence could be felt on university campuses, and a sweeping, albeit disorganized, plan of agrarian revolution was in the works. Fanon was frequently commemorated. Frantz Fanon Day was instituted to mark the first anniversary of his death; Ben Bella, then president of the Algerian Republic, inaugurated the event by paying homage to "the brilliant psychiatrist, the comrade-in-arms and guiding figure who delegated us a doctrine that will guarantee the success of the Algerian Revolution!"[1] All the same, the Constitution that had already been drawn up did identify Islam as the state religion, and an openly Muslim-based code of nationality had been voted in. The women who had fought in the resistance returned to their homes, and those who had been better off to start with went back to running their businesses. They stayed away or were discouraged from a political arena that bore little resemblance to the one they had fought for.[2] Now and again, a quote by Fanon would crop up in admission examinations for students who were seeking entry to a variety of management schools and programs. With the advent of Houari Boumedienne, Fanon commemorations were a rare occurrence, and by the time Chadli Bendjedid took power, they were seriously on the wane.

It must be conceded that the HPB continued to bear his name. But the hospital quickly lost almost all semblance to the institution for sociotherapy Fanon had tried to create. According to Professor Bakiri, the current head physician at Blida,[3] there was a short period during which a team of Cuban physicians tried to salvage the therapeutic program that Fanon had implemented and to revive interest in the farm as a part of that program. "The farm had become a place where 'one' could stock up on supplies, and the 'patients' were no longer involved in any way whatsoever. I wanted to put an end to the situation." He relinquished the farm to the State. Bakiri also informed me that not even one medical report in Fanon's hand—Fanon was not an avid writer of reports, but he did write some—or, more significantly, not a single exemplar of the minutes that were kept of the daily meetings had been found in the hospital archive. Other psychiatrists, Jean-Louis Poisson-Quinton as well as other *coopérants* who worked at the HPB in 1970 and 1971, tell a different story. It seems that some documents were saved in the nick of time from a wrecking crew, including part of the correspondence between Fanon and the hospital's director as well as a number of placement reports, known as *placements d'office*, dating from the turbulent days of 1956. But aside from a handful of commemorative gestures, not much has survived from that period in the history of the HPB. Most of the players are long gone or have scattered to other places; there has been no real effort to track them down or to retrace this slice of history, which like so many others has not been recorded or transmitted to the new generations of post-Independence Algerians.

There is a boulevard as well as a high school for girls that bear the name of Frantz Fanon. Young people, for the most part however, know next to nothing about him; a very representative young girl at the high school that bears his name ventured that "he must be some kind of French general, I bet." Even though his books continued to be widely available in bookstores, by the 1970s, most people, if we exclude academics and their students, did not have a very clear idea what he stood for. People who do read him are convinced, to a degree that Fanon, himself, could never have anticipated, that "The Pitfalls of National Consciousness" is an accurate portrayal of what Algeria has become. He was becoming a troublesome legacy, however, inside official political circles where collective accountability and adminis-trative collegiality were long forgotten. Oil revenues were now being used to pacify the population, and with the exception of a handful of diehard uni-versity professors, Fanon's message had given way to the omnipresent shadow of the military security forces. Even in Marxist circles, especially among the old guard of the Algerian Communist Party, Fanon had more or less become irrelevant. Some people in the universities were still interested in his works, but he had ceased to serve as an inspiration or a point of refer-ence for the situation in which the country now found itself. Moreover, Fanon was not a Communist, and in the eyes of the old school Algerian Communist Party, his itinerary was extremely atypical and had nothing to do with their history, past or present. The official leadership was irked by his atheism and by his views on women, his belief that their liberation was as pressing as that of men—a position he would argue in both *Studies in a Dying Colonialism* and in *The Wretched of the Earth*. Fanon, they claimed time and again, had underestimated the power of Islam. Would it not be more accurate to say that he had intentionally underestimated it? That, for him, the creation of the nation would have resulted in the cultural evolution of Islam? Envisioning Islam as a political force organized into parties was an unthinkable proposition during his lifetime. One should also note that the Algerians he had come in contact with during the struggle, even the devout ones, did not consider Islam as a source of revolution. They may have de-fended its moral values and may have relied on them as a means of persua-sion and to impose order in the *maquis*, but the operational ideas behind their motives and their rhetoric were democracy and social and economic reform. Even their relationships to other Arab countries were tenuous; they were restrained with the Gulf countries and angered by Egypt's claim that it had played an influential role in Algeria's Revolution. They were Algerians first and foremost, and that's how they wanted it, just as the Palestinians would later see themselves as Palestinians first. That the Constitution de-clared Islam as the official state religion struck most of them as an unavoid-able corollary, but the decision to base the Constitution on Islamic founda-tions did not really reflect the attitude of the times; even when the Evian accords were being drawn up, the key issues had been the "economy," "oil," "minorities," and "nationalities."[4] In point of fact, we shall never know if the Constitution would have declared "a state whose religion is Islam" if, in the immediate aftermath of Independence, the matter had been put to a na-tional vote. Throughout the seven years of struggle, in the cities as well as in the countryside, the concerns, in those times of great upheaval, had al-ways been of a different order. How do we rebuild our villages, recuperate our lands, raise our children in dignity, have access to hospitals and medications? These were the concerns, and as someone who returned to the region as early as March 1962,[5] and had opportunity to have substantial contact with the modest majority, I can attest to this firsthand. (I realize, of course, that a single testimony has its limits and partialities.) In July 1962, when the women of the Casbah, fearing the threat of civil war, took to the streets of the capital shouting "seven years is enough," the idea that they had to stay inside their houses or wear their veils outside them was not prevalent in their minds; as a matter of fact, many of them forgot to wear their veils on that day. Thirty years later, Karima Berger, an Algerian Muslim who was an adolescent at the time, speaks with the privilege of hindsight about a missed opportunity "In the name of God the Clement and Merciful, Algeria shall be a Democratic Republic founded on individual freedom and social justice, on total respect toward different ethnic groups and on the equality of all citizens regardless of religion or race."[6] In 1962 Algiers, Algerian Muslims, across class lines, were not expecting the massive exodus of Europeans and Jews.

The official discourse has repeatedly emphasized the importance of minimizing the influence of Fanon, whose international renown, especially in the West, annoys the Algerian leadership. After all, he was neither Arab nor Muslim, not even an Algerian for goodness' sake. And the general line became something like this: "Fanon owes his experience and the opportunity to develop his ideas to the Algerian Revolution. He owes much more to it than it does to him. And while he may have been a devoted militant and acquired a certain stature, he did not influence our leaders in any way and has never been a theorist of the Revolution." Fanon's aspirations never included becoming a theorist of the Algerian Revolution. Not to mention that in those days I never came across anyone who was a *theorist of the Revolution.*

Irene Gendzier writes that the representatives of the Algerian leadership she met with in 1971 consistently sought to avoid any discussion of Fanon's political ideas, to deny any influence he may have had on the leadership—especially on Ben Bella and Boumedienne—to protect the pure Algerian character of the revolution.[7] They seemed annoyed, she reports, by Fanon's popularity in the West, especially in the United States, that "bastion of imperialism." While we may grant that the Algerians were reluctant to discuss internal affairs with a foreigner who was American, no less, the conclusions arrived at by Gendzier strike me as being very much on the mark. The official line was certainly not shared by everyone but differing views did not have too many means of expression at their disposal. Much later, in December 1987, a significant decision was made to hold an international conference on Frantz Fanon in Algiers. It is worth mentioning that the conference took place during a period of great discontent and that six months afterward the 1988 riots took place. Despite being violent and disorganized, these youth riots that the Islamists tried to co-opt and the State tried to stamp out did manage to raise a brief hope for the democratization of Algerian society. Although the Conference did finally take place in 1987, it cannot be forgotten that Manville and others in the Antilles had been working hard since 1982 to resurrect Fanon from oblivion.[8]

Curiously, the "forgetting" of Fanon in Algeria coincided with a similar response in France, albeit for different reasons. In France, where he was more closely associated to decolonization and Third World solidarity than to questions of race, Fanon became increasingly sidelined to the point of almost disappearing from the debate by the 1970s.

Immediately after his death, the tributes that had been published in the first trimester 1962 issue of *Présence africaine*, combined with the flurry of reviews and responses to *The Wretched of the Earth*, had created an immense stir around Fanon and his work. As far as the European Right was concerned, things were clear-cut: Fanon was the enemy. The Left was in a much more ambiguous and uncomfortable position. Wasn't this book proof of Fanon's blind faith in the Third World? Was it not injudicious of him to cast himself as the apologist of violence? As Maspero would point out in the tribute that was published in *Présence africaine*,[9] the only thing that French readers took away from the book's section on Europe was its ironclad verdict on the violence and failures of European civilization.

In the 1960s, French society viewed the War in Algeria as a closed chapter. Most of the old colonies in Africa were "independent" by then. The history of decolonization was buried, encrypted to be precise. Television had made its massive entry and a culture of consumerism was settling in for the long haul—it mattered little that, in the process, the less fortunate were increasingly being shut out. The subject and history were no longer on the agenda. Structuralism was on the rise and the idea of man as a conscious actor in his own fate in decline. The anti-imperialist and Third World movement that was still in place and had evolved out of the anticolonialist struggle was not politically focused on France. Maspero's publishing house, *La joie de lire*, the *Cahiers libres* collection in which *L'An V* and *Les Damnés de la terre* had been published, the journal *Partisans* that had devoted its third issue to Fanon form an important axis in the movement. While they provide a context for the diffusion of Fanon's ideas, they also create a perception, widely shared by the French public, wherein Fanon's ideas are grouped with those of Che Guevara and Fidel Castro.

In the immediate aftermath of Fanon's death, Lanzmann, acting separately from Jeanson and Maspero, who had a similar project in the works, wanted to publish a book about Fanon, but both projects came to naught.

Maspero had explicitly requested that Jeanson collaborate on a book about Fanon that would also include a selection of excerpts. In the meantime, *Peau noire, masques blancs* was reissued with a new afterword by Jeanson that succeeded in convincing Maspero that his views about Fanon and his work were radically different from Jeanson's. "I must tell you that your Afterword did not include any of the things I was expecting and many, including your wordplay on leukemia, that I was surprised to find, and this is the reason why I do not plan to pursue the project." Maspero tried instead to collect Fanon's unpublished writings, especially the articles that had been published in *El Moudjahid*.

He recalls how difficult it was to compile them. He even traveled to Algeria, where he met with Josie Fanon, who gave the project her approval but who did not have any of the relevant documents in her possession. With her help, they went through *El Moudjahid's* archive and tried to determine which articles Fanon had indeed written. Rheda Malek, who was the Ambassador to Belgrade at the time, forwarded a list of the articles on which Fanon had worked. In keeping with the spirit of the paper, he reminded Maspero that writing for the paper had been a largely collective and anonymous activity. That being said, there were, judging from the style, the favoring of certain expressions and images, articles that gave every impression of having been written primarily by Fanon. Furthermore, there were other articles that he had conceived of but had not written himself, having merely edited and supervised the work of others—"Throughout the liberated zones of Algiers,"[10] written at the end of August 1957, as well as the article on the Christian community and Independence are two that were written in this way.[11] The articles were nonetheless compiled and the collection, though incomplete, was published as *Pour la révolution africaine*,[12] appearing in 1964 as Fanon's last and final work. The book, which received high marks in Africa, was not exclusively *political* in that it retraced Fanon's journey, beginning with "The North African Syndrome" and ending with his writings on the Southern front, and it barely caused a stir in France. By then, there was an overwhelming tendency to view Fanon's work as a reminder of a history of decolonization that France had put behind it and which it felt no longer concerned it. There was, furthermore, an effort afoot to cast Fanon's assessment of this history as a mistaken one, and this view was gaining ground.

In 1970, Fanon's work became the subject of a wave of biographies, or critical essays to be precise, that were all published simultaneously. The first round was British and American: David Caute, Peter Geismar, Irene Gendzier.[13] Geismar's book was never translated into French; the translation of Gendzier's book managed to capture some attention in France but not enough for a second edition. The subsequent round of works written by

Renate Zahar, Pierre Bouvier, and Philippe Lucas drew a limited audience and not one of them resulted in a second printing.[14] Despite Fanon's books being reissued on a regular basis after 1965, despite the increasing perception of *Black Skin, White Masks* as a prophetic essay on racism, despite the high sales (even without the foreword by Sartre) of the 1968 paperback of *Les Damnés de la Terre*, by the 1970s, Fanon had fallen into oblivion, or, as Michel-Antoine Burnier accurately put it in 1971, had been pigeon-holed as a *philosophe maudit*. News about new editions of his works or the appearance of a new biography drew a small response from the likes of Burnier, who in 1971 wrote a piece that appeared in *Le Magazine litéraire* that revisited the reality of the Algerian War and pointed out the applicability of Fanon's analysis of the colonial situation to the situation in which African and European countries now found themselves; there were also articles by Juliette Minces, who had traveled to Algeria in the early days of Independence and who had known many of the writers at *Révolution africaine*. In her review of Irene Gendzier's *Fanon* for *Le Monde diplomatique*, Minces reminded readers that Fanon was not precisely a political theorist and that the main and invaluable purpose of the gaze he had turned on colonial society was the awakening of consciousness.[15] Third World supporters in France had stopped expecting a revolution in Africa. Pascal Bruckner's *Le Sanglot de l'homme blanc* had put an end to that debate. While 1968 may have grown out of the period of self-reflection that followed the end of the colonial wars, it did not draw its impetus from recent events in the Third World. It was preoccupied, rather, by an internal debate and with effecting changes of mentality and mutations in the quotidian within French society, a project which, in all likelihood, would have been very much to Fanon's liking. At the beginning of the 1970s, the Left was primarily focused on China and much more interested in "cultural revolution" than in Fanon's writings. France under Pompidou became France under Giscard. The history of decolonization was buried and forgotten—*la guerre d'Algérie n'a pas eu lieu*. The deaths of Lumumba and of Moumié and the responsibility of the West in these assassinations were consigned to oblivion. This was a denial of history and of the assistance of the United States and the governments of Europe that were behind the emergence of new dictatorships in Africa. Dealings with African countries were conducted at an intrastate level, and as long as there were profits to be had, the principle of noninterference was fiercely defended. The expert studies and reports that recommended funds for nongovernmental African organizations or institutions were carefully stowed away in drawers. The *harkis*, those problematic witnesses to a history that is best left unmentioned, were placed in camps in southern France. Workers from the Maghreb were now being brought in to assist the Portuguese when their numbers became too small to fill the great number of subaltern jobs that are essential to economic success; once more, North Africans were being objectified and manipulated. Their presence is a mere parenthesis, stripped of name, family, history, and language, viewed as a pure instrument of the industrial machine.

Fanon's ideas were seen as belonging to a past that had ceased being relevant to the concerns of the day. The term "Fanonism" that was increasingly being bandied about was, if anything, a mislabeling of his work; his writings were increasingly associated with the importance of spontaneous movements, the idealization of rural, peasant masses and their assimilation of a Maoist model, and subverted as an apology for violence. The label was also a kind of shorthand for humanist idealism, an ideology whose time had passed.

By now, the very person of Fanon had become a disturbing one. The tendency was to explain him away, along with the historical period he had tried to elucidate and that no one wanted to consider anymore; he was viewed as someone who had made not only an ideological miscalculation but a personal one as well. In September 1971, Albert Memmi wrote "La vie impossible de Frantz Fanon," a very long article that was published in *Esprit* and that perfectly captured the tone and mood of France during this period.[16] Why, one wonders, did Memmi choose to write about Fanon? One possible answer is that the two almost invariably appeared side-by-side on the syllabi of American universities. Memmi and Fanon never met. They could have very easily, however: Memmi was from Tunis, a contemporary of Fanon's, and, like him, interested in the impact of the colonial situation on the individual. And even though Memmi's article may have given the opposite impression, the two men never crossed paths. I vividly remember the indignant stupefaction with which I read Memmi's 1971 account of Fanon's "impossible life." In the context of the great silence that typified this period of postdecolonization, I was glad to discover that Albert Memmi had indeed never met Fanon. Before this article, no one—including Jean Ayme, Lanzmann, and even Jeanson (despite the reservations about Fanon's character he may have voiced in the afterword to *Peau noire, masques blancs*)—had felt compelled to write that Fanon had orchestrated his own downfall.

If Memmi had known Fanon, he would never have used the word "rage" in connection with the man. "Enraged, Fanon decided that he wanted to be neither French nor Antillean, but Algerian," Memmi wrote. There is no doubt that Fanon was an angered man, but that's a far cry from the childish rage, the tantrum in the face of being denied the desired object, the infantile impotence, that Memmi attributes to him. These statements could only have been made by a person who did not know Fanon. He continued to write about what he calls Fanon's "self-rejection," his denial of his Antillean roots and of his blackness. One is forced to wonder if this reading of Fanon represents an instance of pure projection on Memmi's part. Memmi, a Tunisian Jew, did not choose to live his life in either Israel or Tunisia and chose to study in France. How do these choices add up to a failure, to a refusal of who one may be? Would it not be more accurate to describe them as a kind of reaching beyond the self? What's more, Fanon never dismissed the Antilles; he was pained by their decision to not opt for the path of decolonization. "Blood Flows in the Antilles under French Domination," one of his last articles for *El Moudjahid*, written in 1961, commemorated the first congress of the Antillean-Guyanese Front. Fanon, who was already ill at the time, had sent a message of encouragement and congratulations in which he expressed all his pride and joy at seeing "the motor of history beginning to turn" on the shores of the Caribbean. With his family and with his friends Manville and Juminer, whom Memmi cites, Fanon shared an affectionate complicity, an intimate Creole language, and a powerful bond. Juminer, who was working as a biologist in Tunis when the two men met up again, went everywhere with Fanon, who was keen on introducing him to his French, Tunisian, as well as Algerian friends. When Olivier met Juminer's son and asked, "is he French?", and his father informed him he was Guyanese, which made the boy then ask, "is he as strong as an Algerian?" and the amused father answered, "he is also very strong." Even Manville, who had wanted Fanon to stay and become part of the Guyanese-Antillean movement and had gone to such lengths to convince him in 1956, supported the choices Fanon had made. In Manville's eyes, it was Martinique that had failed, not Fanon. It would take him twenty years of hard work to get the Martinicans to break their silence on that "traitor" Fanon—traitor to France, not to the Antilles—and honor the man. Memmi maintains that Fanon should have returned and fought in his native Antilles. In addition to pinning him with the ubiquitous badge of "purifying violence," Memmi argues that Fanon, culturally a Christian, was fundamentally out of step with Islamic-Arab culture. The debate about identity that would come into its own and become paramount in the 1970s and 1980s was laid out by Memmi—the project of being exclusively identified with one's origin was at odds with Fanon's conception of what it meant to be a free subject. Fanon was, furthermore, wary of the political and cultural trap implicit in a project of return to origins. No one disputes that he underestimated or tried to ignore the power of Islam, but he was also operating on the assumption that the society was in transition, that identity was in flux and could be guided by the evolution of the situation on the ground—be it in Algeria, the Antilles, or anywhere else. Fanon, furthermore, who had difficulty absenting himself from the gaze of others, never lost sight of his own confrontation with and reflection on negritude. He was attentive to the implicit danger of withdrawal proposed by negritude, which he understood as an essentialist value, a return to the "one and indivisible" origin that is impervious to both time and history. Fanon was apprehensive about the consequences of this mindset. He was, as Guy Sitbon wrote in his tribute, one of the last internationalists.

Édouard Glissant's analysis of Fanon, appearing in the *Le Discours antillais*, is more subtle.[17] Glissant writes that "the most important example of the effect of *diversion* is the case of Frantz Fanon" (CD, 25). *Diversion* is understood as the "ultimate resort of a population whose domination by an Other is concealed: it then must search elsewhere for the principle of domination, which is not evident in the country itself" (CD, 20).[18] "Caribbean intellectuals have exploited this need . . . to find another place: that is, in these circumstances, to link a possible solution of the insoluble to the resolution other peoples have achieved" (CD, 23). The Jamaican Marcus Garvey took the "plight of black Americans" upon himself in the United States. The Trinidadian George Padmore, who inspired the Pan-Africanism of N'Krumah, found himself by N'Krumah's side and stayed there (CD, 24). Glissant describes Fanon's *diversion* as "grand and intoxicating," adding that in Martinique, at the time Glissant was writing his book in 1981, "years go by without his [Fanon's] name (not to mention his work) being mentioned by the media, whether political or cultural, revolutionary or leftist . . . An avenue in Fort-de-France is named after him. That is about it" (CD, 25). Glissant continues by asserting his certitude that Fanon "would no doubt have confronted [the Martinican problem] if he had lived." Glissant adds that

> it is difficult for a French Caribbean individual to be the brother, the friend, or quite simply the associate or fellow countryman of Fanon. Because, of the French Caribbean intellectuals, he is the only one to have *acted on his ideas*, through his involvement in the Algerian struggle. [. . .] It is clear that in this case to *act on one's ideas* does not only mean to fight, to make demands, to give free rein to the language of defiance, but to take full responsibility for a *complete break*. The radical break is the extreme edge of the process of diversion. (CD, 25)

For Glissant, diversion does not exclude the possibility of return. "Diversion is not a useful ploy unless it is nourished by reversion: not a return to the longing for origins, to some immutable state of Being, but a return to the point of entanglement, from which we were forcefully turned away"

(CD, 26). This crossroads, where the original parting of the ways took place, must find its expression. Fanon died too young for us to speculate about the geographies of his life after the 1960s. But, if we understand *return* to mean, as Glissant does, not a homecoming to the point of departure but the ability to express the relationship to that point of departure, then Fanon was well on his way home and even Martinique was within his sights. Still, the problem for Fanon may have had more to do with the in-betweenness and the acceptance and understanding of this in-between state as a necessary condition for anyone seeking to reach the fullness of becoming. "I do not identify with my origin, nor do I deny it, but my trajectory as a subject pushes me elsewhere." Fanon was more of a psychoanalyst than he or we were led to believe. Finally, to qualify Fanon's death as "typically auto-destructive" is to pronounce a trenchant diagnostic that would be unthinkable for any psychoanalyst to utter. Fanon burned his life like many others did at that time, but he lived, made mistakes, rebounded, created, invented.

Peau noire, masques blancs and *Les Damnés de la Terre*, Fanon's first and last books have enjoyed a long life of publication in France and continue to be reissued on a regular basis. The same cannot be said of *L'An V* and *Pour la révolution africaine*, the two works that are more overtly linked to decolonization; their importance has steadily diminished over the years, and 1982 marks the year of their respective last editions. Elsewhere in the world, however, first *The Wretched of the Earth*, then *Studies in a Dying Colonialism* followed by *Black Skin, White Masks* have been translated into numerous languages: Italian, Arabic, English, Japanese, German, Spanish—in some cases, as early as 1962.

As early as July 1962, Giovanni Pirelli, always the unconditional friend, convinced Einaudi to publish and distribute *The Wretched of the Earth* in Italy. In addition to the collection of texts and drawings by children that he had compiled with Charby, Pirelli also put together a book of letters and firsthand accounts from the Algerian War: *Le Peuple algérien et la guerre*; he entrusted the manuscript to Patrick Kessel, who edited it. At first, Fanon had expressed doubt about the project: "These are just little stories, little, personal stories," he had said to Pirelli at the time. But by the time he had started writing *The Wretched of the Earth*, he had a change of heart and conceded that he had been deeply upset by some of the letters. These were all anonymous and mostly written by prisoners in French and Algerian prisons; the editors had made a conscious decision to keep anything that hinted at journalism, literary or official-sounding prose out of the book. In addition to the prison letters and accounts, there were others written from the internment camps, from the major cities as well as the Algerian hinterland,

and a handful from the Algerian community in France. They talk about personal privation and suffering, inscribing these in the collective experience. Published in 1963 by Maspero, the book was greeted with widespread indifference in France. It mattered little that this was the first book to afford a glimpse inside the realities of the Algerian War as told by the people who had endured them. Algeria was a closed and shuttered chapter.

Pirelli, in the meantime, remained committed in his effort to introduce Fanon to Italian readers. After the publication of *The Wretched of the Earth*, he made prompt arrangements for the translation of *L'An V*, and in 1970, he began to work on an anthology of Fanon's writings; this time around, Pirelli wrote a foreword to introduce his own translations of the Fanon texts, which were also accompanied by a relatively exhaustive biographical account. In 1963, he founded a Frantz-Fanon Circle, designed to furnish documents and provide information on African, Asian, and Latin American liberation movements to the relatively uninformed Italian Left. Pirelli, who was in contact with a number of liberation movements, tried, whenever possible, to gather materials that were directly supplied by the movements. The Center published a widely diffused bulletin that was circulated to the entire Left, organized debates to which it invited such notable figures as Amilcar Cabral and Agostinho Neto. It was also an important and early resource in the Italian movement against the U.S. intervention in Vietnam. In 1967, however, the Center and Pirelli, himself, were mired in internal controversy. Pirelli thought that the Center should operate primarily as an archive that would be available to the various parties traditionally associated to the Left, syndicates, students, and the workers movements that were beginning to emerge at the time. Other members, belonging to a small group calling itself the Revolutionary Communist Party, wanted to appropriate the Center as an exclusive organ for their particular ideology and accused Pirelli of intellectualism and academism. In 1968, the Center closed its doors. It was launched anew in 1970, but under a different name and with a newly stated objective to study *socioeconomic structures* in all societies, including Western ones.

When Pirelli died in 1972, Fanon's name disappeared for a second time. Pirelli, who had shared Fanon's ideas about the legitimacy of violence and armed struggle in wars of national liberation, disagreed with their simplistic application to the Italian situation. Fanon had held a similar position during his lifetime. It is impossible to say more, to extrapolate, for example, how Fanon would have viewed the Red Brigade had he lived.

In the United States, where Fanon became known slightly later than in Europe, his influence was and continues to be considerable. *The Wretched of the Earth* was the first of his books to be translated into English, and in 1963, through the intermediary of *Présence africaine*, it was published. Alioune Diop, the journal's editor-in-chief, wrote a letter to Maspero, in which he informed him that Fanon had entrusted him with a copy of the manuscript in order to ensure the book's distribution in Africa and America. Fanon reassured Maspero that his understanding with Diop only involved the English translation. In 1965, a new translation of the book published by Grove Press appeared in the United States. The book made a great impact in black America. White America was not far behind, and the book's reputation as a work of capital importance was quickly established. The book's publication triggered a vast response in the American press. Leaving aside the small number of Beijing-inspired negative articles that took Fanon to task for his lack of realism, the majority of reviewers hailed the book as an important study of colonialism and registered their indignation at the horrors of colonial wars. They also described Fanon's position as nonpartisan, taking neither the side of the East nor the West, and concluded with questions about the nature of the aid that was being distributed to the Third World. They concurred with Fanon that the aid was not a matter of generosity but reparation, and they raised questions about who should get it and to what end. The subject of violence did not strike the same nerve it had in Europe and raised far fewer reservations and less indignation: American society, it seems, was quite aware of its own violence. While America was ready to accept the application of Fanon's main ideological principles, the right of nations to self-governance, for example, it underestimated the subversive power of this idea in relationship to its own society. Nowhere was Fanon's impact more felt than in black American movements of the 1960s. *The Wretched of the Earth*, his other works were not as widely read—some, not at all—became the *Little Red Book* or the Bible as the case may be of black America. It has almost been conclusively ascertained that even before Fanon started working on *The Wretched of the Earth*, both Malcolm X and Robert Williams, the founder of the armed black American revolutionary movement, had met with him in Africa. Fanon also had a major influence on black political organizations, namely the two most important groups: the Black Panthers and the Black Power movements. Whereas the Black Panthers understood the personal dimension of Fanon's involvement in the Algerian struggle, Black Power did not. One of their leaders reportedly claimed in private that "Fanon was the representative of the Caribbean in Algeria." Be that as it may, the important thing was that these movements found themselves reflected in Fanon's writings and that his works served to illuminate their own colonized situation in the United States: how to fight against exclusion and not succumb to negative self-image, how to disassociate from the values imposed by the dominant society and use the struggle as a means to human dignity. Huey Newton and Bobby Seale, the founders of the Black Panthers, viewed *The Wretched of the Earth* as a seminal text. They identified completely with Fanon's assessment of colonialism and described their own situation in America as "domestic colonialism." They believed in the necessity of creating a well-organized party whose main aim would be the raising of consciousness. They followed Fanon's lead and expressed a similar vigilance toward the black bourgeoisie and distanced themselves from the cultural nationalism they perceived as an unavoidable phase but not as an end in itself. They no longer considered the struggle as a straightforward black/white proposition. These were the principles that led to the program that clearly delineated their situation, in a far more incisive manner than the Marxist literature that was being produced by the Third World and with which they were familiar.

Black American movements felt submerged in a dichotomized world ruled by alienation, negritude, and violence. Questions having to do with the inferiorized and negative image of the self, the option of paralysis or violence, and the decision of resorting to cultural nationalism, the negritude of origins that is a necessary but transitional phase in the evolution of consciousness were their daily fare. The idea of using violence as a revolutionary means to put an end to oppression and especially as a conduit for the restoration of dignity also took hold. Malcolm X had already spoken of the "failure of nonviolence," and in 1962, Robert Williams stated that "in the short term, nonviolence will be one day equivalent to suicide. This violence is used in a measured fashion as self-defense and as a means of revalorization. To be able to handle a weapon to defend oneself and not only when fighting alongside the White man." Much as Fanon, this American leadership did not see violence as an end in itself.

A more complete discussion of the influence that Fanon and his work wielded in the United States falls outside the purview of this work. Suffice it to say that in subsequent years Fanon's books continued to be published and translated. *Studies in a Dying Colonialism* appeared in 1965, it was followed in 1967 by *Toward the African Revolution*; that same year saw the publication of *Black Skin, White Masks* by Grove Press. This last book, with its discussion of the position of blacks in a white society, of a politically problematic class struggle, and with its refusal to embrace white values wholesale, also struck a chord in black America. Nor can it be underestimated that this was a book written by a black man whose analysis of what it means to be black was directed to a black audience as well as to a white one. Fanon's influence, though it may give the impression of waning at times, held steady in the United States; his books became a fixture on American campuses; and later, in more politically correct times, his works finally became a mainstay of university curricula. It is difficult to know if this would have pleased Fanon.

The only thing that can be said with any certainty is that Fanon lived his life in a state of perpetual motion and invariably left his texts behind him. By 1955, *Black Skin, White Masks* was far from his mind, and by the time he was working on *The Wretched of the Earth, Studies in a Dying Colonialism* had fallen into a similar oblivion; on several occasions, with respect to *Studies in a Dying Colonialism*, he showed little inclination to act on the initiatives suggested by his publisher. At the December 1987 colloquium in Algiers, the degree to which young black American intellectuals admired and respected Fanon was evident; he had become such a hero in their eyes that they had difficulty believing they were in the presence of people who had actually known him while he was alive. In the end, they simply marveled. As for the distortions that were introduced on that occasion to cast Fanon as a black Lacan—they were the product of pure delusion.

Black Skin, White Masks, hailed in the United States, is the only one of Fanon's works that the Arab world has not deemed necessary to translate. *Studies in a Dying Colonialism* and *The Wretched of the Earth*, have, on the other hand, enjoyed a rich life in the Middle East where they have been used and interpreted to suit the needs and agendas of different periods.

Fanon found especially fertile ground in Iran, where the Iranian intellectual Ali Shariati introduced his works. Shariati, a former student of Berque, is a historian and sociologist who was removed from his post and imprisoned on several occasions in the late 1950s under the Shah. He is committed to Shi'a Islam as a progressive force and to the possibility of investing modernity with traditional Islamic values that have been co-opted by the clergy and dismissed by the West. During his time in France, he read Fanon's works and felt they touched on concerns that were akin to his. Fanon's atheism did not stand in the way of the possibility of dialogue and the ensuing short-lived correspondence that took place between the two men. "Even if I do not share your views with respect to Islam," Fanon wrote,

> I respect your view that in the Third World (and if you don't mind, I would prefer to say in the Near and Middle East), Islam, more than any other social and ideological force, has had an anticolonialist capacity and an anti-Western nature. I hope that your intellectuals will be able to instill life in the inert and drugged body of the Muslim East so as to raise the consciousness of the people [. . .] in order to found a different kind of man and a different kind of civilization. I, for one, fear that the fact of revitalizing the spirit of sectarianism and religion may result in a setback for a nation that is engaged in the process of becoming, of distancing it from its future and immobilizing it in its past.[19]

Fanon's words of caution did not dissuade Shariati, who was especially keen on promoting Fanon's ideas about challenging the West and creating the possibility for the advent of a new man in the Third World. As early as 1962, he set about translating *The Wretched of the Earth* himself and making arrangements for *Studies in a Dying Colonialism* and the rest of the works to be translated by others. By the time he died in 1977, a mere two years before the Iranian Revolution, Shariati's ideas were omnipresent in revolutionary Iranian circles. Fanon's reputation grew as a consequence of Shariati's popularity. In the early days of the Iranian Revolution, posters bearing Fanon's image and the message that "The chador is a thorn in the eye of Western imperialism" with an additional caption at the bottom that read "our brother Frantz Fanon" began to appear. To the question "who is this Frantz Fanon?", the man on the street in those days would have probably answered: "I don't know, but he is one of us."[20] This vulgarization, instrumentalization even of Fanon's ideas, would, in subsequent years, and certainly by 1981—the year that marks the victory of the conservatives in Iran—lead the powers that be to interpret Fanon's essay "Algeria Unveiled Itself," as a plea for a return to the veil (*Studies in a Dying Colonialism*).

In 1982, Fanon would reemerge in the Francophone world via the Antilles, where Marcel Manville had worked long and hard to ensure the long overdue acknowledgement of Fanon and his contribution. In the spring, an international conference in the form of a memorial was held in Fort-de-France; the roster of participants included people from everywhere, and an especially great number of Caribbean politicians, sociologists, psychiatrists, and psychoanalysts who had gathered to discuss Fanon's writings.[21] Concurrently, *Sans frontière*[22] published a special issue that compiled first-person accounts by Joby Fanon, Manville, André Mandouze, Mongo Beti, Mario de Andrade, N'Krumah, Mannoni, Jeanson and Ben Bella. "Fanon was not a Che Guevara, and we should not turn him into a Camus," Ben Bella wrote. "He was a committed intellectual who shared the same responsibilities of other Algerian intellectuals: Benhabylès, Lacheraf, Omar Oussedik, Redha Malek, and Ben Yahia." After the memorial at Fort-de-France, a Frantz Fanon Center was created, and plans for a number of subsequent meetings and forums went into effect.

There would, indeed, be other meetings—Brazzaville in 1984,[23] and Algiers in December 1987.[24] But Fanon was no longer present to answer, explain, expand. . . . His work belonged now to its readers and to their times in history.

Fanon Today

An unresolved destiny. A child of the times. A mind in action and restoring the tragic. Fanon's fears corroborated by political developments. Where do Fanon's ideas on violence, shame, and the real stand today? Fanon, language smuggler.

To imagine the country, the context, the circumstance, and the personal life that would have been Fanon's had he lived is to indulge in pure speculation. Had he stayed in Algeria, which would have been, at least in the immediate aftermath of the Algerian War, the most likely scenario, what kind of influence would he have wielded today? Given his proximity to those in power, would he have been in a position to direct the course of events, or would there have been a point in time when irreconcilable differences would have triggered a complete break? Even as early 1962, one can only guess how he would have reacted to the bloody battle between the OAS and the French army, or, more significantly, to the second autonomous zone that formed inside Algiers and wanted to challenge the OAS and also take control of the city, acting quickly to make the most of the power struggle that the leadership in Tunis had predicted. His friend Omar Oussedik, following in the footsteps of his relative Boualem Oussedik, had already joined the second autonomous zone. The two, former members of the old guard of *Wilaya* 4, were determined to return to Algeria as soon as possible and reestablish their connection inside the country. Fanon who, throughout it all, had paid close attention to developments inside the country probably would have applauded their decision. But what would he have made of the civil war between the Tlemcen group and the Tizi-Ouzou group?[1] It is more than likely that he would have supported Ben Bella's ascent to power, at least at the beginning—his revolutionary values did not demand that he be a legitimist—but his approval probably would not have extended to the party's role in the proceedings. Would he have supported Boumedienne's July 1965 coup d'état? Would he have assented to serve as an ambassador to an African nation? A number of young militant intellectuals, Rheda Malek, Ben Yahia, and many others, were sent to represent Algeria in the various corners of the globe. Or would he have acquiesced, at Che Guevara's request—who had never met Fanon but who had read his books with passion—to play a part in Cuba?

Two things remain certain. At least on a part-time or temporary basis, he would have most certainly resumed his psychiatric work because he valued his relationship to the mentally ill whose physical suffering touched him profoundly and because he was driven by a desire to do his part to help relieve alienation. He had a score to settle with what had passed for psychiatric medicine in colonized Algeria. He was committed to putting his ideas to the test, to implementing his plan for decentralization, to increasing the number of open clinics, to supervising the training of qualified nurses. Would he have succeeded? It is difficult to say, given the grim lack of a trained personnel and a system in which professional qualifications counted far less than other factors and where initiatives for change were frequently brought to a standstill. Psychiatry, furthermore, does not rely entirely on technical capacities, in the way of, say, surgery or radiology, and Fanon would have wanted to pursue his research on other forms, both old and new, of violence and alienation.

The second certitude is that he would have continued to write. He would have written in French, and his writings would have come out of his experience, because regardless of whether it was his life, or his actions, or his writings, there had always been only one Fanon. The attempt to apprehend him under his diverse facets—the Antillean, the Algerian, the psychiatrist, the writer—belies the profound unity of his person. He would have continued to write and to ask questions about the evolution of events. Could he have affected developments in Algeria, in Africa? It is impossible to determine what political impact he may have had. There is little doubt that some would have listened, but would it have been enough?

Though worthy, these questions, like the hypothesis of Fanon's return to the French Antilles, belong to the realm of fiction. The truth is that Fanon was dead before his time, and for those of us who knew him, he and his message, his call to conscience and for a vigilance of mind and body, remained forever young. To reflect and proceed, to act and think—this, more than anything, is what young people who read Fanon today identify with, even before understanding the substance of his ideas. Above all else, they are susceptible to his call for motion. They do not see him as an ideologue or a political theorist but as an idea on the move. Furthermore, because his writings reengage the tragic, restoring it as a dimension of human experience, he is able to cut to the quick of their innermost and most inadmissible questions. They carry this tragic dimension as well as the prospect of overcoming it within them, despite French society's refusal to entertain such considerations.

At the age of thirty-six, an age which today would qualify as the beginning, a man's life was cut short, and a body of work that grew out of a profound ability to experience the world and internalize that experience was stopped in its tracks. Meditations on this experience were spurred by an embodied understanding of oppression and violence, even when it does not appear to be the case. Fanon lived his experience; he internalized and pondered racial, political, and cultural oppression, and revealed the continuity between the human body and the body politic; identifying the bottomless alienation and the violence that perpetuated it and resulted in the depersonalization of individuals and entire peoples, he searched for ways to reverse it, to furnish new points of reference. This is what was at the heart of Fanon's work, at the center of his life and actions, outweighing any and all political contingencies.

It is, nonetheless, true that these meditations are rooted in a specific Cold-War era, a history of colonization and national liberation movements, and the violent demise of colonial and imperial certainties. They hark back to a political climate when the lawful State resorted to repression, police brutality, and prison sentences, as it did in the heart of Paris on October 17, 1961, to suppress anticolonial militancy. Those times, or so we are told, are behind us, accounted for even in history textbooks. The forewords and epilogues that accompany the new editions of *Black Skin, White Masks* and *The Wretched of the Earth* account for them as well. The pages of these books bristle with warnings. Already, in his epilogue for *Black Skin, White Masks*, Francis Jeanson had registered his disappointment in the new Algeria. This independence was not at all what he had envisioned; the new epilogue, unlike the 1952 foreword, is outspoken about its ambivalence toward Fanon, going so far as to find him excessive even in the manner of his death. Much more recently, Gérard Chaliand, bent on distancing himself from *The Wretched of the Earth*, wrote that except for the "analysis of the trauma of the colonized, who rely on an auto-gratifying violence to free themselves, and the discussion of African national bourgeoisies," the ideas are as "remote and out-of-step" as Ferhat Abbas's 1936 statement that the Algerian nation does not exist. Chaliand, to his credit, has tried to situate the writing of *The Wretched of the Earth* in its historical context, but he maintains that Fanon was mistaken in his idealization of mass mobilization and allowed himself to be deluded about the FLN. He urges us to look no further than where things stand in Algeria today. He, nonetheless, adds that Fanon's optimistic voluntarism is the stuff of dreams, and while "the level-headed [. . .] stay at home," "the stimulating function of utopias is one of the engines of history." There is little doubt that at the level of realpolitik, Fanon made mistakes, as when he picked Roberto Holden over Amical Cabral and overestimated the power of popular movements over that of bureaucracies, engrained regionalism, and other weighty considerations. But—and I hope that this short essay has demonstrated as much—he was quite lucid with respect to the leadership of the FLN, its heterogeneity, its lack of a real revolutionary program. When he wrote *Studies in a Dying Colonialism* and "The Pitfalls of National Consciousness," he was also addressing Algerians. Were not the French militants who had idealized Algeria equally at fault for holding on to their extreme, albeit hazy, illusions? I am thinking of certain *pieds-rouges*, who, arriving between May and September 1962 to find a devastated country in the grip of severe setbacks, were not deterred from their dream of turning Algeria into a model of revolution, and an exportable model at that.

Dream for dream, does it not fall to the intellectual to express the contradictions of the real without necessarily resolving them? Is it not also the intellectual's function to fan the dream of that which is possible, of the creative utopia that is not the same thing as illusion, if we understand the latter to mean a complex of suggestions to which one clings in order to avoid self-awareness. Our epoch abounds with examples of illusion: the promise of eternity, the reproduction of sameness, the end—thanks to biological and technological advances—of human incompletion. Illusion can provide a temporary structure, in time and space, for all and sundry in their encounter with the world, with the other of this world. The creative utopia, the dreamy utopia in whose service Fanon had tirelessly labored to the delight, enthusiasm, or annoyance of those who knew him belongs alongside it.

Leaving aside Fanon's analysis of the contradictions of the real and his effort to make the possible imaginable, are his conclusions, including those about violence, as obsolete as some would have us think? Politically, the world has lived up to the fears against which he warned. Take Algeria as an example. It is led by a patriot who fought in the war of independence; it has a single political party that is depleted of content, bureaucratized, bowing to orders from the top; it has a regime bolstered by its army and police, lacking

parliamentary institutions, incapable of controlling corruption and even fa-
cilitating it; a blighted agricultural resource has been discarded for the
benefit of a deficient industrialization program that does not see beyond oil
revenues; there is evidence of an alibistic or muzzled intelligentsia; there is
the invention of a heroic past that is not subjected to scrutiny of any kind, a
false past based on exclusion from the agora and on the myth of historical
homogeneity that will bar generations to come from recuperating the traces
of their history; there has been a mishandled Arabization of the educational
system that is often mistaken for its Islamization; and finally, one sees the
dwindling minorities and the flouting of human rights, despite the noble
promises that were made at Fanon's graveside. Is this not the sum of everything that Fanon had feared and foretold? Did he not warn about these very
consequences? Any political system that severs individuals from their history and memory, that assigns them trumped up origins, forbids them to express the complexity of their identity and identification, and prevents them
from being the actors of their political future will eventually be faced with
violence, erratic or organized as the case may be. Fanon wrote about the re-
lentlessness of a narrative that is relegated to oblivion until it is time for it to
unfold, to play out the final act before the eyes of powerless spectators. The
past ten years in Algeria serve as a tragic illustration of this, and those who
had known Fanon, or had carefully read his works, were in a position to understand these events as they were unfolding.

In 1981, Édouard Glissant, the Martinican writer and intellectual, wrote
that Fanon had wanted to come up with a universal theory of colonization,
but the theory, he argues, begs to be updated, but what parameters does he
use to qualify the Antillean situation? Glissant denounces the political parties modeled on the French template and the bourgeoisie he describes as
"crumb-picking profiteers." He also states that while there is no system of
autonomous production, all artisanal trades have been dismantled, and there
exists no relationship between the population and the economic system that
is totally out of its reach. Furthermore, the Martinican nation, subjected to
muffled but persistent racism, is periodically shaken by uncontrollable and
violent eruptions that, in the absence of a leadership to give them direction,
never go anywhere. In addition to this, there is the emergence of a new form
of alienation, one that did not exist in Fanon's day; namely, a welfare model
in which the social benefits are a direct reflection of those in the metropolis.
The parallels are to be expected, but the foreign aid, in this context, inhibits
the poorer classes from responding in a responsible and collective manner
and becoming active participants in the future of their society. Glissant concludes his summation, by drawing our attention to the psychological misery—not the deep pathologies that express themselves as schizophrenia and

delirium, but the psychological suffering that accompanies privation. After a lapse of twenty years, Glissant's update of Fanon's theory of colonization, written in a prose that is not a jot more modern, reiterates the same parameters stipulated by Fanon and calls on the same need for rupture. Rupture should not be necessarily equated to armed struggle,[2] but its underlying assumption is that the inherent violence of the situation has to be organized, be it as street demonstrations, strikes, or as testimonies of political violence[3] that function as refutations of the inadmissible.

It is equally interesting to listen, after thirty years have elapsed, to the account of Tekeshi Ebisaka.[4] Fanon, he reminds us, was an important figure in social and political movements of the late 1960s in Japan, at a time when the country was swept by the same cultural revolution as the one that swept student movements in the United States and West Germany. This was also the time of the Prague Spring, of Che Guevara and the tough battles he helped wage in Latin America. These were times that were predisposed to the Fanonian message, and this predisposition was particularly apt in Japan, where the student Left carried out violent demonstrations against the Vietnam War that were especially targeted at the presence of the American military bases inside the country. The figure of Fanon would recede in the ensuing years that saw the economic boom that resulted in the social appropriation of the leftist parties and the implementation of a neocolonialist model of exploitation of other Asian nations. But in recent years, this discriminatory society ruled by competition has seen a reemergence of Fanon's ideas. In this technologically advanced society, where every person is expected to be a cog in the machine, even children and adolescents are not spared from the culture of competition and expected to keep apace with a frenzied rhythm of schooling and training, the sole aim of which is productivity and efficiency. These pressures have produced a violent backlash and a society where suicide and, especially, parricide among the young have reached worrisome numbers. Rereading Fanon's work is a way for this society to contemplate anew the possibility of a human being whose *brain* has not been cleaved into separate *muscles*, a human able to participate in every step, from conception to realization, of any undertaking, a human who is entitled to work at a rhythm imposed by his or her own body and not by a principle of productivity that is imposed by bureaucracy, routine, and death.

Ulrich Sarter's account is more or less similar even though it pertains to an altogether different set of circumstances.[5] In Germany, too, Fanon was linked to student and anti-Vietnam War movements. His ideas have resurfaced in a Germany that is realizing that its position is, in the best of cases, a paternalistic one: "You are my brother, but I am much bigger than you." Or one ruled by a culture of fear toward Third World countries: "We have helped them with the money of European wage workers, but there are too many of them, they're going to have too many children." These are arguments that help hasten the weakening of the North-South axis and that stifle European social conflicts and strengthen widespread racism. Fanon's writings, according to Sarter, are especially relevant and enlightening in times like these.

And what is Europe doing, exactly? In what way has it changed its attitude? This Europe has insisted on its place at the table, has refused to be counted out, but what is its role and how does it carry it out? Fanon has shown how both European economic power and guilt-free Western universalism are founded on a principle of exclusion. He also warned against ethnic and religious rivalries. If the law is enforced by "a master, a living god," there will be a descent into uncontrollably violent and self-destructive religious and ethnic rivalry, he wrote. He saw the necessity for a third party. At the end of his life, he was looking for a new place in which to share and develop logos and shared aspirations, a place far removed from the Europe he continued to call out to all the same. What was Europe's reaction to the ethnic and religious rivalries against which he had railed? More often than not it had been reduced to inertia and impotence by the extremity of the violence, but as soon as an opportunity availed itself, it would be among the first to rush in with loan proposals and products to peddle. Europe has agreed to sit at the table as a third player, but under the cover of impotence, it has bent international law to the advantage of the powerful with such frequency that this law has all but ceased to exist.

What are the images and revelations shared by young contemporary filmmakers with moviegoers and television viewers? Audiences are learning that when Sékou Touré rejected internal autonomy, it took France all of 48 hours to pull out of Guinea and that it did not even leave behind the manuals for the operation of the telecommunications and railway systems. That the decision to assassinate Lumumba had been made by the United States and Europe, and that Mobutu's rule in Zaire had the complicity and support of Western heads of state. That Léopold Senghor, whose power was founded on autocracy and repression, was a "political chief" who commanded the respect and admiration of Europe. That the memory of Felix Moumié is kept secretly alive by the youth of Cameroon, and the youth of Zaire want to know why their parents were not free to support Lumumba.[6] In documentary after documentary, Europe's participation is exposed not only in its actions but also in its complicity in the erasure of evidence.

There may be no more colonies, but is the world really all that different from Fanon's portrayal of a mutually exclusive world that has been cleaved in half and where the only interlocutor between both sides is the soldier or the policeman? Is the problem of violence as a self-gratifying act obsolete, behind the times? Has our understanding of violence progressed at all over the past thirty or forty years? The violence has spread, redistributed itself and settled even closer; it has relocated itself out of the colonies and to the great metropolitan centers or their peripheries to be exact. In its new locales it reproduces the same mechanism of two worlds that have been split in half without the benefit of a conduit for truth and with security forces as the sole intermediary. Where do we stand with respect to violence today? We denounce it, while we participate in a society that secretes it in a seemingly milder form that is, in fact, more extreme by virtue of being denied. We denounce, deplore, and condemn it. There may be savages in other parts, but here at home, at the heart of our pacifist societies, inside our supposedly lawful nations—impossible! But is not our refusal to consider violence a refusal to understand it as the site where life refuses to cede to death, to individual or collective death as the case may be? Is it not, as the refutation of a framework, in which the modes of violence may not be so readily apparent but succeed, nonetheless, a means of preventing the subject from reclaiming his or her history, temporality, and future in the society with others? Should we not recognize it as a call for change? A call to which someone has to answer? Not answering with slogans or slick and well-appointed establishments that are deadly and emptied of meaning, but by *answering for*. . . . Answering for oneself and for one's own internalized violence and for one's own limitations. The answer is also in allowing, instead of denying, that historical violence be replayed so that those traces that are shared by all can be identified and elevated to the status of the memory of a potentially universal legacy. No one is more affected in France, today, by this necessity to understand violence, in both its historical and contemporary manifestations, than the descendants of the old colonies, the Algerians in particular. Although colonialism may no longer exist in its explicit and historical form, the effects of its irreconcilable two-partite structure continue to thrive under different guises. The divide between African and Arab, which Fanon discussed at great lengths, must also be addressed and the old conflicts between these two groups revisited. The transmitted imaginary still dictates the African view of Arabs as invaders who dismantled African empires and as stigmatized by their involvement in the slave trade. In the Arab imaginary, Africans are viewed as black, bastardized Muslims outside the ken of civilization. If this piecemeal memory is not afforded the possibility of unfolding, of playing itself out in order to be historicized, then the shorthand of insignias and labels will remain forever affixed.

To speak of the possibility of enactment is to speak of spaces of mediation open to those very actors who have been excluded because of violence.

Open spaces for the dramatization of their history. Fanon used to say that exchanges between a representative of the political power and a peasant enabled the peasant to understand by increments that oppression could wear the face of a black man or a white one, of an Arab or a European. Fanon, working at a specific historical juncture and with the tools that were available to him at the time, was a precursor in his understanding of violence as an expression of the psyche that cannot be ignored: when laws cease to protect, and an exclusive and dominant discourse annuls all bearings, and self-image is forcibly devalued, and the subjective transaction between "mind and body" intercepted, then, there is no choice but to rebuild, beginning with the body, with images, with words, to rally the violent, because violated, self in order to reinscribe it in time and language. Fanon, writing in his time, has already laid out the essential features of this argument. Indeed, when we speak of the violence in the city's outposts, especially when what we really mean are the children of immigrants, many of them from poor, peasant backgrounds, we are speaking of people who have been locked out, banned from the agora. The children of the immigrant bourgeoisie and intelligentsia are able to bridge the gap despite their psychic wounds. They successfully create places of passage because they have not been deprived of their points of reference or of linguistic spaces of negotiation. They identify themselves to the plurality, and they successfully inscribe themselves in the perception of the other; they interject their difference, tackling the problem incrementally—one person at a time—casting themselves as something other than terrifying specters. The heirs of the disinherited, on the other hand, end up in the slums of Nanterre, in the outskirts of Lyon, and, of course, in the projects; they are the ones who have been repeatedly dispossessed,[7] repeatedly relegated to lives of privation, and who, despite it all, have retained their dignity and refused to give up without a struggle. "Where is the line of force, the direction?" Fanon would ask. Where are the symbolic landmarks? What happens to a subject who has to consult two opposing symbolic systems in order to orient him or herself? What happens when these systems are founded on mutual ignorance and reciprocal devalorization and rejection? Paralysis happens or there is violent rupture. Paralysis, of course, may take the form of submission to a cultural schema that has been defined a priori.

With respect to cultural anthropology, Fanon was again light-years ahead of his time. His views diverged sharply from the current regressive ethnopsychiatric approach that leans so heavily on the culturalism Fanon found suspect and always kept at arm's length. The culturalism that is practiced in France today attributes specific mentalities to cultural spheres and engages in the a priori identification of individuals to the cultures to which they purportedly belong, thereby assigning them a preconceived identity. This is a formula that works hand in hand with the prescriptions associated with the *retour identitaire*. Though Fanon, true cultural anthropologist that he was, may have alerted us to the ways in which the oppression that follows from the need for political domination results in the hemming in and "mummification" of a subjugated culture with devastating consequences to the individual psyche; and though the brand of sociotherapy he practiced in Blida may have drawn on referents that were culturally meaningful to his patients, he never accepted the idea of a nexus between specific mentalities and cultures. In those instances when the cultural points of reference had been effaced by the dominant culture, he did not, as ethnopsychiatrists do today, counsel his patients to consult their cultural legacies in order to reconstruct the appropriate symbolic spaces that would furnish a stepping stone to freedom.

Fanon was a tireless militant for the idea of culture in motion and continually altered by new situations. Even as early as his critique of Mannoni, Fanon had argued that that there was no such thing as an intact traditional world, that the transformation was already underway and that this world in transition had to locate its own humanity and universality in its modernity. Conservatives and traditionalists continue to find this reading disturbing. It is too culturalistic for some, too universalistic for others. This double-pronged understanding that seeks to widen the points of reference at the same time that it moves on to something new in order to achieve a potentially universal outcome points, yet again, to Fanon's contemporaneity. His approach is far too universal for psychoanalysts and thinkers who maintain the importance of a return to origins while others fault him for differentiating, for attaching too much importance to cultural difference, not fully realizing, perhaps, that for Fanon this difference provided entry to cultural and historical points of reference that had been delegated to the subject by previous generations. As our century draws to a close, the passage from the particular—not to be confused with individualism—to the universal with the questions it raises about the failure of universal values and the place of the subject as actor has been at the center of the debate that has placed the disappearing subject, on the one hand, and the acting, hence politicized, subject on the other. By progressing from the freedom of the individual to a larger, political freedom, Fanon broached a problem that has never ceased preoccupying our modern societies.

In the field of psychiatry, Fanon's ideas continue to be innovative. Would he have been one of the instigators of antipsychiatry? The answer to this question would have to be "no." Fanon did not think that the cause of mental illness was purely or directly political. The idea that there would be no

schizophrenia, delirium, or even neuroses under different political conditions was not one he entertained. He subscribed to institutional therapy as
François Tosquelles, Jean Oury, Félix Guattari and a handful of others have
understood it. He believed in the efficiency of sites that could function as
stages on which conflicts could be played out, in the mise-en-scène that allowed for the expression of conflicts that had already declared themselves
psychologically as well as for those that had been denied, the ones that had
been edited from the narrative, the more violent, half-remembered errata,
to become organized and acknowledged as conflicts.

In *Black Skin, White Masks*, Fanon chronicles his own experience of the
passage from pain to conflict. He describes how a child reacted to him by
pointing a finger and exclaiming, "Look, a Negro!" He describes the child's
gaze and the initial wave of awe it triggered, followed by the shame, and
then, he remembers "making a scene." In his account, Fanon dwells on the
importance of that gaze and points to shame as affect, or more precisely as
an emotional experience that occurs in between the private and the social,
on the cusp between the psychological and the cultural, linking the intimate
and the public, immobilizing the body whose only wish is to disappear
below ground or achieve transparency, assaulting the integrity of the body
image and robbing it of words. Anthropologists, who resolved the problem
by dividing the world into Christian guilt and the shame of other civiliza-
tions, and psychoanalysts, who are content to attribute the emotion to latent
childhood memories linked to parental images or to conflate shame and
guilt when, in fact, they exist in an antithetical relationship, have only recently started to understand shame in a different way. Shame is a reflection
of the temporary or permanent dissolution of social ties, a rupture of subjective continuity that results in a confused self-image and in the loss of spatial and temporal bearings and makes the collapse of prior investments seem
imminent. Guilt, on the other hand, related to the internalized self and its
endless pursuit of fantasy, does not endanger the integrity of the subject and
his or her social integration. The guilty are able to think, to imagine, that
they have a hand in their own fate whereas shame is always linked to a situation outside the self, often pertaining to the gaze, that results in humiliation and impotence. In the 1950s, Bruno Bettelheim had a difficult time
convincing his fellow psychoanalysts of the importance of understanding
the centrality of shame in the experience of deportees. He failed to persuade
his colleagues that the experience of being subjected to a gaze that divested
one of humanity and to a physical and psychological violence that used any
means necessary to reduce one to an abject state was a shameful one that
stripped away subjectivity, and it could not be addressed by way of resurfacing childhood images.

In the past fifteen years, and especially in the past year or so, the topic of shame has become an increasingly important subject of study, to which even psychoanalysts are paying attention. Shame is no longer consigned, as had been the case in the 1950s, to an existential status derived from the philosophy of the subject and phenomenology. There has been a steady stream of conferences and publications on the topic because shame, in much the same way as violence, now occupies an incontestable place in the psychopathology of everyday life, especially in contemporary French society. The *shame* of the 1980s has given way to the *hate* of the 1990s; in youth lingo, the sentiment is expressed in the possessive—*j'ai la honte* (literally, I have shame)— making of shame (and hate) an object to be appropriated and identified as an object of *jouissance* that is rooted in the body and functions as the constant companion of public lives lived under the gaze of others. The experience of shame has also been felt by European society as a whole as it sits and watches the procession of tragedies unfold before its eyes: Bosnia and Rwanda are just two examples. For the young, from almost every social sector, albeit in varying degrees, the emotion of guilt, which makes allowances for some form of social connection, is overshadowed by the shame to which they feel enjoined, the feelings of exposure and social isolation, the feeling of being fingered because one is unemployed, or unwilling to become a cog in the economic machine, or because of a physical appearance that is registered by the eye as a *délit de faciès*. The relationship to the gaze is invariably at stake, the ubiquitous gaze that inhibits and burns. . . .[8] From the moment the gaze makes contact with its object, the physical appearance or trait in this case, any possibility of appellation is suspended. The gaze engulfs its object in a real that is devoid of linguistic space. The ensuing linguistic void is registered either as a paralysis spiraling toward death or as an escalating and open-ended violence. Fanon has underlined the significance of this gaze that *inhibits and burns* and identified the ways in which it is an assault on the image of the self. Drawing on his own experience of this gaze, Fanon tried to unravel it, to break it down together with the emotional indices that accompany it, to penetrate it by means of language in order to give form to a complex of relationships that are difficult to apprehend even though they may be overt. By transposing this relationship on to the page, Fanon rehearses it on the stage of language, reinscribing it in the process. The writing proceeds from a piece of the real, a perceptual trace, an emotional sign that insists on its form and its entry into congress with others. Fanon's personal experience is the occasion for a kind of writing that does not rely on a structured argument but persuades by virtue of its movement, by becoming a reenactment of the gaze and the shame. He does, however, draw on the works that were available to him at the time. This is a disparate collection that includes Jacques Lacan on the mirror stage, Merleau-Ponty and Sartre's theories on the self and the other, and the somewhat outmoded writings of L'Hermitte on body image. These were the books that informed his own ideas about how the body's inscription in time and space is conditionally linked to its action in and on the world. Pedagogues, social workers, psychologists, and a host of others continue to be befuddled by the way in which spatial and temporal circumscription prevents young people who reside in the projects from connecting with their futures. This is yet another situation that speaks directly to the disjointed relationship between the image of the self and the image of the other that is articulated, albeit in a nascent and stalling manner, by Fanon. While we may ascertain that the black man does not enter into the white man's image, the same cannot be ascertained for the Antillean black who is not certain if he considers himself black. Many young Caribbean students in Europe have reported that they have felt blackened or washed out as a result of their encounter with the European gaze, that the image they have been assigned was circumscribed by the color of their skin, even though they may have been spared the experience of shame. The instability of this image—is it specular? or is it an image of the self? of the other?—is at the heart of the questions that face us today. What happens, therefore, in the case of a second encounter with this tyrannical identification, to the earlier image of the self and the other, in which the "I" was already constituted with the complicity of the other to sidestep a psychotic outcome? The intrusion of the dominant figure as an imposed identification creates a rupture in the image of the self. This tear is all the more difficult to heal when language does not intervene to rectify the situation, and when it intervenes in the form of the dominant language, it can reenact the imposed identification. Consequently, the appropriation of time and space become extremely difficult.

It may strike us as curious that Fanon did not develop his discussion of the gaze in his "Algerian" texts, especially in "Algeria Unveiled."[9] Should he have done so, he would have had to address and dissect his relationship to the North African gaze. This gaze, which thought of itself as white at the time, was not white in quite the same way as the colonizer's gaze. The latter gaze was an unseeing gaze, a slippery in-between gaze, that landed on its object as it would on a darkened mirror, a gaze that deliberately refused to see or reflect the colonized in any way whatsoever in order to ensure their absolute exclusion from the subjective realm. The particular attention that Fanon brought to the subject of shame and the gaze derived from the fact of his blackness as well as from a specific historical context. The past in the Antilles begins with the disappearance of a prior civilization and the arrival of the first black slaves. For the descendants of black slaves, there is no Antillean precolonial past; history in the islands begins under the burning and humiliating gaze of the white master. The situation in Algeria was of a different kind insofar as Algerians laid claim to a precolonial past that was responsible, despite being censored and damaged, for myths, signifiers, and a deeply engrained tradition of resistance against the occupier. The Algerians were colonized, subjected to the gaze (or its absence) of the colonizer who may have sought to objectify them and deny them their singularity, preventing them from inscribing themselves in their own destiny, but they were not enslaved. Their history should not be confused with the history of slavery. Fanon had intuited this difference, but he did not have the opportunity to pursue it or to undertake a comparative historical study of Algeria and the Antilles.

Yet, as I write this, the experience of shame that Fanon detailed, refuted, and disarmed in his account of it threatens to permeate Algerian society as a whole. The problem can be formulated only with difficulty at this point. Again, we first meet it in the victims, themselves, in their expressions of shame for the things they had to undergo and shame for the criminals who refuse to acknowledge their actions. But the problem extends beyond the individual victims to include the whole of civil society. Torn between the "recommended amnesia" and the desire for truth and acknowledgement of the acts that have been committed, it runs the risk of becoming entrapped inside its own self-reflexive gaze. If the outcome should be a denial of the things that have taken place, then access to guilt and the work of mourning shall be obstructed, thereby creating a fertile ground for the reemergence of violence. Despite this, a great number of Algerians wish to be free of the traumatic event and to relegate it to its rightful place in memory, ideally a collective memory. In recent years, there has been a bounty of works—books, journals, visual and other creative works, as well as the formation of new groups and associations. It seems that Fanon was not entirely mistaken, after all, and that the Algerians are on the whole a people who want to live, understand, create.

Technically, Fanon was not a psychoanalyst, having never undergone psychoanalysis himself. But the evidence that has been advanced to point out this *shortcoming* is, on closer analysis, further proof of the unwitting contemporaneity of Fanon's ideas. In 1999, David Macey, writing about the "Look, a Negro!" episode, claims that psychoanalysis would have enabled Fanon to formulate the offending gaze as a "narcissistic wound" or as a "castration experience." Instead, Macey writes, Fanon remains imprisoned in a gaze that refers him to how he is perceived by the other in a strictly phenomenological sense.[10] But the gaze was precisely the thing that Fanon wanted to capture; its bewildering immediacy and the ensuing collision with a real in which language is ruled out, the mounting need for action, for the mise-en-scène that, ideally, precedes representation.

The gist of the argument of those who claim Fanon misconstrues and distorts psychoanalysis is that the unconscious is directionless, structured around fantasy and desire, and not related in any way to the real that Fanon persists in arguing for.[11] Fanon, it is also tirelessly repeated, only focused on Freud's theory of trauma and totally overlooked the theory of fantasy, when, in fact, Freud abandoned the theory of trauma that attributed neuroses to real events in favor of the theory of fantasy that was unrelated to real events and relied on how experience is organized in the imaginary. The final point calls Fanon to task for his first work, in which he claimed that the Oedipus complex did not apply in the Antilles, where psychological problems only arose after one left the family home and entered a white society that was organized according to different norms that broke with the traditional family structure. There is some truth to the claim that in his earliest writing, Fanon did, in fact, look to Freud for ways of thinking about subjective rupture and that he did not look beyond the idea of trauma. Later, in Tunisia, Fanon was very much taken by Ferenczi, reading everything by him that he could get his hands on. Now a mainstay of any psychoanalyst's library, Ferenczi proposed an approach to the complexities of trauma that did not necessarily attribute these to exclusive categories ("everything is trauma or everything is fantasy"). Lacan, for his part, has claimed that for all speaking creatures the entry into language is always structurally traumatic. Today, this debate has been laid to rest, and psychoanalysts are no longer preoccupied by the opposition between utterance "only fantasy pertains to the unconscious" and the pertinence of traumatic events as causal psychological factors. The event, itself, is not generally viewed as the traumatic thing, rather it is the way in which its potential inscription may have been thwarted—the trauma is the thing that happened before the words to describe it availed themselves in order to represent it and recast it as a memory which could become forgettable, given time. More attention is also being paid to the repercussions of historical traumas suffered by previous generations and the ways in which these have affected subjects who have been entrusted with the responsibility of working toward some form of resolution for themselves as well as for those who came before them. These repercussions embody a failure to proceed to the commonplace Oedipal conflict that characterized nineteenth-century neuroses. The entire enterprise of clinical psychoanalysis today is to listen for the gaps, the lapses, the search for words and meaning, in an effort to defy psychosis and help the men and women who have been delegated the difficult psychological challenge of transforming walls into passageways, not only for themselves but for their predecessors as well as their descendants. Fanon, as I have already said, was not a psychoanalyst in the strict sense of the term. He was a child of the times, however, who had the foresight as well as the temerity to place his cards on the table; using the words that were available to him at the time, he made a case for the real that one "slams up" against and for the desperate necessity of making it symbolic and narrative in order to become a subject. In France today, this "real" that language cannot dislodge comes knocking at our doors in the person of those whose grandparents died in the Holocaust and of the children of immigrants who have lived not in exile so much as immured in their bodies.

What is there to say about the immense shame that installs itself and cleaves to the body, presents itself as the prow of a stage that cannot be breached, and that, today, has become as germane as violence? If only we could find a way to make it more bearable, to mobilize it as guilt. The problems facing us today were signaled by Fanon, even though he may not have had the tools to pursue them as far as one may have hoped. Aside from the philosophy of the subject, which we know he was familiar with, psychoanalysis in the 1950s did not offer any real direction for the problems he was trying to tackle. Curiously, when he does directly engage the theories of the day, the result is difficult to assess. His claim in *Black Skin, White Masks* that the Oedipus complex, as it is understood in Europe, does not apply in the Antilles and that the first trauma is a consequence of leaving the family home and confronting the white gaze of the other raises certain questions. Is this a defense of the moral order? a way of preserving the idyllic universe of early childhood? of denying the pain of being born? of repressing impulses? of resisting lost childhood illusions? Probably, yes, and why not? What we do know is that by the time he arrived in Blida, and later in Tunis, he had stopped maintaining that trauma begins when one leaves the family home, and he never again referred to the irrelevance of the Oedipus complex to the Antilles. There is more than a grain of truth, however, even in his pithy and impatient 1952 formulation, and in this, too, Fanon was a child of his times. He was, in fact, trying to make two points, the first being, namely, that the unconscious cannot be bracketed by personified Oedipal figures, the "mommy-daddy" pairing that appears on birth certificates. The Lacanian conception of the paternal function as a break, as a symbolic third element that superimposes itself on culture and nature, would have served Fanon better and been closer to his own idea of what he termed the "line of force that organizes," the image that he used to talk about symbolic points of reference. Fanon was not afforded the time to pursue this line of thinking that was still novel even for Lacan. The second point, perhaps more important, has to do with the particularities of the Antillean family and the sociological absence of the father, a dynamic that is currently being studied in the

Antilles. The white master usurps the figure of the father, and another fills the space that should have been occupied by the father in the maternal imaginary. In addition to ousting the father and taking over his place, the inherited paternal figure of the white master is indifferent and unresponsive, fails to answer when called on. With respect to homosexuality as well as to the Oedipus complex as a means to symbolic representations mediated by a paternal figure backed by a real father, Fanon was not entirely mistaken in noting this relative absence and its relationship to the "white signifier."

Finally, Fanon makes a case for the connection between trauma and the real. He proceeds intuitively, with the conviction that there are some elements of the real that are undeniable and that refuse to be "unconscioused," resist, in other words, their transformation into traces that would be receptive to repression and to the pull of oblivion. This real, with its staggering experiences and violence, that cannot be "unconscioused," to use the same obsolete but eloquent word as Fanon, has become, today, a major concern of the daily praxis of psychoanalysis. It is the real of the individual, subject to parental abuse, rape, and all the other forms of violence that result in memory lapses, paralysis, and a bottomless rage toward the self and the other. It is also the real of the wars and the exterminations for which the Holocaust is the paradigm of our century. It is the real of painful experience that, for generations on end, cannot be integrated as unconscious memory. In the face of this real, words become impoverished, emptied of meaning, and one has to allow the sensations and perceptions to come to the fore. "The real is the camp, life after that is just a dream," as Primo Levi said toward the end of his life. Fanon, at thirty, was engaged in an endeavor to transform the real of the camp, to reinstate temporality to life and inscribe the dream.

How does one set about deconstructing a language to make it resonate in a different way? Antillean, Algerian, and African Francophone writers owe much to Fanon, even though awareness of this debt may not be common knowledge. The debt has less to do than one would expect with what Fanon had to say about language, as when he famously stated at the Second Congress of Black Writers that was held in Rome in 1959 that language had "to speak the nation, the sentence composed to express the people, to become the mouthpiece of reality through actions." Much later, Glissant would say that the only place where Creole was easily installed as the national language was Haiti because it had been the language of the nation's creation almost from the start. That is a Fanonian statement if there ever was one. But in the French Antilles of the 1950s, Creole did not enjoy a similar status; in fact, it does not enjoy such status to this day. Fanon, who always spontaneously switched to Creole whenever he found himself in the company of Guyanese or Antillean friends and was always amused by the surprise with which the rest of us registered this spontaneity, was, in those years, very out-spoken about the way in which Creole had been relegated to its lowly status. It was the forbidden language, looked down on by the Antillean bourgeoisie, treated as the language of camouflage and derision by the lower classes. At that time especially and in the hands of a colonial enterprise that was still convinced of its superiority, Creole was maliciously used as a pretext for marginalizing and demeaning those who spoke it. *Toi parler petit nègre* was also a way of saying "stay in your place." And there were times during the colonial period when the phrase was an absolute expression of truth; it is a truth that continues to be alive and well today: "You, with your funny robes and your witchcraft, stay in your place or go back to where you came from."

Fanon's pronouncements on the function of language, though significant, are not the important thing. Momentum was what really distinguished him as a speaker and writer. Becoming the *mouthpiece* of a nation or defining the *language of the nation* are secondary considerations. The imperative thing was to make the language speak, and this is precisely what Fanon achieves in his writings. Fanon turns the French language on its head through a semiotic infiltration of the language itself. The rhythm, the beat, the images stretching for the words that will extend them as metaphors . . . ideas are coaxed, deriving from instinct, from the scraps of language that are entwined with the body, from perceptions that belong to the senses. A language, unburdened by the distinction between oral and written, a language that forces the limits of punctuation, that is studded with images that are anchored in the body and its senses. A language that proceeds by breaking ideas down and putting them back together again as robust metaphors. A language that proclaims itself as here to alter things, to turn the French language upside down. Kateb Yacine, who was already an established writer when he and Fanon crossed paths in Tunis, was engaged in a similar undertaking. Yacine spoke of seizing the French language as though it were a *war trophy*, of using scansion, and rhythm, and metaphors that were alien to it to infiltrate it. The writer Fanon, not unlike the writer Kateb Yacine, did not theorize about any of this. He wrote the way he did because he could not do otherwise. Today there are a great number of Antillean, Algerian, and African Francophone writers who deliberately engage in linguistic *métissage*, slipping their smuggled goods into the dominant language so as to make it resonate in a different way. This project is the obverse of the stance that maintained that it is necessary to master a language that is transparent to itself and opaque to others in order to express oneself. One cannot rule out Fanon's importance, albeit unacknowledged, to this movement. Though these writers may not realize it, the freedom of hybridizing French with

Creole, Kabyle, Arabic, or Wolof, of releasing language from its subjugation to the monolingualism of the other, is one they owe more to Fanon than to any of his predecessors. Senghor and Césaire wrote in a language both admirable and lyrical, but their works remain cloistered in an elitist literature of description and dissent that makes a clear distinction between the language of abstraction and the language of affect and the body. Contemporary writers, regardless of which side of the colonial fence they may have found themselves on, owe the very possibility of reflecting on and recounting the status of language to word runners like Fanon. In addition to reminding us that the real must take up residence in the language, this linguistic freedom pertains to another time that could just as well be today. Finally, there is the freedom that results when languages interact, seeping into each other until both are joined in the same condition, one in which origins are impossible to designate.

Restoring the Tragic
(in lieu of a conclusion)

Fanon, it has been said, was excessive. Fanon, it has been said, was mistaken. He has been charged with cultivating an erroneous Third World ideology that has been overturned by worldwide political developments. And which wide world is this may I ask? The one in which the discourse of "globalization" exists side-by-side in the utmost tranquility with the retrograde but all too real one of circumscription by nationalism, regionalism, lethal ethnic divisions, and frosty border relations? Colonialism is behind us. The colonial situation and the relationship, more precisely the nonrelationship, it engendered between colonizer and colonized, a relationship that Albert Memmi and Frantz Fanon, writing from their respective subjective positions, tried to elucidate in the 1950s, are a closed political chapter. The legacy of this encounter has remained with us, however, and the residual effect of the relationship between oppressor and oppressed persists in muffled form. Neither the oppressor, whose impulses have remained unchanged, nor the oppressed have been spared from its lingering impact. More time, say the practiced hands, the situation needs more time, an immeasurable amount of time before we can extricate ourselves from the assignation with oppression.

The preoccupation may seem quaint in a world saturated with verbiage about the single market economy, globalization, quality of life, and fear of germs that somehow manages to harmoniously co-exist with malnutrition, massacres, and the labor and sexual exploitation of children. Within this framework of neutral pacification, violence is more than ever present. So present, in fact, as to merit manifold expression, its variety and proliferation great enough to require pluralization: the violence of collective mass atroci-

220

ties, the muted violence of economic domination, state-sanctioned violence garbed in a threadbare legitimacy, and the run-of-the-mill violence of the strong on the weak. Our newspapers speak of little else, and it is curious to note how their pens have unwittingly revived the expression "wretched of the earth." The ones they designate with this term are more or less the same as the ones whom Fanon wanted to see live, released from lives in which death is always at the door; they are the destitute: the anonymous men and women who die in clandestine vessels that do not make it to shore or in the bellies of airplanes; and they also are the ones who have been serenely globalized under the rubric of "exclusion." Globalization of exclusion is the mirror image of economic globalization. It is no secret that economic globalization today is creating a greater inequality not only between North and South but also within Western societies.

Studies in a Dying Colonialism and *The Wretched of the Earth* are not outmoded texts when we choose to read them as an appeal to the future and what it could hold. They only appear dated if we read them in the indicative mood, as simple assertions. If we pause to compare Fanon's words of warning to the analysis of political realities that is being proffered by "soft" experts, or if we place them alongside the unending spectacle of horror upon horror, to whom does the violence point? Where does the blame for the annihilation of the political fall? Overwhelmingly, the view today is to fix the responsibility on the collapse of ideologies and the end of political utopias. Is this demise really equal to the task of snuffing out the dream, of ridding us of the tragic dimension that inheres in all of us? But then our modern "democratic" societies are not overly preoccupied with dreams or with the tragic impulse; these have been edged out of the public sphere in favor of efficiency and competence. We dismiss these concerns in our young who, fittingly, are still consumed by such matters and assign them to the same social categories as our artists and marginalized citizens. The denial of death, violence, and unhappiness is roundly approved; the inclination to equate revolution with criminality and to prefer exclusion to conflict is widely accepted. This is the utopia in which we live today, the underhanded utopia that dares not even speak its name.

Fanon's reflections on humankind and its evolution are, we are told, anachronistic in this era of economic globalization, cognitive assertions, and exclusionary subjectivity. The subject has been neutralized, disposed of in his or her incompletion, and deprived of the tragic dimension that Fanon wanted to awaken. All that remains is the individual who more often than not views the other as absolute bogeyman or victim, in other words as the least possible sum onto which the unique, satisfied, and omnipotent narcissistic self can be projected. Fanon's ideas, his analyses, and words of caution that have been left to slumber for this long while are now resurfacing, emerging like a sea serpent out of the history of individuals and nations, to help us understand violence and racism, ethnic regression and the rise of fundamentalism, and to show us how to defy the defeated norms and expose the discourse and the acts that are devised to turn subjects into objects.

Modernity has profited from the diminishing of the subject while proffering negotiation and language as the tools of democracy. Fanon, too, believed in the power of negotiation and language as subjective and collective aspirations, but what good are they in the absence of subjects? How can human beings who have been objectified or reduced to an animal-like existence contemplate their inscription in this space? What is at issue today is not a question of qualifying the other as inhuman; that practice has already had its day and has seen itself condemned as a "crime against humanity." Rather, it is the relegation of the other to a subhuman status that has become not entirely unthinkable, a practice that paradoxically lends itself to endless repetition. The other is repeatedly assigned to a less-than-human status, until such time as the other can be entirely excluded from humanity. Unlike Engels or Sorel, Fanon insists on the fact that the relegation to a less-than-human status engenders violence. In his wake, it has become evident that this violence, repeatedly denied by societies that are, or proclaim themselves to be, "pacified," can be erratic, cruel, and as destructive to the self as it is to the other. This is the thing that states fail to understand as they adroitly balance violence against counterviolence; or, in the case of the more enlightened ones, alternate condemnations of violence with ritualistic calls for dialogue. In fact, the refusal to take these matters into account is at the root of their failure. History's lesson is one of the negation of other human beings, despite the keen awareness of the precise measure of humiliation, shame, and insults this negation involves.

Abbreviations and Notes

Abbreviations Used in Text

BSWM   Frantz Fanon. *Black Skin, White Masks*. New York: Grove Press, 1967.

CD   Édouard Glissant, ed. *Caribbean Discourse: Selected Essays*. Trans. J. Michael Dash. Charlottesville: University Press of Virginia, 1989.

CS   Irene L. Gendzier. *Frantz Fanon, A Critical Study*. New York: Random House, Pantheon Books, 1973.

P&C   Octave Mannoni. *Psychologie de la colonization*. Paris: Éditions du Seuil, 1951.

TAR   *Toward the African Revolution*. Trans. Haakon Chevalier. New York: Monthly Review Press, 1967.

TWOE   Frantz Fanon. *The Wretched of the Earth*. Trans. Constance Farrington. New York: Grove Press, 1966.

Major Works of Frantz Fanon

Peau noire, masque blancs. Paris: Éditions du Seuil, 1952. *Black Skin, White Masks*. Translated by Charles L. Markmann. New York: Grove Press, 1967.

L'An V de la révolution algérienne. Paris: François Maspero, 1959. Reissued in 1966 as *Sociologie d'une révolution. Studies in a Dying Colonialism*. Translated by Haakon Chevalier. New York: Monthly Review Press, 1965.

Les Damnées de la terre. Paris: François Maspero, 1961. Copyright 1963 by *Présence Africaine. The Wretched of the Earth.* Translated by Constance Farrington. New York: Grove Press, First Evergreen Edition, 1966.

Pour la révolution africaine. Paris: François Maspero, 1964. *Toward the African Revolution.* Translated by Haakon Chevalier. New York: Monthly Review Press, 1967. (There is some debate as to whether all of the articles collected in this work were actually written solely or even primarily by Fanon. Many of the articles first appeared in the newspaper *El Moudjahid.*)

Before Blida

1. Olivier Fanon, born in 1955.
2. Marcel Manville is responsible for the creation of the Cercle Frantz-Fanon in the Antilles. He suffered a fatal stroke on December 2, 1998. He died in his robes at the Palais de Justice while awaiting an audience related to a court case seeking reparations for the victims of October 1961. A week before, he and I met for the last of many times. Fanon and Manville never met again after 1957.
3. "Mulatto," "mulatta" are terms that designate a mixed black and white lineage. "Creole" and "béké" designate the white inhabitants of the Islands: the powerful whites who were the owners of the vast tracts of land known as *habitations.* Hierarchy in the Antilles was based on skin color and the quantity of landholdings.
4. Irene L. Gendzier, *Frantz Fanon, A Critical Study* (New York: Random House, Pantheon Books, 1973), chap. 1.
5. From a conversation with Fanon that took place in Tunis in 1958.
6. Aimé Césaire, born in 1913, is the great Martinican poet, playwright, and essayist who was also one of the founders of the *négritude* movement as his early writings, especially *Cahiers du retour au pays natal,* attest. From the mid-thirties until 1956, he was an active member of the French Communist Party. In 1945, he ran on the *départamentaliste* platform and became the mayor of Fort-de-France and a deputy at the National Assembly. In 1950, he wrote *Discours sur le colonialisme* and in 1956, he resigned from the French Communist Party and founded the Martinican Popular Party (PPM).
7. "The ten families": one of the terms used by Martinicans to refer to the békés.
8. The main boulevard where strollers convened in Fort-au-France.
9. In fact, the *Surcouf* was never in Martinique.
10. The expression *l'entrée en dissidence* (joining the dissidence), spoken with the words run together as if it were one word, referred to the organized resistance of Martinicans to the Pétain administration.
11. Marcel Manville is largely responsible for relating the details of this episode; Fanon spoke of it only in the vaguest of terms.
12. Oral testimony by Manville supported by Joby Fanon's account in a special February 1982 issue of *Sans frontière.*
13. For a more lively and detailed account of this uprising, see Marcel Manville, *Les Antilles sans fard* (Paris: L'Harmattan, 1992).

14. Quoted by Manville.

15. Bougie, currently known as Bejaïa, is a small port city in eastern Algeria.

16. Cited by Manville. Paul Bourget is a French author whose works include *Démon de midi*. In the period between the wars, he stopped writing comedies of manners and started writing psychological novels. Praise of traditional bourgeois values is the distinctive hallmark of his works.

17. This letter was discovered after Éléonore Fanon's death in 1981. It had been carefully put away in a box.

18. *Dachin:* Antillean vegetable dish. In his letters from the front, Fanon often reminisced about the foods of home.

19. An Algerian-born French psychiatrist and psychoanalyst of Algerian-Jewish descent. Under Fanon's supervision, he wrote a thesis on the practice of sociotherapy in Blida. There will be more about him later.

20. In the immediate post-War period, a great many abandoned structures were turned into student housing.

21. J. Postel and C. Razajano, "La vie et l'œuvre psychiatrique de Frantz Fanon," *L'Information psychiatrique* 51, no. 10 (December 1975): 1053–73.

22. In his essay *Sociologie de Frantz Fanon* (Algiers: SNED, 1971), Phillipe Lucas discusses a third play entitled *La Conspiration*.

23. A psychiatrist who was a pioneer in the area of institutional psychotherapy, Tosquelles was a Spaniard and anti-Franquist who immigrated to France in 1939. He died in 1996.

24. "The North African Syndrome" was published in the journal *Esprit* in February 1952. We may wonder how a young psychiatry student living in Lyon managed to have his essay published in *Esprit*. Fanon was pursuing a degree in legal medicine and psychiatry under Professor Michel Colin. Jean-Marie Domenach, the editor-in-chief of *Esprit*, happened to be Colin's brother-in-law. Colin is the one who brought Fanon's writing to Domenach's attention. Colin remembers Fanon as conscientious but awkward, not very skilled at conducting autopsies, and not particularly interested in scientific accuracy. He remembers asking him a very concrete question about legal medicine and Fanon answering him with a long and involved narrative, worthy of a detective novel. He also remembers him as endearing, extremely curious, very romantic, but often capable of being quite distant, even untrusting.

25. Fanon, like many other young students from the colonies, attached a great importance to university credentials. The important thing was to acquire degrees from universities, and Fanon wanted to have several—one in philosophy as well as a few more in medicine, psychiatry, and criminology. In the eyes of the family back home, each degree represented a further proof of success.

26. In a letter dated July 23, 1973, Madeleine Humbert writes: "I have no recollection of Fanon ever deigning to note down observations. He couldn't have left us with a more disagreeable impression, behaving toward the nurses like . . . a colonialist." It is true that Fanon never took down observations. He did not want to because he despised it as a quasi-inquisitorial protocol of traditional treatment. For him, a psychiatrist was first and foremost a therapist. To call Fanon a colonialist is . . . surprising, to say the least. What is certain is that he was absolutely intolerant of prison guard

behaviors in his medical staff. He was unsparing toward anyone who failed to consider the mentally ill as subjects.

27. Frantz Fanon, *Troubles mentaux et Syndromes psychiatriques dans l'hérédo-dégénerescence spinocérébelleuse: un cas de malade de Friedreich avec délire de possession,* medical thesis, Lyon, 1951.

28. See *Partisans* 10 (May–June 1963).

29. He was equally skeptical about the Mouvement contre le Racisme, l'Antisemitisme et pour la Paix (MRAP) and similar organizations that were beginning to emerge in Europe at the time. When Manville, who had founded the organization in 1949, asked him to come along to a movie about racism that was being shown in one of the studios on the Champs-Élysées, Fanon resisted and criticized the event as a social frivolity but went anyway. That night they were showing *Mozambo,* a film that was, coincidentally, featured at the Blida ciné-club when Fanon happened to be in attendance and about which he held forth vivaciously after the screening.

30. F. Tosquelles, "F. Fanon à Saint-Alban," *L'Information psychiatrique* 51, no. 10 (December 1975).

31. Ibid.

32. This was the term used to differentiate between training and personal analysis. The training analysis was conducted under the supervision of analysts who had qualified as "titulaire" (licensed). Numerous psychiatrists who were involved in institutional psychiatry chose to go into analysis. The term *didactic analysis* is no longer used in France, where the overriding consensus today is that any analysis is always first and foremost personal.

33. Normopathy: a term that is frequently used by institutional psychotherapists to describe people who shield themselves from their neuroses by claiming their "normality." A very widespread symptom.

34. Terms used by Fanon himself.

35. Jacques Lacan, *L'Envers de la psychanalyse* (Paris: Éditions du Seuil, 1991).

36. Frantz Fanon, "Sur quelques cas traités par la méthode de Bini" (On several cases treated according to the Bini method), paper presented at the 51st *Congrès de psychiatrie et de neurologie de langue française* (Pau, 1953), pp. 539–44.

37. I never did manage to obtain a clear response from Fanon about this.

38. Léopold Sédar Senghor was primarily known as a poet and an activist during this period. He was also the deputy for Senegal, a position he occupied until 1960 when he became the first president of the Republic of Senegal. At the time of Fanon's letter to him, he had recently published *Anthologie de la nouvelle poésie nègre et malagache de langue française* for which Jean-Paul Sartre had written a preface, L'Orphée noir. Senghor was the first African to receive a graduate degree in French literature from a French university (1933). During his student years in Paris he befriended Damas and Césaire. All three were responsible for founding the journal *L'Étudiant noir* and for launching the Negritude movement. After World War II, during which Senghor spent two years in a German prison, Senghor became, in his poetry as well as in his political activities, a committed witness to the dawning era of independence, *les soleils des indépendances.* For him as for Césaire, it is difficult to know where poetry ends and politics begin. Senghor was the poet of *la négritude de-*

bout (negritude on its feet). He came from a mixed cultural background and became the theorist of cultural métissage. In much the same way he had with Césaire, Fanon would later part ways politically with Senghor.

39. For a more detailed account, see M.-C. and E. Ortigues, *Oedipe africain* (Paris: Plon, 1966; 3rd ed., Paris: L'Harmattan, 1984).

40. Interview with Jeanson, November 1998. After Fanon had left for Blida eighteen months after this interview, Jeanson, who did not travel to Algeria during this period, only met with him on two subsequent occasions.

41. In 1982, Octave Mannoni claimed that his *Psychologie de la colonisation* was published by Seuil at the same time as Fanon's book and that he is the one who suggested the title to Fanon. This is a revised memory. Mannoni's book was actually published two years before Fanon's, and the title *Peau noire, masques blancs* was proposed by F. Jeanson.

42. Interview with Jean Daniel, June 1999.

43. *Le Premier Homme* by Camus (Paris: Gallimard, 1994) and *Le Monolinguisme de l'autre* by Derrida (Paris: Galilée, 1966) attest to this.

44. *Black Skin, White Masks* (New York: Grove Press, 1967), pp. 228–31.

45. L'Orphée noir, Sartre's preface to Léopold Senghor's *Anthologie de la nouvelle poésie nègre et malagache de langue française*, Paris: Presses universitaires de France, 1948.

46. *Peau noire, masques blancs* (Paris: Éditions du Seuil, 1953), p. 12. The English edition does not include Jeanson's introduction.

47. Léonard Sainville, "Le Noir antillais devant la littérature," *Les Lettres françaises*, August 1, 1952.

48. A paperback edition is warranted after a minimum sale of 2,000 copies.

49. The dependency complex discussed by Mannoni is not entirely unrelated to La Boétie's idea of voluntary servitude, a system that is not entirely alien to the West and that encapsulates the various forms of individual or collective subjugation as these pertain to everything from totalitarian systems to cult phenomena.

50. By the author's own admission in 1975 (*Le Racisme revisité* [Paris: Denoël, 1997, p. 242—new edition of *Psychologie de la colonisation*, Paris, Éditions du Seuil, 1950]).

51. When Mannoni interprets the dreams of young Malagasies who have been traumatized by Senegalese sharpshooters who killed their family members, he resorts to the very conventional view that the guns are simply phallic symbols and nothing more.

52. We can also wonder if Fanon's rebuttal challenged Mannoni in ways that his analysis did not.

53. Culturalism is associated to the "culture and society" school of anthropological thought that views cultures as typified by particular personalities, psychologies, ideas, mentalities, and modes of behavior.

54. The rise of Nazism forced a great many German and Austrian psychoanalysts to leave a Europe they did not wish to leave behind and immigrate to the United States in 1939.

55. Interview with Jacques Azoulay, September 1998.

56. Some of the pioneering figures of this view, which later would become widely

held, were: François Tosquelles, Louis Le Guillant, Lucien Bonafé, Sven Folin, and, somewhat later, Jean Oury and Félix Guattari.

57. Tosquelles on Fanon: "F. Fanon à Saint-Alban," cited article.

Algiers, 1953

1. The term *pieds-noirs* was not used in colonial Algeria. It was a term that came into usage in France after 1962 and conveniently grouped native-born Algerian Jews with Europeans. Its usage has now become de rigueur, an inevitable shorthand that flouts historical accuracy.

2. The 1870 Crémieux Decree granted French citizenship to Algerian Jews. We shall return to this decree and the subsequent controversy that surrounded it.

3. In 1949, there were 6,300 Jews, 700 of them in Algiers and its vicinities, who were not French citizens.

4. Géronimi was born in Algeria to Corsican parents. He was Fanon's intern in Blida and later in Tunis. When Algeria gained its independence, he became an Algerian national. He became a professor of neurology and now resides in France, where he moved in 1992.

5. MTLD (Movement for the Triumph of Democratic Freedom), the main Algerian nationalist party.

6. Interview with Charles Géronimi.

7. Sétif massacres, May 8, 1945.

8. In November 1954, Algiers proper had a population of 360,000: 165,000 Algerian "Muslims" and 195,000 "non-Muslims." If we include the inhabitants of the outlying areas (Maison-Carrée, Hussein-Dey, El Biar, Kouba, Saint-Eugène, Birmandreis, Bouzaréah), however, the number is closer to 590,000: 300,000 Algerians and 290,000 Europeans.

9. The MTLD, created by Messali Hadj, was one of the early major parties in Algeria's complex and thwarted history of national liberation. In 1926, Messali Hadj had formed L'Étoile nord-africaine (ENA), a group whose aims were North African unity and the independence of the three North African countries (Tunisia, Algeria, and Morocco). After the dissolution of the ENA by the French government in 1929, the party resurfaced as the PPA in 1937 only to be banned in 1939, at which point it went underground. In 1946, it reemerged from the shadows and presented candidates in the Algerian elections; it was the PPA-MTLD that split up in 1954. The hotly debated issue of armed struggle resulted in the decision by a faction of the MTLD to take up arms. This decision became a reality on November 1, 1954, which marks the beginning of the insurrection. On December 1, 1954, Messali Hadj founded the Algerian Nationalist Movement (MNA) to set himself apart from the Front de Libération Nationale (FLN).

10. My description of the city owes much to Pierre Chaulet. See Pierre Chaulet, "Parti pris," *Majallat-el tarikh*, second semester 1984.

11. Interview with Charles Géronimi.

12. Ibid.

13. Ibid.

14. In 1950, the union movement started gaining momentum. Unions representing railway, telecommunications, and gas and electric workers were especially successful at recruiting a significant number of "indigenous Muslim" workers, thereby laying the ground for a nascent dialogue.

15. *Consciences maghribines* wanted to fill the void that had been left by the short-lived *Consciences algériennes*. The editorial board that came together in 1953 to launch the journal consisted of Françoise Becht, Réda Bestandji, Pierre Chaulet, Mhaffoud Kaddache, Mohammed-Salah Lounchi, Jean Rime, and Pierre Roche. Three issues were published prior to November 1, 1954, and two appeared after this date. The journal's political position was made more overt with each publication, and by the last issue, in which all the tracts that had been circulated by the FLN were published, the journal was operating entirely underground.

16. In fact, one of its best-known productions, "La famille Hernandez," only became successful after it was performed in Paris in 1957.

17. *Algérie, l'œuvre française* (Paris: Robert Laffont, 1984).

18. In 1953, there was only one Algerian staff physician at Mustapha hospital!

19. A professor of pneumo-phtisiology who was famous for his liberal views.

20. After Independence, it became the Lycée Descartes.

21. Important figure of Francophone Algerian literature. In 1956–57, while attending the L'École normale supérieure in Sèvres and to the great displeasure of school authorities, she complied with the general order to strike that had been issued to Algerian students. In 1957, she published her first novel *La Soif* with Éditions du Seuil. A great many other books would follow. *Le Blanc de l'Algérie* (Paris: Albin Michel, 1996), *Oran, langue morte* (Arles: Actes Sud, 1997), and *Les Nuits de Strasbourg* (Arles: Actes Sud, 1997) are some of her most recent works.

22. I met Fanon in the framework of this organization when it invited him to give a lecture on fear in Algeria.

23. A review of Algerian Jewish history is not the purpose here. The aim, rather, is to give a sense of the specific situation of the Algerian Jewish community during the colonial period in which Fanon came to know it.

24. The *senatus-consulte* of July 14, 1865, allowed Jewish and Muslim "French subjects" to apply for French citizenship on an individual basis. An insignificant number of Muslims applied, and an equally small number of Jews, most of them residents of Algiers.

25. When Daniel Timsit writes about his family history or the author Rolland Doukhan, who was born in Constantine, relates the story of earlier generations and the saga of his family's emancipation, there is *always* a sense that in this journey toward modernity, the parents are the transitional figures and the grandparents the witnesses to an ancestral and profoundly human time. See D. Timsit, *Algérie, récit anachronique* (Saint-Denis: Bouchène, 1998).

26. Pierre Vidal-Naquet went to great lengths to shed light on the disappearance of this young teacher who was a member of the PCA and had been arrested on June 11, 1957, by a French parachute unit and accused of desertion. It later surfaced that he was executed after he had been tortured for several days. See Pierre Vidal-Naquet, *L'Affaire Audin* (Paris: Éditions de Minuit, 1989).

27. Interview with Jacques Azoulay, October 1998.

28. Ibid.

29. Internment camp that was intended primarily for the detention of "French" citizens who, in a variety of capacities, were supporters of the 1954 movement.

30. *Les Juifs d'Algérie* (Paris: Éditions du Scribe, 1992) (collective work).

31. In the author's note that accompanied his 1989 work on the Algerian War, the observations that Jean-François Lyotard had shared in private in the 1970s about his 1950–52 sojourn in Constantine are expressed in the following manner: "My experience in Constantine was and continues to be responsible for my rude awakening. The *différend* announced itself in a manner so radical that the consolations that were generally available to my contemporaries—vague notions of reform, pious Stalinism, futile leftist views—had become unthinkable where I was concerned" (*La Guerre des Algériens* [Paris: Galilée, 1989], p. 39).

32. Interview with Rolland Doukhan, November 1998.

33. An equanimity that had already shocked many French travelers in Algeria: Robert Barrat, Colette and Francis Jeanson, Mandouze and many others.

34. Interview with Charles Géronimi.

35. Nor did they heed the call of Monsignor Duval, the newly appointed Archbishop of Algiers who had succeeded Monsignor Leynaud in February 1954, when he argued for a policy of rapprochement between Muslims and Christians. It did not take very long before the European population started to refer to Monsignor Duval, who remained in Algiers after independence, as Mohammed Duval—a name that stuck from 1954 to 1962.

36. One of the roads between Blida and Algiers cut across a place that was known as the Chiffa Gorges, where one could indeed see apes at play in the small waterfall.

37. The little rose.

38. Jean-Robert Henry and Lucienne Martini, "La vie culturelle d'une guerre à l'autre," *Autrement* 56, Alger 1940–62, *"Une ville en guerres," Autrement* 256, March 1999.

Blida

1. "Aspects actuels de l'assistance mentale en Algérie," *L'information psychiatrique* 31, no. 1 (1955): 11–18. Publication of L'Hopital psychiatrique de Blida-Joinville.

2. Report submitted by Henry Reboul and Emmanuel Regis at the XXIIᵉ Congrès des médecins aliénistes et neurologues de France et des pays de langue française (Tunis, 1–7 avril 1912). Paris: Masson.

3. "Lettre à un Français," *Pour la révolution africaine* (Paris: Maspero, coll. "Cahiers libres" 53–54, 1964), p. 55. (Frantz Fanon, "Letter to a Frenchman," *Toward the African Revolution*, translated by Haakon Chevalier [New York: Monthly Review Press, 1967], pp. 47–51.)

4. Movement for the Triumph of Democratic Freedom, the main nationalist movement and the precursor to the FLN.

5. At the time, in Algeria as well as in France, psychiatry and neurology were seen as connected disciplines and courses in "neuropsychiatry," part of the core medical school curriculum, were generally taught by neurologists.

6. The prevailing mentality of the day is reflected in the forensic report of an Algiers-based psychiatrist who writes: "This subject does not appear to have come from a psychiatric hospital but from a concentration camp."

7. The war injury was the only thing he and Fanon had in common.

8. Antoine Porot and Jean Suker, "Le primitivisme des indigènes nord-africains et ses incidences en pathologie mentale." In *Sud médical et chirurgical*, April 1939.

9. Even as someone, who was briefly involved and retains a concrete recollection of this experiment, my recent reading of the thesis Azoulay based on it has, after so many years, renewed my sense of amazement. In and of itself, the thesis sets out to do what one would expect from a thesis in medicine, but rereading this work fifty years after the fact has been a true revelation. I am struck by the way the project combined rigor and humility, by the realizations that were reached as student and teacher progressed in their work and by the language that was used to account for them.

10. Jacques Azoulay, thesis.

11. She even managed to obtain and read *Black Skin, White Masks*.

12. Azoulay, thesis.

13. Interview with Makhlouf Longo in 1987. Longo, with whom we worked very closely, died recently in Blida. He was arrested in January 1957 and sent to the Paul Cazalles camp.

14. In the interest of fairness, a canteen was opened in the European men's pavilion after the creation of the *café maure*. As a result, the Algerian staff could, with good reason, consider itself a precursor.

15. Known today as the Frantz Fanon Hospital.

16. Interview with Charles Géronimi.

17. *Congrès de psychiatrie et de neurologie de langue française*, 53rd session, September 5–11, 1955, p. 657.

18. *Wilaya* was the name that had been formerly used to refer to administrative districts. Subsequent to the uprising of 1954, the term acquired a new meaning, when the Armée de Libération Nationale (ALN) started using it to refer to the areas of the country that were involved in the armed resistance. There were six *Wilayas* operating inside the country's borders: *Wilaya* 1 (the Aurès mountains), *Wilaya* 2 (the area north of Constantine), *Wilaya* 3 (Kabylia), *Wilaya* 4 (Algiers and outlying areas), *Wilaya* 5 (Oran and outlying areas), *Wilaya* 6 (the Sahara).

19. Originally from Azouza in Greater Kabylia, Abbane Ramadane was from a modest family. He joined the PPA after 1945 at a time when he was employed as a civil servant in the *commune mixte* of Châteaudun-du-Rhumel in the region of Constantine. His ties to the paramilitary group the OS (Organisation spéciale) led to his arrest in 1951 and to a five-year prison sentence. In prison, he was repeatedly subjected to special disciplinary measures after he went on a very long hunger strike, but he did not break down under torture. He was transferred to a prison in France, in Nancy, before being brought back to the prison where he had originally been detained in Algeria, El Harrach in Maison Carrée. The prison director, who had heard about Ramadane, wanted to avoid bringing this political organizer together with political prisoners; he decided to adjourn his sentence and Abbane was freed in January 1955. Upon his release, Abbane immediately joined the FLN. (Abbane's name is often transcribed with only one *b*.)

20. *Revue pratique de la vie sociale et de l'hygiène mentale* 1 (1956): 24–27.

21. "Test of projective apperception," familiar to psychologists as a diagnostic and prognostic tool for personality assessment.

22. Cheikh Ben Badis led the Association des Oulémas, which was responsible for the interpretation and reform of Islamic law. This association had been involved in a legal fight to institute a moral reform and Islamic schooling. While it did not whole-heartedly support the November 1 insurrection, it came out in favor of Algerian independence and made a statement to that effect in January 1956.

23. At the Soummam Congress, the FLN posited the supremacy of the political over the military and instituted new structures to that end. In addition to the Army of National Liberation (ALN), based in six national districts known as *Wilayas*, the creation of two new bodies was announced:

(1) The Conseil national de la révolution algérienne (National Council of the Algerian Revolution [CNRA]), a sovereign parliamentary body, made up of thirty-four members (seventeen permanent members and seventeen deputies), was invested with the authority to order the cessation of fighting. The council was expected to hold annual meetings.

(2) The Comité de la coordination et d'exécution (Coordinating and Executive Committee [CCE]), was an executive body made up of five members. All civilian and military structures were under its command, and it was based in Algiers. Abbane Ramdane, Krim Belkacem, Larbi Ben M'Hidi, joined by Ben Youssef Ben Khedda, and Saad Dahlab formed the first CCE.

24. The extremely complex history of this period is beyond the scope of this work. Historians have addressed it in the three-volume *La Guerre d'Algérie* (Paris: Temps actuel, 1981), under the direction of Henri Alleg. The works of Benjamin Stora and Mohammed Harbi are especially recommended as well. But my immediate goal here is simply to recreate the atmosphere of those days.

25. Amédée Froger was the mayor of Boufarik, a little town that was the living symbol of colonization.

26. Mollet had just instated the "Republican Front" government.

27. Fanon struggled with this decision as it entailed revealing information that had been divulged by a patient in a psychiatric setting. But given the enormity of the consequences, he decided to notify his patient about what he planned to do and to alert Mandouze, who was in a position to avert the catastrophe.

28. "Le T.A.T. chez la femme musulmane. Sociologie de la perception et de l'imagination," co-authored with Charles Géronimi. Congrès des Médecins aliéniste, Bordeaux, August 30–September 4, 1956.

29. He was a historian and former professor of political science at Grenoble who specialized in Trotskyism. Pierre Broué is the author of *Trotsky* (Paris: Fayard, 1988).

30. The respected lawyer Ali Boumendjal was arrested in March 1957. He was tortured and died as a result of this torture. His death was officially attributed to suicide by defenestration.

Fanon Transits through Paris

1. In June 1956, two young militants were guillotined at the Barberousse prison in Algiers, despite the promise to the contrary that had been made to Germaine Tillion.

2. Larbi Ben M'Hidi, leader of the Toussaint Movement was a member of the CCE (Coordinating and Executive Committee) in the region of Oran. Later, after he established ties to the external political leadership, he returned to Algiers, where he worked side-by-side with Ben Khedda and especially closely with Abbane Ramdane, to lead the fight inside the city and in its outlying areas. He was captured on February 25, 1957; on March 4, his body was discovered "hanging" in his cell; he had been horribly tortured and his hands and feet were shackled. He was a deeply political man, whose calm and honesty left a lasting impression on the young men and women who had joined *Wilaya* 4. He was ever present and always very attentive to the young people who had joined the fight (account by Safia Bazi, February 1999).

3. The Étoile nord-africaine (ENA), a movement whose platform was the unity and independence of the three North African countries (Algeria, Tunisia, Morocco), was created in 1926 and twice dissolved by the French government—first in 1929 and again in 1937 by the Front populaire. It later reemerged as the PPA (Parti populaire algérien); the MTLD was formed when the PPA split into two groups. The MNA (Mouvement national algérien), the organization led by Messali Hadj, was founded on December 1, 1954 to distinguish itself from the FLN that had just launched the insurrection.

4. "La vie impossible de Frantz Fanon," *Esprit*, September 1971.

5. This view was not welcomed by all. In our June 1999 interview, Jean Daniel informed me that an Algerian pharmacist in Blida who considered himself a "moderate nationalist" was irritated by Fanon's assumption that they were in the same boat. This especially fair-skinned man had claimed that his experience of racism and Fanon's were not in the least similar.

6. Pierre Vidal-Naquet, *Mémoires*, t. II, *Le Trouble et la Lumière* (Paris: Seuil/La Découverte, 1998), p. 37.

7. *El Moudjahid*, 1956.

8. Contrary to the claims made by Jean Daniel and later revived in the historiography of French intellectuals, this book was not the "the revolutionary's breviary, announcing the birth of the revolution." To draw such a conclusion is to dismiss the nationalist movement's long gestation, its long clandestine history, and, especially, the later ties between the heirs of a paramilitary organization, the OS, that had been contemplating the possibility of armed struggle for a long time and a group of militants associated to the MTLD, the "groupe des 22," whose five leaders were Boudiaf, Ben Boulaïd, Didouche, Bitat, and Ben M'Hidi. See Mohammed Harbi, *Le F.L.N., mirage et réalité* (Paris: Éditions J.A., 1980).

9. Vidal-Naquet, *Mémoires*, t. II, p. 32.

10. "Le dossier Jean Muller," *Témoignage chrétien*, February 1957. The posthumously published account of the draftee Jean Muller revealed that certain French military units were relying on police methods that were comparable to the barbarous tactics that had been used by the Nazis.

11. In this book, see Blida, p. 90 n. 30. Also see Algiers, 1953, p. 51 n. 26.

12. *La Cruelle Vérité* (Paris: Plon, 1982). Farès was born in 1911 to a very modest family living in the Kabylia region. He was orphaned at a very young age. After working for many years as a notary's clerk, Farès became the first Muslim notary public in Algeria. In 1953, he became the President of the Algerian Assembly. In August 1955, he signed the motion for the sixty-one elected representatives. He assisted the FLN both legally and financially. In 1957, he tried to impress the importance of negotiations on the French government. In November 1961, he was arrested for colluding with the FLN. After the signing of the Evian Accords he was set free and became the President of the Provisional Executive Branch. After independence, he was placed under arrest by Ben Bella, at which point he withdrew from political life. He died in 1990.

13. In late 1959, early 1960, the escalation of the crisis was hastened by the takeover of the *état major* of the external Armée de libération nationale (ALN) that was under the undisclosed, but ironclad, command of Houari Boumedienne.

14. This information comes from an unpublished work by Anne-Marie Louanchi-Chaulet.

Tunis

1. Ahmed Ben Bella was born into a poor peasant family in the Oran region. He attended secondary school in Tlemcen. After receiving his *brevet* (equivalent to an eighth- or ninth-grade diploma) he reported for military service in 1937. He was demobilized in 1940 and reenlisted in 1943. He was an executive officer in the *tabor* regiment, 14e RTA; he fought in the entire French and Italian campaigns, distinguishing himself at Monte Cassino. In the aftermath of the events of 1945, he left the army and became a member of the PPA-MTLD. After serving as the town councilor in Marnia in 1947, he presented himself as a candidate for the newly formed Algerian Assembly in April 1948. A leader of the Oran OS and a member of the MTLD's central committee, he was arrested in Algiers in May 1950, judged to be a threat to internal security, and sentenced to a seven-year prison term. In 1952, he escaped from the Blida prison and made his way to Cairo, where he joined the external delegation of the MTLD. He was purported to have close ties to Nasser. Twice, once in Cairo and again in Tripoli, he barely escaped being assassinated by the Main Rouge. On October 22, 1956, he was one of the passengers on the airplane that was hijacked on its way to the Tunis meeting; he was arrested and remained in custody until the end of combat. From 1956 on, he was in disagreement with the FLN's positions regarding the conduct of war and alliances. After his release, he became, with Houari Boumedienne's support, an opponent of the Gouvernement provisoire de la République Algérienne (GPRA). In 1962 and 1965, he was the president of the Algerian Republic. He was unseated by Boumedienne, imprisoned, and later held under house arrest until 1980.

2. Omar Ouamrane, not especially politicized and unconditionally loyal to Krim Belkacem, wanted to have Ali Mahsas, a Ben Bella loyalist who was opposed to the CCE and to the Soummam platform, arrested and sentenced to death. Mahsas owes his life to Bourguiba, who saved the situation by exiling him.

3. By decision of the Soummam Congress, colonel was the highest military rank that was conferred on the leaders of the various *Wilayas* (the different Algerian regions and provinces that had been geographically defined on the occasion of that congress).

4. Ferhat Abbas, *Autopsie d'une guerre* (Paris: Garnier, 1980), p. 210.

5. As reported by René Vautier in *Caméra citoyenne, Mémoires* (Rennes: Apogée, 1998).

6. After the serious conflicts between the ALN and the armed forces of the MNA that were led by Mohammed Bellounis and had, in theory, allied themselves to the ALN in 1955, Amirouche Ait Hamouda gave the order for the massacre at Beni Illemane, a village that supported Messali Hadj and Bellounis. In the wake of this massacre, Bellounis went to the French side, taking his men and weapons with him. In August 1957, he had the rank of "general" and 1,500 men at his command. He was manipulated on numerous occasions by the French Army.

7. Provisional Government of the Algerian Republic. There were three governments between September 1958 and March 1962. The first two were presided by Ferhat Abbas.

8. Charles Robert Ageron, ed., *La Guerre d'Algérie et les Algériens, 1954–1962* (Paris: Armand Colin, 1997), p. 267.

9. Interview with Safia Bazi, February 1999.

10. The different versions of Abbane's death continue to be unresolved to this day. What we do know is that the colonels met on several occasions between the seventeenth and the twentieth of December to discuss Abbane's fate. On December 24, Abbane was persuaded to make a trip to Morocco, purportedly to meet with the Moroccan monarch, Mohammed V. He was accompanied by Krim Belkacem and Mahmoud Cherif; Bentobbal chose not to be party to the proceedings, and Colonel Saddek, Abbane's friend, was not included in them. In Tetouan, Morocco, they were met by Boussouf and two other men; from there, they were to travel to Tangier by car. A few kilometers into the journey, the car they were traveling in left the main road and turned onto a dirt road that led to a farm. Abbane was forced out of the car at gunpoint and turned over to the two unidentified men. Rumor had it that Boussouf was the one who pushed for Abbane's execution against the advice of Krim Belkacem who was in favor of "mere" imprisonment. Ferhat Abbas' memoirs, however, claim that Krim had agreed to the execution. But all of these accounts remain unconfirmed. What is certain is that Abbane died on that farm. The official announcement of his death in May 1958 in *El Moudjahid* claimed he had been "killed in action."

11. The new CCE was made up of nine members: five colonels (Krim, Boussouf, Bentobbal, Ouamrane, and Mahmoud Cherif) and four political leaders (Ferhat Abbas, Dr. Lamine Debaghine, Abdelhamid Mehri, and Abbane Ramdane).

12. Ahmed, who was the brother of Ali Boumendjel, was born on April 22, 1906, in Beni Yenni in the heart of the Kabylia region. He, like his father, was a schoolteacher. When he was eighteen, he was sent by the École normale d'Alger on an "educational" trip to Paris. It was during this trip that he met Messali Hadj and became an Algerian militant, committed to being reunited with his past and his civilization.

In 1937, he returned to France, where he studied law, subsequently becoming Messali's legal representative. In 1944, he left the PPA to join the UDMA and later became its general secretary. In 1951, he was an advisor to the French union. He would write for *Esprit* as well as *L'Express;* his debate with Camus was printed in the latter. In his capacity as a member of the French Federation of the FLN, he was able to relocate to Tunis when his brother Ali died in 1957. He became a member of the CNRA (National Committee of the Algerian Revolution), where he became the liaison officer to sub-Saharan Africa in 1959. He took part in the Melun meetings and in the first Evian conference. At Independence, he was appointed Minister of Reconstruction and Public Works in the government of Ben Bella. See Benjamin Stora, *Dictionnaire biographique des militants nationalistes algériens* (Paris: L'Harmattan, 1985).

13. Paper presented by Pierre Chaulet at the Algiers' Conference, December 1987.

14. I remember taking dictation from Fanon and adding my own contribution to a number of these very short articles; I have no knowledge, however, of the titles under which they appeared in the end. They generally did not veer from the major subjects of the time: sufferings and struggle of the Algerian nation, Algerian national unity, France's mistaken assessment of the situation, African solidarity.

15. Compilation of issues 1–91, *El Moudjahid* 3 (1962), t. I, p. 154.

16. Ibid., p. 404.

17. Ibid., p. 408.

18. In this book, see Fanon and Africa, p. 141 n. 3.

19. In issue 39, April 18, 1959.

20. The entire text of this statement appears in *The Wretched of the Earth* in the chapter entitled "Reciprocal Bases of National Culture and the Fight for Freedom." (*The Wretched of the Earth*, translated by Constance Farrington. [New York: Grove Press, 1966], pp. 190–99.)

21. *El Moudjahid*, issue 54–55, November 1959.

22. *El Moudjahid*, issue 88, December 1961.

23. "Dedication to Bertène Juminer: This book illustrates a principle: if action does not transform the individual consciousness then it is nothing more than incoherence and agitation. The intensity of the subjective evidence that has come to light in the Algerian nation's epic struggle against colonial oppression attests to the impossibility of deferring a collective awakening. Have faith in your people and devote your life to their dignity and betterment. For us, there is no other way. Your brother, Frantz."

24. "L'Algérie face aux tortionnaires français," *El Moudjahid*, issue 10, September 1957.

25. *El Moudjahid*, December 1, 1957.

26. Even if Fanon may have given Francis Jeanson the impression that the involvement of the group he led was of no importance, he was, in fact, quite appreciative of Jeanson's commitment.

27. Fanon told us, in the utmost confidence, how in 1956, he and his friend Colonel Saddek had come up with a plan that would speed up the end of the War. The action, which would be timed to coincide with a session of the United Nations that would draw international attention to Algeria, involved taking over the Algiers Admiralty, located at the tip of a jetty that extended to include almost the entire bay

of the city, and bombing the European sectors of the city. Another Fanonian fiction? Algiers in 1956 was not Pristina or Belgrade, and the ALN was not NATO. Even so, the scenario is less far-fetched today than it may have been at one time.

28. In March 1959 (issue 38) and in April 1959 (issue 40), the interviews with Lamine Khène and Ali Kafi, leaders of *Wilaya* 2; in May 1959 (issue 41), the interview with Colonel Lotfi, leader of *Wilaya* 5.

29. Paper presented by Pierre Chaulet at the Algiers Conference, December 1987.

30. There were two of us: Charles Géronimi and myself.

31. In July 1961, Bourguiba wrote a letter to de Gaulle requesting the removal of the French naval forces from the Port of Bizerte as well as a review of Tunisia's border with the Sahara. The fact that France did not respond to these requests, compounded by the fact that plans to expand the existing army base were being implemented by French soldiers on the ground, resulted in civilian and military demonstrations at the site of the French military holdings in Bizerte. The French response was immediate and extreme: 7,000 parachutists, 3 warships, and a 3-day battle. On the Tunisian side, there were 1,200 wounded and 700 dead, almost all of them civilian; the French losses amounted to 24 dead. The residents of Tunis reacted with deep shock. In this town, where summer is usually so promising, that was a summer of violent anti-French demonstrations. Shops were looted. It was the end of an era, about which Michel Martini would write: "I was uncovering another Tunisia, another Tunis, other Tunisians, other residents of Tunis, behaving as if they had been struck by lightening" (*Souvenirs algériens*, vol. 1 *L'Algérie française* [Paris: Biotem, 1997], p. 652).

32. The dish was known as *poisson complet*, and it did not matter who you were or where you came from, eating this meal for the first time was a veritable rite of passage.

33. Interviews undertaken in September and October 1998. I want to extend a special thanks to Marie-Jeanne Manuellan for her vivid recollections.

34. *La Raison, cahiers de psychopathologie scientifique*, was a journal published in the early 1950s by the "Librarie nouvelle"; it was very partial to Pavlov and the Soviet Union and very hostile to psychoanalysis, which it viewed as a "bourgeois science." Many of its contributors would later become psychoanalysts of great distinction.

35. In a note that appears in *Black Skin, White Masks*, Fanon writes: "Let me observe at once that I had no opportunity to establish the overt presence of homosexuality in Martinique. This must be viewed as the absence of the Oedipus complex in the Antilles. The schema of homosexuality is well enough known. We should not overlook, however, the existence of what are called there 'men dressed like women' or 'godmothers.' Generally they wear shirts and skirts. But I am convinced that they lead normal sex lives. They can take a punch like any 'he-man' and they are not impervious to the allures of women—fish and vegetable merchants" (BSWM, 180).

36. See *Souvenirs algériens*, vol. 1, p. Of metropolitan origin, Michel Martini worked as a surgeon in Orléansville (Ech-Cheliff), Algeria between March 1955 and July 1956. He was arrested and sentenced, after one year of preventive detention, to five years in prison as a result of his activities in support of the Algerian struggle for independence. He continued his political involvement in Tunisia until July 1962 and

later embarked on an academic career in Algeria that lasted until his retirement in 1987.

37. In time, even the journalists started to refer to themselves by this name. These representatives of the world press made frequent forays into Algeria where conditions were much tougher than in Tunis. They included Claude Krief, Albert-Paul Lentin and Jean Daniel, all Algerian-born; Robert Lambotte and Madeleine Riffault, who wrote for *L'Humanité*, the Swiss Charles-Henri Favrod, and the American Tom Brady, who wrote for the *New York Times*. Their support of the Algerian cause was a matter of public record.

38. The expression was coined by Jean Daniel. Interview, June 1999.

39. See Rheda Malek, *L'Algérie à Évian* (Paris: Éditions du Seuil, 1959).

40. Nacer, who was a protégé of Krim Belkacem, was not especially well regarded for his intellectual abilities. The rumor that he may have been involved with the Waffen-SS further tarnished his image in the eyes of the young militants.

41. Abbas, *Autopsie d'une guerre*.

42. Rheda Malek reports that Fanon told him: "I am going to go see Houphouët-Boigny [Minister of State of the French government at the time] to tell him that we are ready" (*L'Algérie à Évian*).

43. Sékou Touré, born in Farana in 1922, entered political life by way of syndicalism. He worked as a clerk in the financial division of the PTT (Postal Services) and was responsible for the unionization of this sector. In 1947, he created the PDG (the Democratic Party of Guinea), quickly becoming its leader. He was elected as a regional councilor in Beyla (1953), then in Conakry (1957); the "no" with which he responded to de Gaulle's plan in 1958 sealed his leadership role in Guinean politics. He was the first president of the Republic of Guinea in 1961, a post he occupied until his death in 1984. The hegemony of the PDG, the single party of "national unity," paved the way for personal dictatorship (Sékou Touré proclaimed himself the "Supreme Leader of the Revolution" in 1968); nepotism (his family and his ethnic clansmen, the Malinke, ran the party and the bureaucracy); and a police state: camp Boiro, a prison for political detainees that was built with Czech help in 1964, has become, today, a symbol of resistance to the regime.

44. African American author of detective fiction.

45. Jacques Berque, *Mémoires des deux rives* (Paris: Seuil, 1989). Berque uses the term "Algiers Forum" to refer to the solidarity rally, organized by the watchdog committee for French Algeria, that was held in Algiers on May 16, 1958. One of the figures who was at the forefront of this effort was Pierre Lagaillarde, a former parachutist, who became the president of the new Association générale des étudiants d'Algérie, a group that was allied to the Poujadistes. In the group that had assembled under the French flags that adorned the stage, erected outside the building that housed the *gouvernment général* in the epicenter of the European city, a number of Algerian Muslim women made a statement by removing their veils in public. When news of this event reached Tunis, not by direct satellite to be sure, Fanon found it deeply disturbing. Aside from his political concern about the limitations of the Algerian resistance, he was also shocked by the patent exhibitionism of the gesture.

46. Jacques Berque, "Une cause jamais perdue," *Présence Africaine*, reissued later as *Une cause jamais perdue: Pour une Méditerrannée plurielle* (Paris: Albin Michel, 1998).

47. Diane Weil-Ménard, *L'Oeuvre et la Pensée de Giovanni Pirelli*, Doctoral thesis, 1992, p. 245. Interview with Luigi Nono, October 11, 1987.

48. In this book, see Fanon and Africa, n. 14.

49. A terrorist organization, responsible among other things for the assassination of Lemaigre-Dubreuil, which we now know had links to the French secret service.

50. We owe this detailed information to G. Pirelli, who has written about all this at more length in Fanon 1 and Fanon 2, Turin, Einaudi, "Politica" series, nos. 23 and 24, 1971.

51. Abbas, *Autopsie d'une guerre*, p. 316.

52. Interview with Maspero, April 1999.

53. "Cahiers libres" Collection. *L'An V de la révolution algérienne* was the second book to be published in this series.

54. Fanon had suggested a meeting in Italy in 1960, but Maspero was otherwise engaged at the time.

55. Interview with Safia Bazi, February 1999.

56. This blanket rejection, manifest in the baseless behaviors that the colonized overwhelmingly resorts to when confronted by colonial jurisdiction, his self-imposed opacity, had already been discussed by Fanon, as early as 1955, in the article with Lacaton ("Conduites d'aveu en Afrique du Nord," *L'information psychiatrique* 51, no. 10 [December 1975]: 1115).

57. See *L'An V,* 2d ed., p. 183.

58. Charles Robert Ageron, "Un aspect de la guerre d'Algérie: la propagande radiophonique du FLN et des États arabes," in *La Guerre d' Algérie et les Algériens, 1954–1962*, p. 259.

59. *L'An V de la révolution algérienne* (1959). *Studies in a Dying Colonialism.* Translated by Maakon Chevalier. (New York: Monthly Review Press, 1965), 157.

60. *Studies in a Dying Colonialism*, 25.

61. *Studies in a Dying Colonialism*, 31.

Fanon and Africa

1. Félix Houphouët-Boigny, born in 1905, was a physician before he became the manager of a prosperous plantation. In 1944, he founded the African farmworkers syndicate that gave rise to the Côte d'Ivorian Parti démocratique (PDCI); later, the PDCI joined forces with the Rassemblement démocratique africain, forming the PDCI-RDA that was led by Houphouët-Boigny for the duration of his life. Between 1946 and 1959, he represented Côte d'Ivoire in the French Parliament, where he was initially associated with the Communists and then with the Union démocratique et socialiste de la Résistance (UDSR). He occupied a number of cabinet positions during the Fourth Republic. In 1958, he agreed to the autonomy plan proposed by de Gaulle, whom he considered an ally. The agreement was short-lived, however, and Côte d'Ivoire declared itself fully independent in August 1960. He became the first president of the new republic, a post he held until his death in 1993 by imposing a single-party regime. The welcome he extended to Jean-Bédel Bokassa, the ex-Emperor of the Central African Republic, in 1979 and the sumptuous cathedral he

built in Yamoussoukro, his hometown turned capital, helped fuel the growing opposition to a regime already weakened by economic crisis and accusations of corruption. Demonstrations forced Houphouët-Boigny to accept a multiparty system.

2. The move cost Touré dearly: the French government withdrew in a matter of twenty-four hours, taking all removeable infrastructures and canceling all aid.

3. Chawki Mostefaï was born in Kabylia. He was a medical student who joined the university chapter of the PPA during World War II. Implicated in the events of 1945, he became a member of the central committee of the MTLD in 1946. In 1951, he espoused the plan of action that had been set forth by the UDMA and the Ouléma and withdrew from the MTLD. After a period of political inactivity, he joined the FLN in 1956. In 1958, in his capacity as advisor to Krim Belkacem, he took part in the meetings with sub-Saharan African nations. He was appointed to the "Rocher Noir" provisional government and was responsible, with Abderrahmane Farès, for negotiating the accords with the OAS. In 1963, the Ben Bella government appointed him to the leadership of the Union industrielle africaine.

4. Former British colony: the Gold Coast.

5. *El Moudjahid*, December 24, 1958, issue 34.

6. This is how Algerian militants referred to the War in Indochina.

7. The first one had taken place in Paris in November 1956. See the chapter titled "Blida."

8. Mongo Beti, who also took part in this event, confirmed this in 1982.

9. The term appears only once in his writings, in the April 1960 lecture "Pourquoi avons-nous choisi la violence?" where he uses it in its adjectival form to caution against the peril of "ethnic consciousness."

10. It is not too difficult to imagine that Fanon would have been opposed to ethnopsychiatry and very interested in the *sans-papiers* (illegal aliens).

11. Marie-Pierre Ulloa, *Francis Jeanson, un itinéraire d'engagement*, DEA thesis "Histoire du XXe siècle," Paris, Institut d'études politiques, 1997.

12. In 1952, Mario de Andrade gave a clear summation of the reasons that led to Fanon's change of heart. In 1959, in the immediate aftermath of the Rome meeting, Fanon and Mario de Andrade discussed the concrete possibilities of armed struggle in Angola. Amilcar Cabral, the founder of the African Party for the Independence of Guinea-Bissau and Cape Verde (PAIGC), was working as an agronomist in Angola, where he also had an important part in the creation of the Popular Liberation Movement of Angola (MPLA). Like Mario de Andrade, he believed that political action alone was insufficient and that the Portuguese colonial power could be taken on only through armed struggle. Fanon, acting on his firmly held principle of African solidarity, had advanced a very concrete proposal; he offered to arrange for eleven Angolan cadres to be trained by the ALN in guerilla war. Amilcar Cabral was charged with selecting the men and delivering them to the Tunisian border. He failed to do so. Fanon received word of this failure while he was attending the 1960 conference. He was extremely displeased and attributed it to the hesitation of "assimilated intellectuals" to commit. ("Fanon et l'Afrique combattante," *Afrique-Asie*, July 19, 1982.)

13. "This Africa to Come," *Toward the African Revolution*. Trans. Haakon Chevalier. (New York: Grove Press, 1968), p. 180.

14. Actor, member of the Jeanson network. Detained and incarcerated in Fresnes,

he managed to escape and reach Tunisia with the help of the usual underground networks. For more details, see Hervé Hamon and Patrick Rotman, *Les Porteurs de valises: La résistance française à la guerre d'Algérie* (Paris: Albin Michel, 1979).

15. This paper was published only in Italian in one of the volumes of selected works edited by Pirelli (see *Fanon* 1, p. 47).

16. Serge Michel, *Nour le voilé* (Paris: Éditions du Seuil, 1982).

17. These notes, constituting a veritable logbook, were posthumously published in *Toward the African Revolution* ("This Africa to Come").

18. Ibid., pp. 176–90. In this text, Fanon also writes in an enlightening manner about the task he has set himself: "To put Africa in motion, to cooperate in its organization, in its regrouping, behind revolutionary principles. To participate in the ordered movement of a continent—this was really the work I had chosen" (pp. 177–78).

19. On June 14, 1960, de Gaulle, in an address that was aired on radio and television, extended a solemn invitation to the leadership of the GPRA: "I hereby declare that we await them here to find an honorable solution to the ongoing fighting." The GPRA decided to respond to the invitation. At one point, there was talk of sending Ferhat Abbas in person; then the plan was changed and an exploratory delegation led by Boumendjel and Ben Yahia, the chief cabinet minister under Abbas, was sent instead. The French were represented by de Gaulle's secretary general for Algerian affairs and by Colonel Mathon. The meeting was a diplomatic fiasco, but de Gaulle's recognition of the GPRA as a negotiating partner amounted to a political victory. For a more detailed account, see Rheda Malek, *L'Algérie à Évian; Histoire des Négociations Secrètes, 1956–1962* (Paris: Éditions du Seuil, 1997) and Alistair Horne, *A Savage War of Peace: Algeria, 1954–1962* (London: Macmillan, 1977).

20. Shortly thereafter, we learned that the letter had been composed by Marcel Péju and signed off on by Claude Lanzmann, who was simply doing the bidding of Sartre who did not wish to change his travel plans in South America.

21. Dr. Annette Roger, a brilliant neurophysiologist who headed the Gasteau nuerophysiology laboratory, was working in Marseille at the time as a specialist in electroencephalography. She was internationally renown for her work in infantile epilepsy, but she was not a psychiatrist, and her understanding of psychiatry and Fanon's were leagues apart. A former member of the Resistance, a militant member of the PCF until 1956, she assisted the FLN in the Marseille region. She was arrested when she was caught transporting a member of the leadership in her own car. She was a few weeks pregnant at the time of her incarceration and managed to obtain a postponement of her prison term. She claimed that a little known Tunisian network had helped her make her way to Tunis.

22. UGEMA is the General Union of Algerian Muslim Students. UNEF is the National Union of French Students.

The Last Year of Fanon's Life

1. Personal correspondence between the author and Michel Martini, also cited in M. Martini, *Souvenirs algériens*, 2 vol. L'Algérie algérienne, 1962–1972 (Paris: Glyphe et Biotem, 2000).

2. Ibid.

3. The observation is not surprising in light of what we found out in the 1960s about Soviet psychiatry. The diagnosis of "disassociative personality disorder" was routinely used to justify the internment of "dissidents" in the camps.

4. Interview with Pierre Chaulet, February 1999.

5. In August 1961, Fanon was in Italy waiting to be summoned by Ben Khedda to attend the meeting of nonaligned nations that was scheduled to take place in Belgrade in early September. The summons never came and not just because of political reasons. The state of Fanon's health was becoming cause for great alarm among his Algerian friends.

6. "You mustn't stay in Tunis, you have to go there," he told me feverishly at a time when, unbeknownst to me, the subject of how to best use my "qualifications as a psychiatrist" was being discussed by the Army and the Ministry of Social Affairs. In light of my gender and my minority status, the solution, in the end, was neither fish nor fowl: my job entailed working with the victims of "war trauma" in the Tunis area. I learned a lot from my patients and learned even more about improvisation.

7. Arguments that capitalize on native authority generally serve to bolster the view that "he/she is not one of us, he/she cannot know"; this is the belief that is at the heart of all ethnic identification, regardless of where in the world it may occur. Why not ask instead: "Who is this other who is not I but who is also I?"

8. As witnessed by the author and confirmed by Simone de Beauvoir in her memoir, *La Force des choses* (Paris: Gallimard, 1963; reissued "Folio" collection, 1977), vol. 2, p. 409.

9. Interview with Claudine Chaulet, February 1999.

10. Here Fanon alludes in a much more direct manner, than in the talks between the GPRA and France, to the Troisième Conférence des peuples africaines on the topic of neocolonialism that was held in Cairo between March 25 and March 31. Even though the conference concluded on a note of forceful denunciation, Fanon, in an interview with Giovanni Pirelli, described the position taken by a number of governments and newly independent African nations as a "betrayal of Africa."

11. Simone de Beauvoir, *La Force des choses*, vol. 2, p. 420–27.

12. Alas, this was all too true. When one consults the works that have been written about the French intelligentsia in the final years of the Algerian War, Fanon's name is always indexed in the context of Sartre's foreword. While Sartre correctly states that Fanon's book is not addressed to Europe, he communicates little about the tone of the book and its message. What's more, he misses the point of Fanon's dialectical reading of violence. If we were to go by Sartre's foreword, we would be inclined to conclude that redemption follows from the individual act of murder. The idea of murder as an act of redemption is not at all a central one for Fanon. His idea of violence is much more linked to a symbolic impasse. (See "Fanon Today" in this book.)

13. In March 1961, when preparations were underway for the first Evian talks and Krim had been appointed to lead the Algerian delegation, Fanon stepped in to do him a very good turn. Krim, who had been unwell, was diagnosed as suffering from anxiety. Fanon was entrusted with his care, and both men were whisked off to an isolated Italian villa where Krim was supposed to undergo a sleep cure, to which he had not been made privy, under Fanon's supervision. After Fanon had spent a few hours with

his illustrious patient, he became increasingly convinced that the medical problem was not at all emotional in nature. At daybreak, Fanon walked for more than two kilometers to alert the surgeon Michel Martini. Krim was suffering from a severe gall bladder infection and incipient peritonitis and needed immediate surgical attention.

14. I came across this expression in an interview about Fanon that Jeanson gave for a special issue of *Sans frontière*, February 1982.

15. Her real name was Colette Grégoire. As a supporter of the FLN, she was arrested and tortured. When she was released, she came to Tunis with her husband, Jean Melki. She returned to Algeria at independence. She died at a young age in 1963.

16. The reasons for this delay have never been fully explained. Bureaucratic problems—Fanon's passport was still in a fictitious name—or a practice of conducting preliminary tests on an outpatient basis? The second hypothesis seems the more likely one.

17. Myself included.

18. Interview on Radio Alger on the second anniversary of Fanon's death (December 1963).

19. Reported by Simone de Beauvoir in *La Force des choses*, vol. 2, p. 440; confirmed in an interview with Josie Fanon in December 1987.

20. *El Moudjahid* 3, issue 88, December 21, 1961.

21. Ibid. Also as quoted by Irene Gendzier, *Frantz Fanon: A Critical Study* (New York: Random House, Pantheon Books, 1973), p. 235; cited hereafter as CS.

22. Reproduced in its entirety in *El Moudjahid*.

23. "Frantz Fanon, le journaliste," speech delivered at the Algiers Conference in December 1987; unfortunately, the proceedings from this conference were never published.

24. Author of *Dernier Quart d'heure* and *La Lutte tricontinentale;* later, he was a contributor to *Politique Hebdo* and one of the founders of the first *Politis*.

25. Guy Sitbon, who lived in Tunis, was for many years the correspondent for *Le Monde* before joining the team at *Jeune Afrique*. He and Fanon met several times and had more than one occasion to indulge in mutually enjoyable bouts of verbal sparring.

The Wretched of the Earth

1. On the assassination of Lumumba, see Serge Michel, *Uhu Lumumba* (Paris: Éditions du Seuil, 1982), and the recent documentary by Thierry Michel, *Mobutu, roi du Zaïre*. Production: Les Films de la Passerelle, 1999. See also G. Heinz and H. Donnay, *Lumumba Patrice: Les cinquantes derniers jours de sa vie* (Brussels: CRISP and Le Seuil, 2nd ed., 1976).

2. Frantz Fanon, *The Wretched of the Earth*, trans. Constance Farrington (New York: Grove Press, 1966); cited hereafter as TWOE.

3. A title of the Holy Spirit, taken to mean "the advocate."

4. Fanon is alluding to the Algerian militants who were behind November 1, 1954.

5. Gilbert Comte, "Un *Mein Kampf* de la décolonisation," *La Nation française*, March 21, 1962.

6. *Les Temps modernes*, April 1962.

7. *Esprit*, February 1962.

8. "*Les Damnés de la Terre*, de Frantz Fanon," *Le Monde*, January 1962.

9. *L'Express*, November 30, 1961.

10. "Frantz Fanon et les problèmes de l'indépendance," *La Pensée*, February 1963.

11. Many years later, Maspero reported that Fanon had written to him that "after the War, when times would have been more propitious for such things, he would have liked to clarify and, in all likelihood, revise certain positions that had been raised by those who had taken part in the debate and with whom he had been unable to discuss matters under normal conditions."

12. Sartre had taken the side of Israel in the Six-Day War.

After

1. The Constantine *El-Asnar* and *La République d'Oran*, December 27, 1962.

2. Interview with Safia Bazi, February 1999.

3. Interview October 11, 1999. The psychiatric hospital is in the process of being transformed into a CHU departmental.

4. During the initial preparation of the Tripoli program, the reference to religion was included at Ben Bella's request. He argued for Islam as a force of the poor against the rich and questioned the premise of the secular State and FLN. Mostefa Lacheraf had other views and argued that conservative forces would use religion to spread reactionary values that would affect the family, women, and social dynamics. See Mohammed Harbi, *Le FLN, mirage et réalité* (Jeune Afrique, 1980), 333.

5. Between March and July 1962, in the city of Algiers under attack by the OAS, the deuxième zone autonome d'Alger (ZAA) was established under the direction of Omar and Boualem Oussedik and Ali Louinci. After an attack by the OAS on the Beau-Fraisier clinic, situated in the Algiers hills, in which twenty Algerian patients lost their lives, the Muslim population stopped seeking treatment in establishments that were situated in the European neighborhoods. Work began on the creation of a health facility for Algerians, and an additional effort was underway to turn the Ermitage clinic into a psychiatric center for Algiers and its surrounding areas. The history of the second autonomous zone that existed in Algiers between March and July 1962 has yet to be written.

6. Karima Berger, *L'Enfant des deux mondes* (La Tour d'Aigues, France: Éditions de l'Aube, 1998).

7. Irene Gendzier, *Frantz Fanon: A Critical Study* (New York: Random House, Pantheon Books, 1973).

8. As my work on this book was coming to an end, the name and memory of Fanon were making a comeback in Algeria. An *El Watan* December 23, 1999, editorial about the *Larousse* entry under Fanon's name protested that he had been classified as "a French psychiatrist and sociologist," reminding readers that he had "personally and of his own free will chosen to be an Algerian," and stressing that he was a "worthy son of the Algerian nation."

9. *Présence africaine*, first trimester 1962.

10. *El Moudjahid*, issue 9.

11. *El Moudjahid*, March 1958.

12. As far as I have been able to determine, there are only a handful of articles that were written in their entirety by Fanon that are missing from this grouping: "Le conflit algérien et l'anticolonialisme africaine" (#11), "Encore une fois, pourquoi le préalable?" (#12), "Le calvaire d'un peuple" (#31), and the first articles that were published in *Résistance algérienne*, one in March 1957 on French Algerian urban militias, the other on the role of women in the liberation struggle, that was published as an appendix in *L'An V de la révolution algérienne*. "Les Antilles, naissance d'une nation," however, was not written by Fanon.

13. David Caute, *Fanon* (London: Collins, Fontana, 1970); Peter Geismar, *Fanon* (New York: Dial Press, 1971); Irene Gendzier, *Frantz Fanon: A Critical Study* (New York: Random House, Pantheon Books, 1973).

14. Renate Zahar, *L'Oeuvre de Frantz Fanon* (Paris: Maspero, 1970); Pierre Bouvier, *Fanon* (Paris: Éditions universitaires, 1971); Phillipe Lucas, *Sociologie de Frantz Fanon* (Alger: SNED, 1971).

15. Juliette Minces, "Frantz Fanon, vu par Irene Gendzier," *Le Monde diplomatique*, August 1973.

16. *Esprit*, September 1971, p. 248.

17. Édouard Glissant, *Le Discours antillais* (Paris: Éditions du Seuil, 1981), p. 35 (*Caribbean Discourse, Selected Essays*, translated by J. Michael Dash, Charlottesville: University Press of Virginia, 1989).

18. Ibid., p. 36.

19. This letter appears as an epigraph in Ali Shariati's *Eslâm-Shenâsi* [Islamologie].

20. Interview with Nouchine Yavari d'Hellencourt, October 1999.

21. *Frantz Fanon. Actes du mémorial international*, March 31–April 3, 1982, Fort-de-France, *Présence africaine*.

22. *Sans frontière*, special issue, February 1982, previously cited.

23. *L'Actualité de Frantz Fanon. Actes du colloque de Brazzaville*, December 12–16, 1984 (Paris: Karthala, 1986).

24. The conference proceedings are unpublished.

Fanon Today

1. This is how the inner circle referred to the two factions: Boumedienne, the Frontier Army, Ben Bella and a handful of others, constituted the Tlemcen group, and the GPRA and a few others constituted the Tizi-Ouzou group.

2. Contrary to a general and abused perception, Fanon did not think that sporadic acts of terror were an end in themselves. He thought armed struggle needed a set of conditions to be in place and its objectives had to be clearly defined.

3. All political usages are based in some way on violence. But when violence is legitimized by the State, it fails to perceive itself as violence.

4. "Présence de Frantz Fanon," *Frantz Fanon. Actes du mémorial international*, *March 31–April 3, 1982*, Fort-de-France, *Présence africaine*.

5. Ibid.

6. See the documentaries, *Pourquoi la Guinée a dit non,* 1998; *Mobutu roi du Zaïre,* by Thierry Michel, 1999; and the televised program on *Léopold Senghor,* 1998, narrated by Jean-Noël Jeanneney.

7. The legacy of dispossession is a long one in the history of the peasantry, especially in Algeria, even before the French colonial era.

8. Imre Hermann, *L'Instinct filial,* translated into French by Georges Kassai (Paris: Denoël, 1972).

9. First chapter of *Studies in a Dying Colonialism.* Trans. Haakon Chevalier (New York: Grove Press, 1967).

10. David Macey, "Fanon, Phenomenology, Race," *Radical Philosophy* 9 (May–June 1999).

11. Jacques André, "Fanon entre le réel et l'inconscient," *Frantz Fanon. Actes du mémorial international.*

Index

247